ROUTLEDGE LIBRARY EDITIONS:
SMALL BUSINESS

Volume 3

FINANCE FOR GROWING ENTERPRISES

FINANCE FOR GROWING ENTERPRISES

Edited by
ROGER BUCKLAND AND EDWARD W. DAVIS

Routledge
Taylor & Francis Group
LONDON AND NEW YORK

First published in 1995 by Routledge

This edition first published in 2016
by Routledge
2 Park Square, Milton Park, Abingdon, Oxon OX14 4RN

and by Routledge
711 Third Avenue, New York, NY 10017

Routledge is an imprint of the Taylor & Francis Group, an informa business

British Library Cataloguing in Publication Data
A catalogue record for this book is available from the British Library

ISBN: 978-1-138-67308-3 (Set)
ISBN: 978-1-315-54266-9 (Set) (ebk)
ISBN: 978-1-138-67993-1 (Volume 3) (hbk)
ISBN: 978-1-138-67994-8 (Volume 3) (pbk)
ISBN: 978-1-315-56355-8 (Volume 3) (ebk)

Publisher's Note
The publisher has gone to great lengths to ensure the quality of this reprint but points out that some imperfections in the original copies may be apparent.

FINANCE FOR GROWING ENTERPRISES

Edited by Roger Buckland and Edward W. Davis

ROUTLEDGE

London and New York

First published 1995
by Routledge
11 New Fetter Lane, London EC4P 4EE

Simultaneously published in the USA and Canada
by Routledge
29 West 35th Street, New York, NY 10001

Typeset in Times by
Mathematical Composition Setters, Salisbury, Wiltshire.
Printed and bound in Great Britain by
TJ Press Ltd., Padstow, Cornwall

British Library Cataloguing in Publication Data
A catalogue record for this book is available from the British Library

Library of Congress Cataloguing in Publication Data
Finance for growing enterprises/edited by Roger Buckland and Edward W. Davis.
p. cm.
Includes bibliographical references and index.
1. Small business – Finance. I. Buckland, Roger. II. Davis. Edward W.
HG4027.7.F553 1995
658.15'92 – dc20 94–44949

ISBN 0-415-08233-1

CONTENTS

FIGURES

TABLES

Finance for Growing Enterprises
Preface to the 2016 edition

The articles in this volume address the perennial question of where small, growing firms can find the finance they need to innovate, expand and thrive. Lord Young's report for the UK Prime Minister in 2015 highlights the critical issues: the reliance on bank debt and the need for alternative sources; the failure of banking markets and the growing intervention of government in supporting – even subsidising - funding for growth (Lord Young, 2015). Banks are not necessarily the optimal choice for the funding of small growth firms, as Keasey and Watson point out (this volume, chapter 4). Indeed, UK banks have been criticised heavily for their attitude towards commercial lending in the aftermath of the financial crisis of 2007-8. Despite explicit government subsidies to lending by the banking sector to small firms, the typical flows of credit in 2015 have been net repayment of bank borrowing by the commercial sector, not positive flows of credit from the banks to growing firms.

While there have been many studies of the small firm funding 'gap' over the years, the critical issues in corporate finance remain the same: how well do financial markets and institutions provide appropriate finance for entrepreneurs; how the inevitable agency issues between 'insider' owner, manager and 'outsider' financier can be resolved; how the transactions costs involved in reaching public financing markets can be overcome; how firms balance their independence with the use of external venture capital, equity issues, mergers and acquisitions and corporate takeover.

Several of the authors writing in this volume continue to explore these issues in their research. For example, in Keasey (2015), Professor Keasey addresses the complicated issues involved in balancing financing requirements with the entrepreneur's control over the business. Professors Mason and Harrison (2015) bring their analysis of 'Business Angels' up to date, illuminating the agency problems attendant upon outsiders taking on risks in small firm financing. Buckland et al. (2011) consider how contemporary emerging equity markets transfer information and handle risks. The field continues to grapple with the core problems of aligning entrepreneurial management with risk-averse finance.

One significant shift since 1995 that is not represented here lies in the place of what is now known as 'Private Capital': intermediary investing partnerships that select and invest in small and fast-growth firms as part of a portfolio of investments which may also include distressed firms, management buy-outs and buy-ins, or firms with equity already listed on public exchanges such as the London Stock Exchange or NASDAQ. A complex and fast-growing finance sector, private capital also embraces non-bank debt, real estate, infrastructure and natural resource financing. While the 1980s and 1990s might have viewed the target of stock exchange listing as the culminating phase of growing enterprise financial status (see Davis, this volume chapter 7), in the 21st century private equity houses have displaced banks and public equity markets as a critical force in growth firm finance. Estimates put the global private capital market at some US$550 billion in 2015 (Prequin, 2016). Gompers et al. (2015a, b) provide an excellent contemporary analysis of how these markets operate. Thus, they find that private equity look for investment returns over 5-year horizons; that they aim for internal rates of return on their investments in the mid-20s percentage; that they take equity stakes of over 80 per cent on average; that private equity exits predominantly through strategic sales to other firms (50 per cent), financial sale (30 per cent) and only 12 per cent by an initial public offering (Gompers et al. 2015a, figure 1, tables 8, 16, 27).

The key to understanding private equity is, again, the manner in which that source of finance overcomes the transactions costs, information availability and agency issues attendant upon small growth firms. By excluding the public, the man-in-the-street, who are expensively protected from their deficient knowledge by regulation of markets, private equity houses aim to have privileged access to inside knowledge, which can be assessed by professional investment managers and where investments can be monitored by active professionals.

References

Buckland, R., Williams, J. and Chen, J (2011), 'Regulatory Changes, Market Integration and Spill-Over Effects in the Chinese A, B and Hong Kong Equity Markets', Pacific Basin Finance Journal, vol. 19, no. 4, pp. 351-373 http://dx.doi.org/10.1016/j.pacfin.2011.01.002

Gompers, P., Kaplan, S.N. and Mukhalyamov, V. (2015a), What Do Private Equity Firms Say They Do? Working Paper 15-081, Harvard Business School. Accessed 18-1-2016 at http://www.hbs.edu/faculty/Publication%20Files/15-081_9baffe73-8ec2-404f-9d62-ee0d825ca5b5.pdf

Gompers, P., Kaplan, S.N. and Mukhalyamov, V. (2015b), What Do Private Equity Firms Say They Do For The Companies They Buy? Harvard Business Review, June. Accessed 18-1-2016 at https://hbr.org/2015/06/what-private-equity-investors-think-they-do-for-the-companies-they-buy

Keasey, K., Martinez, B. and Pintado, J. (2015), 'Young Family Firms: Financing Decisions and the Willingness to Dilute Control ', Journal of Corporate Finance, 2015, 34, pp. 47-63. http://dx.doi.org/10.1016/j.jcorpfin.2015.07.014
Mason, C. M. and Harrison, R. T. (2015), 'Business angel investment activity in the financial crisis: UK evidence and policy implications', Environment and Planning C: Government and Policy, 33(1), pp. 43-60. http://dx.doi.org/10.1068/c12324b
Prequin (2016), 2015 Private Capital Fundraising Update, Accessed 18-1-2016 at https://www.preqin.com/research/private-equity/1/

1

INTRODUCTION

Roger Buckland and Edward W. Davis

The particular objective of this book is to provide a research-based critical review of the sources of finance available to small and growing firms within the UK. The phenomenon is of long-standing but continuing interest and has been reinforced within the 1980s by a range of financial innovations, such as management buy-out or changes in the Stock Exchange itself, designed specifically to cater for the smaller, growing firm. Small and medium-sized enterprises (SMEs) that are growing and developing are commonly described as 'growth small firms', or, more graphically, as 'emergent firms'. Such firms have particular requirements for development financing during their rapid internal and external growth and also have a particular requirement to manage their transition. That transition relates both to the emergence of their internal management and organisation and to their relationships with external investors and stakeholders: typically involving a shift in status, from that of private enterprises to public and eventually quoted businesses.

The prosperity of the 1980s – as exemplified by the public image associated with USM (unlisted securities market) millionaires and the impact of venture-capital intermediaries in broking successful management buy-outs – has helped create an impression of a transformation of the prospects for a critical sector within the UK economy. The subsequent severe recession inevitably had a radically different effect, inspiring trenchant criticisms of small firms' problems with banks, liquidation and, within firms newly quoted on the USM, a high rate of attrition, primarily by take-over (Cowling et al. 1991). So the downside of smaller firms' more recent economic performance again rehearses the impression that finance is of critical importance for those smaller potentially high-growth enterprises at the margin.

The overall economic role of smaller firms within the UK is clear enough. In terms of numbers of firms and proportion of population employed, their value has long been recognised (Stanworth and Gray 1991). What particularly matters, of course, is their contribution to the rate of growth of the economy. In this respect, therefore, our attention is directed towards a relatively narrow subset of smaller firms, those with growth potential, for which the question of an adequate financial market able to supply services without excessive cost is of major importance. That is not to dismiss the significance of the more typical small firm, growing at a relatively modest rate, financed by its own cash flow and marginal 'external' funding, primarily derived from bank overdrafts. Smaller, more vulnerable firms, experiencing credit rationing, loan defaults and bankruptcy, could transform their prospective growth by better management together with improvements in available capital sources.

In summary, *Finance for Growing Enterprises* brings together a series of empirical studies of how firms finance growth. Inevitably, the various authors have started from common, sometimes overlapping, sometimes differing, definitions or interpretations of the growing firm's 'problem': for example, what constitutes the original Macmillan Gap (Macmillan 1931; Radcliffe 1959; Stanworth et al. 1982). The reader will find here a range of critical perspectives on such 'gap' terminology: sometimes overlapping, always subtly different in angle and attack. The appropriate theoretical model and methodology for subsequent investigation have elements in common as well as substantial differences. In the editors' view that is part of the merit of this exercise. It enables readers of this book to see how different researchers approach a common subject. In the conclusion the editors provide their own summary interpretation of the principal findings, together with an evaluation of the policy implications to be derived from this and other studies, including those drawn from other countries.

TRANSACTIONS COSTS IN LONG-TERM FINANCE

The traditional approach to small-firm finance has been that of identification of difficulties or excessive costs associated with raising capital. There are two elements of theory, at least, which apply in this context, the first based on transactions costs and the second on agency costs. In the case of the former the question of economies of scale in capital markets has attracted the attention of economists since the original 1931 Macmillan Report first identified a potential gap in the supply of long-term capital to smaller firms. The 1971 Bolton Committee of Inquiry into Small Firms analysed financial facilities available to the small firm. The Committee came to the conclusion that there was no corresponding 'Bolton Gap' but did recognise the disadvantage to smaller firms as a result of economies of scale in finance, particularly long-term capital. It is arguable that this is what constituted the original Macmillan Gap; and it is likely to have been reinforced in the post-war period by increased concentration within the capital market.

One of the more visible transactions costs borne by smaller firms is that incurred in attempts to raise long-term capital, particularly if that involves a new issue on the Stock Exchange. Previous research, summarised in Chapter 7, illustrates the nature of costs incurred by smaller entrants to the London Stock Exchange. Further, for those smaller or weaker firms not able to resort to the Stock Exchange for capital, the costs incurred do to an extent serve as a proxy for similar, potentially larger costs incurred by unquoted firms seeking to raise long-term funding. While financing gaps can be alleviated by the presence of specialised venture-capital institutions (as considered in Chapters 5 and 6) the seller of such equity remains in a position of uncertainty and lack of power. Indeed, the growth of institutional venture capital might be ascribed to financial institutions' comparative advantage in profitably exploiting the relatively inefficient market in unquoted equity. The critical question is always whether such costs may be deemed to be excessive. The Bolton Committee research studies, however, failed to find a significant number of deserving firms which were unable to raise finance on reasonable terms. In effect the availability, or lack of it, of funds for smaller firms shades into the existence of an 'information gap' which is discussed in more detail in the following chapters and developed in our conclusion. Indeed, the evidence to the Bolton Committee suggested that most of the unfortunate firms not having obtained finance were experiencing an information gap about appropriate existing sources of finance.

Agency costs also enter the question of the substantive composition of the gap in the provision of capital to smaller firms (Puxty 1985; Eisenhardt 1989; see also Baiman 1990). Relationships with financial intermediaries are central to the question of small-firm funding, particularly for the growth-oriented smaller firm with which we are concerned. The principal–agent problems of small firms are intrinsically limited: entrepreneurial owner–managers (and their families) control equity, while working capital can be provided by the well-informed clearing bank. Investors are 'insiders' with high-quality information about the firm and few contractual problems in relationships with managers of their capital. Virtually by definition the growing small firm outstrips not only its own internally generated capital from retained earnings but also the capacity or portfolio-based risk-aversion of its owner–entrepreneurs. While continued trading by a financially stable enterprise may depend on rolling over bank overdrafts, planned growth will require an investment of 'permanent' capital, whether equity or long-term debt. If recourse to a stock exchange quotation is not feasible, then the supply of external capital will depend on the willingness of banks to extend longer-term loans, or venture-capital intermediaries, individuals as well as institutions, to extend equity and also debt. It is here that agency costs may arise, as the requirements of 'outsider' investors proliferate and their contractual problems become more complex and costly to resolve.

THE SIGNIFICANCE OF AGENCY COSTS

Suppliers of 'external' capital, whether new equity or debt or hybrids and derivatives, may be concerned that the original owner–entrepreneur or owner–managers may seek to transfer wealth from new shareholders to themselves, whether by transformation of the business risk of the firm or by expenditure on abnormal fringe benefits. So financial intermediaries, for example banks, will set conditions upon the provision of long-term loans embodied in formal contracts which mean that the effective cost of such finance is increased. One example of this is where the bank requires conformation with specific restrictions on working capital ratios (for example, on ratios of stocks and debtors to creditors) which effectively increases the firms' cost of working capital. Citron (1992) examines the use of financial ratio covenants in UK bank loan contracts by reference to the attitudes of lending bankers. Another version may occur when prospective new investors set formal conditions for the supply of such capital, by, for example, investing only in participating preference shares, with powers of conversion to voting ordinary shares in the event of default on preference share dividends or capital repayment. The incidence of agency costs is likely to impact more severely upon smaller firms by virtue of their relative lack of power in agency relationships. Jensen and Meckling (1976) put forward three main elements for agency costs: monitoring costs, for example, restrictive covenants; bonding costs, arising from a contractual obligation by the agent (here, the small firm) not to undertake business detrimental to the principal (the bank, or 'external' equity investor); and residual loss, arising, for example, from economic opportunity costs as a result of the impact upon full economic potential of the resolution of the problems in monitoring and bonding.

Therefore, for the smaller firm agency costs assume a similar effect to that postulated for larger firms within the theory of the firm. Fear of take-over obliges managers of larger firms to look to defend their stock market valuation by, for example, 'satisficing' dividend policies; this in turn constrains those firms' ability to use retained earnings to finance growth. For smaller firms dependent upon retaining continued bank support, which is the mainstay of their 'external' capital sources, the relevant constraint is that embodied in the performance requirements of essential lenders. Their support for client firms has traditionally been facilitated by the provision of security, whether based on the corporate assets of the borrower or the personal guarantee of the director or sole trader. As the Wilson Committee's investigations revealed, 'The most common complaint ... was that the level of security demanded by the banks was excessive' (Wilson 1980).

Compounding that, particularly for prospective new entrants to the Stock Exchange but also clearly applicable across all firms, is the issue of accounting conventions of prudence (Buckland and Davis 1990a). This conservatism in book values may be particularly inhibiting for the growing small firm, where such conventions will impact upon the treatment of intangible assets and goodwill. At the margin the quality of security would determine the bank's attitude. Under severe trading conditions therefore, such as those evident in the UK recession of 1990–93, there could be a perceived imbalance between the longer-term prospects of a given enterprise, its current trading experience and the quality of security. Under such circumstances it is hardly surprising that the banks, with their cultures and traditions oriented towards the shorter-term lending proposition, should seek to foreclose when security appeared vulnerable.

A variant but complementary interpretation may be found in the 'pecking order hypothesis' (Myers and Majluf 1984). The essence of this theory is that capital is raised in a sequence designed to minimise dilution of equity and control. In effect, therefore, retentions and debt would be preferred to new issues of equity. Indeed, evidence from the UK (Cosh and Hughes 1994) is consistent with this interpretation, under which owner–entrepreneurs' reluctance to dilute equity but willingness to incur debt may also act as a signal to prospective suppliers of capital. The question of the demand for capital and the attitude of owner–entrepreneurs to external equity is, of course, very important. Virtually by definition, fast-growth smaller firms are more likely than others to exceed their internally generated cash flow or, indeed, the willingness of owners to incur greater specific risk by further increasing the weight of equity investment from their own personal capital. Transactions costs for raising new external equity capital on a public stock exchange particularly discriminate against smaller issuers by virtue of administrative and market pricing costs. This, however, does not take account of the greater 'compliance' or in effect, agency costs incurred by a public quoted company compared with a private firm, arising from more exacting legal and reporting requirements. By comparison the transactions and agency-based compliance costs of borrowing from one's local banker may seem more attractive.

The attractions of an ordered preference for retained earnings and debt must also reflect the long-recognised (King 1977) significance of tax, personal as well as corporate, which has undeniably influenced UK companies in this direction. While changes in UK personal and corporate tax systems in the 1980s will have reduced the scope of this effect, fiscal considerations can still provide an explanation for the continued attraction of borrowing and the reluctance to create new shares.

SECONDARY CAPITAL MARKETS AND THE EMERGENT FIRM

In their preparation for quotation, firms put themselves into novel financing and information arenas: they also expose themselves to searching appraisal of their organisation and business. In researching the implications of this change in status for the growing firm, attention needs to be paid both to the firm and to the market within which the firm moves. In the former, there are issues of strategic and organisational maturity. As the firm grows, it shifts from immature organisational structures and naive strategic planning mechanisms, moving towards adoption of robust and sustainable management structures and planning processes. Chapter 13 by Buckland and Davis examines some of the issues that are seen to arise within entrants to the UK quoted equity markets.

In the markets themselves, the quotation 'product' has to be designed to be attractive to the range of interests in equity financing. The overwhelming bulk of investment in secondarily quoted equities comes from institutional investment funds, professionally managed in a competitive marketplace in funds management: such securitised and managed funds adopt different perspectives and monitoring structures than do private and insider equity holders (Ashton et al. 1991). As the risk-management, information-handling and transactions-costs economies of securitisation spread through capital markets the share of institutional intermediaries in the funding of emergent firms is likely to increase rather than diminish; and the newly quoted growing firm needs to adjust to the perspectives and financial attitudes of that community. The quotation must also serve the interests of the remaining and the vendor shareholders of the growing enterprise: investors who may be realising part of their personal wealth or their commercial portfolio of venture-capital investments, and investors who remain involved as insider investors, closely associated with the newly quoted firm's strategy. The market's operators are also interested in the quotation process: brokers and issuing houses which wish to secure options on the valuable future business in the growing firm's financing and secondary securities business, and arbitrageurs who hope to benefit from perceiving disequilibrium in the issuing processes themselves.

Consequently, there is continuing intense academic attention to the workings of markets in newly quoted shares, not only in the United Kingdom but across the world: in the USA, in continental Europe, in the emerging stock markets of the Far East and, latterly, Eastern Europe (for example, Ibbotson et al. 1988; Aggarwal and Rivoli 1990; Ritter 1991). Academic models of the quotation process revolve around asymmetric information economics, where intermediaries seek to interest informationally estranged outsiders into becoming shareholders in the place of, and often alongside, the long-standing insider owner–managers of the emergent business. The process has been variously modelled: by price–pressure hypotheses (for example, Scholes 1972; Ibbotson 1975); by deployment of option theory, as in Dimson's (1979) contribution; and in the adverse selection analysis of Rock's (1986) asymmetric information model.

In the latter, now dominant as the foundation of new-quotation pricing behaviour, it is suggested that imperfectly-informed outsider applicants for equities tend to bid in the expectation of introductory gains, but that the better-informed insiders will abstain from bidding where gains do not exist, while crowding out the outsiders when gains are in evidence. Hence, if newly quoted shares are fairly priced at entry, the outsider will have no incentive, on average, to bid; in turn, Rock argues, issuers must underprice initial public offerings (IPOs) at entry in order to provide incentives to the outsider.

Rock's model is attractive, and borne out in practice (see, for example, Muscarella and Vetsuypens 1989; Levis 1990): however, it does not explain discounting in all pricing environments (in tendering procedures or in the dominant UK method of the placing of shares, for example). Chapter 10, by Buckland, on UK pricing procedures, and the subsequent examination of continental European models of innovation in new quotation for the growing firm contributed by Anolli, Buckland and Dubois, together with the fascinating case-study approach developed in Steele's chapter on the Sock Shop International quotation of Spring 1987, throw critical attention on the continuing debate over pricing procedures and how they affect the growing firm during quotation. They also provide insights into the experiences and the problems faced by growing firms when making the transition from the semi-private world of the unquoted company to the exposed informational marketplace of quotation.

These chapters on the innovations in marketing growing firms' equities also point towards the international dimension of the problems of financing growing firms. The UK preoccupation with financing gaps would be familiar territory in other economies (for example, the Rapport Dautresme in France, Dautresme 1983), and the relationship of growth financing to the 'short-termism' of financing systems is one which underlies innovation, experimentation, and especially the state's involvement in the financing of industry (Cox 1986; Marsh 1990). The contributions here throw light upon these issues, and we return to them in the conclusion to the volume.

FINANCING METHODS AND THE STAGES OF GROWTH

Our preceding analysis sets out the domain for the subsequent chapters which constitute this book. These provide a review ranging from the financing behaviour and performance of fairly small firms to the significance of the capital market for new entrants to the Stock Exchange. One omission, deferred until now, is that of a definition of the population of firms under review. This is not a book about the financing of small firms nor a survey of modes of or attitudes towards the financing of the small- or medium-sized enterprise. What concern us are the issues surrounding the transition of the growing firm: the financing problems raised by its emergence into growth and maturity as an organisation. Therefore we are not concerned with any technical classification of firms based on size, whether assets, profits, market capitalisation or number of employees. The critical factors about the firms in these studies are: first, their relative lack of economic power in the financial marketplace; and second, their potential for growth.

The first of these very general descriptions implies that most of these firms are small, but also typically relatively young, perhaps distinctively innovative, and generally growing relatively quickly. Thus in this book we will necessarily be concerned with facets of small-firm finance. Chapters 2–6 by Bovaird, Hems and Tricker, Binks and Ennew, Keasey and Watson, Harrison and Mason, and Murray tend to concentrate on financing and banking relationships for relatively smaller firms. The potential for growth, however, identified under our second description invites us to examine financial innovations, markets and corporate financing behaviour more commonly associated with larger firms – that of the financing behaviour of companies able to resort to a stock exchange quotation. Chapters 7–11 by Davis, Hall and Hutchinson, Buckland and Davis, Buckland and Steele, consider this category of 'successful' firm which has attained the status of a stock exchange quotation.

The book, therefore, covers a range of financing choices available to the growing small firm according to their evolutionary process, from complete dependence on owner's capital (plus bank finance) through interim states involving participation by venture capitalists to that of the fully fledged stock market quotation. Inevitably there is some overlap of the various chapters involved. Firms considered under the final category, growth firms obtaining a stock exchange quotation, continue to have banking relationships, which may indeed be just as critical to them as to the relatively smaller firms in the first category. Amongst the unquoted firms, questions of external equity capital may be vital both to their immediate survival and to the longer-term growth potential of the firm. In sum the book comprises a span of research dealing with:

(a) critical financing relationships, policy choices and costs for the growth-oriented small firm; and
(b) a range of financing innovations generated within the UK in the 1980s of particular relevance to the finance of growth.

A SUMMARY OUTLINE OF CHAPTER CONTENT

Chapter 2 by Bovaird, Hems and Tricker focuses upon the smaller firms within the SME category. Their contribution derives from an extensive study conducted by the Public Sector Research Unit of Aston Business School, which reviewed not only financing constraints but also problems associated with the quality of management and availability of labour. In their chapter Bovaird et al. provide useful founding definitions of the concepts of market failure in the supply and demand for finance, while also establishing an operational concept of market failure linked with a review of previous research into financial constraints on fast-growth small firms.

On this basis, Binks and Ennew (Chapter 3), followed by Keasey and Watson (Chapter 4), consider the role of bank finance for small businesses. As with Bovaird et al., the orientation of both these chapters lies more with the smaller firm, not yet able to command a stock exchange quotation but whose financing behaviour involves banking relationships. In the evolutionary progression of the smaller firm the relationship with banks is of particular importance, given that for many of the smaller firms considered by Bovaird et al., Binks and Ennew, and Keasey and Watson, bank borrowing constitutes the immediately accessible form of low-cost external capital. Within their review of the theoretical framework affecting small-firm financing behaviour, Binks and Ennew consider how information asymmetry poses problems for debt finance, the implications of which they further consider from the perspective of adverse selection and moral hazard. In terms of practical implementation in particular, they comment upon the role of collateral or security in bonding issuers of debt and the traditional reliance of the UK deposit banks on a capital-gearing approach to loan evaluation.

In their chapter Keasey and Watson provide an illuminating background to the development of UK bank policies towards small firms. They go on to consider small-firm debt and equity finance and those characteristics of small firms that tend to produce inherent conflicts with lenders. On this basis they then proceed to investigate, through published accounts, the financing behaviour of 110 UK small firms in the second half of the 1980s. Of particular interest is their discussion of the principal difficulties that banks experience in assessing small-firm risk.

Chapters 5 and 6, by Harrison and Mason, and by Murray respectively, consider 'informal' equity markets, embracing within that definition both individual and institutional forms of venture-capital investment. The importance of these developments (or the related management buy-out market) is not just a matter of the scale and impact of the funds raised. What may matter far more is the impact of a process whereby the owner–entrepreneur has to confront and reckon with the performance requirements of external equity investors, whose realisation of prospective gain will depend on strategies and systems directed towards growth. While the process of bank borrowing will have at least sharpened small firms' attention to cash flows, planning and control, the interests of 'informal' external equity investors will lie more in the exit values to be derived from a successful investment, whether that exit is by trade sale or during stock exchange flotation. That objective will in turn depend upon the growth of maintainable real profits. Focus upon the management requirements necessary to achieve that is likely to be enhanced by the intermediation/transaction processes involved in raising 'external' equity capital.

When new external investors are sought on an equity basis, the issues of changing principal–agent relationships are brought to the fore. While debt contracts will involve the management of bonding and monitoring between the lender and the firm's owners and management, new equity partners will introduce complexities of shared control, distinctions of inside and outside equity, systemic impacts upon existing and future borrowing relationships, and potentially valuable option elements in rights issues and future financing activity. In the traditional Anglo-US corporate growth model the apex of the growth of the SME may be considered to be that of a stock exchange quotation. Through quotation the emergent firm gains informed access to a free market in outside financing, with potentially unlimited volumes of long-term financing for growth projects, whether they be organic or in growth by acquisition. While non-quoted firms may continue to grow and prosper they are unlikely to maintain high growth trajectories, or to become global, multinational enterprises. By studying firms which have attained the particular growth stage of quoted status we can consider not only the particular financing methods involved, but also the historical perspectives of the financing and real strategies behind firms' growth.

Chapters 7–10 by Davis, Hall and Hutchinson, Buckland and Davis, and Buckland, involve cross-section surveys of large numbers of firms obtaining stock exchange quotations in the 1970s and 1980s. They address the traditional mythologies surrounding quotation: the nature of financing problems experienced by firms around quotation, the costs of attaining the new status, and the pricing processes imposed upon entrants by stock exchanges. We also include in contributions by Buckland and Davis in Chapter 9, and in particular by Steele in Chapter 11, the use of case-study methodology. While the survey methodology clearly affords greater opportunity for more robust conclusions with regard to general financing behaviour of such firms, the case studies examined in these chapters provide insights into corporate growth and in particular the substance of the relationship between entrepreneurs and financial intermediaries and markets.

2

MARKET FAILURES IN THE PROVISION OF FINANCE AND BUSINESS SERVICES FOR SMALL AND MEDIUM-SIZED ENTERPRISES

Tony Bovaird, Les Hems and Mike Tricker

INTRODUCTION

In this chapter we explore the meaning and empirical importance of the welfare economics concept of market failure in the specific context of the markets for finance and consultancy services for small and medium-sized enterprises (SMEs). In the empirical work reported in this paper, small firms are defined as those employing up to 50 (full-time equivalent) workers and medium-sized firms as those employing up to 500 workers.

We consider whether the long-suggested 'funding gap' for small firms is important in current economic circumstances in the UK. The chapter then looks at the likelihood that such market failures which exist on the demand side might be put right by the appropriate use of business consultancy services.

The empirical analysis consists of two sections. The first reviews the main conclusions from the literature of the last twenty years relating to constraints on the growth and innovation of SMEs in order to identify previous estimates of the incidence and likely extent of market failure. Secondly, the results of two recent major surveys by Aston Business School are reported, with a description of the methodology which was developed specifically to pinpoint the level of market failure in finance for small firms and the extent of the barriers to using consultancy services.

TONY BOVAIRD, LES HEMS, MIKE TRICKER

THE CONCEPT OF MARKET FAILURE IN FINANCE AND CONSULTANCY SERVICES FOR SMALL FIRMS

The concept of market failure in welfare economics denotes a situation in which goods or services are not made available to those demanding them at the lowest possible social cost. Thus Stiglitz (1988) defines market failure as occurring when 'the market is not Pareto-efficient' and Jackson (1993) suggests that it occurs when there are information asymmetries and principal–agent problems in markets.

Market failure can arise from two different sources in any market: from the behaviour of either the suppliers of goods and services or from the demanders of those goods and services.

Supply-side market failure in finance occurs when financial institutions turn down proposals for finance for reasons which are not connected with the viability of the proposal itself (e.g. because of the firm's lack of a 'track record'). Such market failure may occur even where an offer of finance is made, e.g. if the terms are more unfavourable than is warranted by the degree of risk in the proposal.

However, supply-side market failure cannot be inferred simply because firms report difficulties in raising finance: if their business propositions are unviable, then the market is justified in refusing to finance them. Again, the need to apply to more than one lender, in order to raise finance for a proposition which is likely to be viable, does not necessarily denote market failure, since individual financial institutions may be fully 'lent up' within their portfolios in the particular class of risk represented by the proposal concerned. (For example, Schaeffer and Pulver (1985) found that an initial credit denial rate of 25 per cent for new small firms in Wisconsin fell to 5 per cent after they approached a second or third source.)

Market failure in the provision of finance occurs when finance is refused for projects which can be expected to be commercially viable. In order to make this concept of market failure operational, a definition is needed which is precise enough to allow detailed empirical investigation. This raises the question of who is to determine when market failure has occurred. Clearly, there will always be two sides to every potential identification of market failure. A firm may believe its application for finance for a potentially high-profit project has been turned down simply because the bank manager is prejudiced against female (or black, or Jewish, or disabled, or working-class) entrepreneurs; from the bank's perspective, however, the refusal may appear to have conformed to its normal commercial criteria.

This discrepancy can arise from a number of areas of judgement which are necessary in identifying market failure, areas where the judgement of different actors (or analysts) might reasonably differ. In this sense, market failure is and must remain a social construct, the application of which is determined by the social and economic conditions of the time. This does not lessen its value as a conceptual category in any way, as its basic purpose is, in any case, to demonstrate the essentially negative point that outcomes determined in the course of market processes are neither inevitable nor necessarily socially desirable.

These areas of judgement in the identification of market failure revolve around the perception of the commercial viability of the project. The main ways in which different judgements can emerge about this viability are:

- differing projections of market demand;
- differing projections of production cost;
- differing projections of management adaptability in dealing with unexpected outcomes;
- differing minimum rates of return required;
- differing tolerance towards risk and uncertainty levels.

Clearly, differences in judgement on all of these factors in a project are to be expected in all markets; they are not in themselves sufficient evidence for market failure. Supply-side market failure will only arise when *each* of the following conditions is met in this market environment of differing expectations:

- no financing source shares the overall view of the project held by the project proposer;
- the projections made by the proposer are consistent with the range of past available data for such a project or closely parallel projects;
- the projections made by the financing sources differ from those made by the proposer solely for reasons which do not relate to this project, taken alone, but for other reasons which essentially derive from 'averages' (i.e. stereotypes) derived from past experience with such projects, firms, entrepreneurs etc. (often codified or embodied in 'rule-books' or 'lending criteria').

Demand-side market failure in finance occurs when firms do not properly make use of the financial opportunities available, through lack of knowledge, poor management or inadequate presentation of proposals (for example, failure to provide an up-to-date business plan including the proposed innovation or investment).

One method by which firms might respond to minimise the consequences of market failure in financing would be to use appropriate management consultancy services in order to find funding sources, to make convincing cases to potential funders and, in addition, to make external funding less essential by raising the level of profits available for internal investment.

Parallel definitions can be constructed for market failure in the market for consultancy services:

- supply-side market failure exists when consultancy services are not available to firms which would be prepared to pay a full commercial price for their provision;
- demand-side market failure exists when firms do not properly make use of the consultancy services available to them in the market.

Interestingly, very little attention has been paid in the economics literature to why such market failures, particularly on the supply side, might occur; just as financing problems are seen by SMEs as much more important than problems arising from their own managerial competence, so potential market failures in helping them to alleviate their internal managerial problems are given much less attention.

Operationalising the concept of market failure

Clearly, a two-pronged approach is required to identify potential market failure in empirical investigations; the perceptions of both applicants for and providers of finance should be taken into account and the reasons for the differing perceptions should be explored. However, this is rarely possible within the one study. A fall-back solution is to probe the one side of the transaction about the behaviour of the other, for example, asking firms what reasons banks gave for turning down proposals or asking banks what were the main weaknesses which they identified in the firms making proposals. This highlights *potential market failure*, without demonstrating finally that actual market failure has occurred. This was the approach adopted in the recent government-sponsored research reported here and in Aston Business School (1991) and in Cousins Stephens Associates (1991).

In the survey-based research recently carried out by Aston Business School, potential supply-side market failure was identified as existing when the reasons given to firms for refusing their applications for finance included such non-commercial criteria as:

- the firm lacked a track record;
- the project was 'too novel';
- there was inadequate security for a loan;
- the project was viable but the firm is at the limit of its borrowing;
- the business was poorly located;
- the type of entrepreneur (for example, ethnic origin or other characteristics);
- the industrial sector;
- there were poor financial figures in the previous year;
- the project was 'high tech' and therefore too risky;
- there was unwillingness to support purchase of second-hand (as opposed to new) machinery;
- 'expansion of the firm is too rapid'.

Clearly some of these responses would not be taken in all cases as indicating actual market failure. Since they highlight *potential* market failure, as seen from the perspective of the firm seeking finance, they may therefore overestimate the *actual* level of market failure. In order to explore the level of demand-side market failure, the first Aston Business School survey asked SMEs about their awareness of alternative financial sources (including public-sector sources of grants and loans) and about their use of financial advisers in making loan applications. In the second ABS survey on consultancy services, SMEs were asked a series of detailed questions on their knowledge of help available in putting together business plans, market plans and other improvements to their management practices; their past use of such services; and their attitude to future use of such services. Market failure was directly identifiable in certain instances but more often it was inferred from comparing responses to different questions.

EVIDENCE FROM PREVIOUS STUDIES

In this section, we review the findings of previous studies into the main characteristics of growth-oriented and innovatory small and medium-sized enterprises and the constraints which have inhibited their development, particularly those arising from labour, premises, managerial and financial factors. In each case we examine the extent to which the evidence indicates that market failure may have been a reason for the problems experienced by the SMEs and whether this market failure arose from the behaviour of the SMEs or from the behaviour of the financial and consultancy services sectors.

Growth orientation of small firms

Much of the research into small and medium-sized enterprises has assumed that all such firms wish to grow larger. This assumption also lies behind much government policy which tries to demonstrate to small firms how to overcome the barriers constraining their growth. Yet there is clear evidence that many small firms do not wish to grow and this needs to be borne in mind when designing and interpreting questionnaire surveys of small businesses (such as the surveys reported in later sections of this chapter).

Falk (1978) outlined the following phases in the development of a typical business:

- embryonic (hobby or part-time enterprise);
- infant (full-time employment for one or more people);
- youthful (basic work processes mechanised);
- institutionalised (management and production roles clearly separated).

However, there are no studies which have estimated the relative numbers of small firms in these different phases, nor the rate at which firms typically move between phases. A parallel model for declining firms is also lacking.

One research study carried out for the Bolton Committee in 1971 concluded that small firms were roughly evenly divided on whether growth was desirable, although it also suggested that many of the firms which expressed a positive view were perhaps only indicating lip service to the idea of growth, rather than a commitment (Golby and Johns 1971). These estimates are roughly consistent with those of Hakim (1988), who reported that about 50 per cent of all small firms in Great Britain regard themselves as 'growth-oriented'.

Indirect evidence for a lower level of growth-orientation is supplied by Hankinson (quoted in Curran 1986), whose examination of a sample of small engineering firms concluded that typically owner–managers of small firms did not optimise investment, investing rather only out of necessity when survival depended on the purchase of new equipment. The owner–managers, as in many other studies, were found to be loath to plan ahead to any marked extent. However, a European study of 600 small manufacturing enterprises in Britain, France and West Germany reported that majorities of SME owners in all three countries expressed a desire for growth, either in a new product or their existing line (Watkins and Morton 1982).

One recent smaller-scale survey has also arrived at much higher estimates; but its sample composition is not strictly comparable. Turok and Richardson (1989) found that almost two-thirds (64 per cent) of a sample of 196 small firms in West Lothian in Scotland were expecting to grow, but fairly slowly and steadily, while a further 16 per cent of small firms were seeking fast growth. The firms in this survey were, however, fairly new (started either in 1984 or 1987) and therefore arguably more likely to be seeking expansion.

Innovation in small firms

Given the risks attached to innovation and the likelihood that all actors will have difficulties in managing it – from the initiation to the implementation and dissemination stages – it is especially important to establish the extent of market failure for those small and medium-sized enterprises which set out to be highly innovative. Unfortunately, the literature does not help us much in establishing the dimensions of innovation activity in SMEs. The Bolton Committee did not analyse separately the levels of process and product innovation in small firms. Instead it sought to compare the contributions made by small and large firms to manufacturing inventions and innovations. The debate has continued without resolution since that time.

A CBI study in 1983 suggested that larger firms show a greater tendency than smaller firms to invest in order to replace capital and to increase efficiency but that a higher proportion of smaller firms invest to expand capacity (CBI 1983: based on about 850 small firms, defined as having 200 employees or fewer). Moreover, the recent West Lothian study of 196 fairly new firms found that more than two-thirds (69 per cent) of firms had taken some deliberate action in the previous six months to improve performance or growth prospects, through expanding their product range (38 per cent) or developing new markets (45 per cent) or investing in major new equipment (45 per cent) (Turok and Richardson 1989). Of those 22 firms which were categorised as 'growth firms' in this study, 57 per cent had expanded their product range, 62 per cent had developed new markets and 81 per cent had made major investments in new equipment.

However, a very different picture is painted by Curran (1986), who stresses that the vast majority of small firms play virtually no part in technological and other forms of business innovation. Most small businesses are 'straightforward replicas of existing enterprises run by those who have neither the ability nor the inclination to innovate' and often do so only reluctantly and as a necessity for survival. At the same time, it is necessary to recognise that innovations by SMEs form part of a larger, interrelated innovation process in which *dynamic complementarities* exist between small and large firms throughout the product/process cycle (Rothwell 1986). Curran emphasises, however, the lack of research on small enterprises and technology transfer.

A very different literature highlights the potential innovative role of small firms in regional business systems and (in some cases) in 'new industrial districts', based on the growth of flexible specialisation and inter-organisational networking (Piore and Sabel 1984; Bovaird 1993). The prime examples of such areas are usually said to be Emilia Romagna in 'Middle Italy' and Silicon Valley, USA (with the possibility that the M4 corridor is generating a UK equivalent), but many others have also been suggested (Scott 1988; Henry 1992). The importance of flexible specialisation, and the role within it of networks of small firms is still highly contentious and few clear conclusions have so far emerged from the debate (Lovering 1990; Tickell and Peck 1992). This discussion, therefore, highlights rather than invalidates the need for an investigation of the relative importance for small firms of innovation in product development and process technology compared with non-innovatory capital deepening.

Labour constraints

The Bolton Committee did not explicitly mention shortage of labour, whether skilled or unskilled, as a substantial problem for small firms (although it was cited as a factor in several of the background research papers, for example Merrett Cyriax Associates (1971) and Golby and Johns (1971). The Committee concluded that small firms were not 'poachers' of trained manpower on a significant scale, nor were they in this respect any worse than large firms. In doing so, it dismissed as relatively unimportant the market failure (externality) imposed upon firms which carry out training by those firms which rely upon poaching ready-trained labour.

Subsequent research in the 1970s and 1980s seemed to confirm that skilled labour shortages were either not important in small firms (CBI 1983) or less important than finance problems (Opinion Research Centre survey, reported in Clifton and Tatton-Brown (1979)). The West Lothian study of recently created firms found that only 10 per cent of firms gave lack of workforce skills as the most important constraint on their expansion. However, a rather higher proportion (14 per cent) of growth-oriented firms stated that this was a problem (Turok and Richardson 1989).

A recent Coopers and Lybrand (1990) survey did not ask direct questions about constraints on firms, but did investigate which forms of assistance firms most required from support agencies. Assistance with training was mentioned by 16 per cent of respondents. Only direct financial advice (at 26 per cent) and business information and advice (at 17 per cent) had a higher rating.

Curran and Blackburn (1990), writing before the current recession had taken hold, suggested that small firms have traditionally recruited disproportionately from male workers under 25 years of age and would find it difficult to switch to recruiting older workers and women, in a period when the numbers of young labour-force joiners would be declining sharply. Since larger companies have more resources to attract and retain young workers, small firms are likely to face increasing skill shortages. The reluctance of small and medium-sized firms to address such problems by positive action is shown by a recent study of 303 such firms in the engineering sector in the West Midlands which found that 40 per cent of firms spent less than £1,000 on training in the previous year (WEMTECH 1990).

Labour constraints may arise either through a lack of availability of skilled or unskilled workers at the going wage rate or due to the unwillingness or inability of small firms to pay the going market wage rate. Most of the research reported above has simply assumed that reported labour shortages have arisen from the former cause and very little attempt has been made to establish the extent and level of the latter problem. The labour constraints on the growth of small firms identified above only constitute market failure if the former cause prevails.

Premises constraints

Although the Bolton Committee did not identify shortage of premises as a general problem affecting small firms which needed legislative redress or policy change, by 1980 a number of reports were suggesting that the market supply of premises constituted a problem. Coopers and Lybrand Associates (1980) argued that 'there is a clear evidence that the shortage of premises has constrained the establishment and development of small firms; the provision of premises on suitable terms has undoubtedly itself had the effect of stimulating the formation of new firms and the growth of existing small firms'. Further studies indicated that premises problems ranked high on the list of constraints perceived by businesses (Thomas 1978; Glyn-Jones 1982; Williams et al. 1980; Tricker and Bozeat 1983). Perry (1986) concluded that without public intervention it would have taken several years for market rents to rise sufficiently to tempt private development of requisite numbers of small units, particularly in Assisted Areas.

However, Fothergill et al. (1987) suggest that recent research has rightly played down the significance of property in the formation and growth of small firms. While, in some areas, shortages of small properties have been so acute that the growth of firms has been stultified, it is perhaps more characteristic of small firms that they continue to operate from a myriad of converted and second-hand premises, rather than go out of business because a suitable property cannot be found. Nevertheless, they go on to conclude ('with some certainty') 'that if in recent years there had not been an explosion in the provision of new, small factory units the expansion of the small firm sector would have been frustrated'.

Coopers and Lybrand (1990) reported that just under 30 per cent of all firms with between 11 and 50 employees needed help with their premises (as compared to 16 per cent of all firms in their sample). For firms of this size, premises assistance ranked equal with direct financial help as the most important area in which support was required.

In summary, while market failure in the supply of premises for small firms seems to have been frequently identified, there is still no clear consensus about its significance in constraining small-firm growth.

Managerial constraints

Curran (1986) summarises the literature on the characteristics of small-business owner–managers as follows: '[They] often display exceptionally high needs for autonomy and independence. In turn, these characteristics influence managerial strategies and styles which show a marked reluctance to delegate authority, to set up well defined role structures within the enterprise or to plan explicitly for the future.'

A study of 600 SMEs in Britain, France and West Germany (Watkins and Morton 1982) found that in each country the three most important threats to a firm's survival were perceived by the firms themselves to be availability of finance, difficulty in complying with new laws and regulations, and marketing problems (though the order of priority varied between the countries). However, the financial institutions interviewed in the same study were much less concerned about difficulties of compliance with new laws and regulations and much more concerned with the managerial capability of the owner, which was given first rank in France and second rank in Britain and West Germany.

A more recent survey of banks and venture-capital sources in the UK concluded that, where lack of funding was apparently a constraint on the development of small firms, many of the problems could in fact be traced to weaknesses in management ability or structure, rather than the inappropriate behaviour of funding sources (Cousins Stephens Associates 1991).

Product planning and marketing have been found to be particular areas of managerial weakness in small firms. Hankinson (quoted in Curran 1986) found that small manufacturing firms accorded a low priority to marketing. A recent survey of 303 SMEs in the engineering sector in the West Midlands indicated that the level of market planning was poor or non-existent in some 42 per cent of firms and that only half systematically collected market information data. Nearly two-thirds of these firms felt that their traditional product ranges were vulnerable to imports, indicating lack of adequate product-range development by the firms. Nevertheless, only 28 per cent had so far introduced procedures to enable them to comply with the relevant British Standards requirements (WEMTECH 1990).

Gill (1985) found that even those start-ups which had received management training were unable rationally to approach their day-to-day problems, let alone plan for the future. Most were 'fire-fighting' and recognised that their management skills were inadequate but hoped to learn fast enough to get by until the enterprise gained a more stable footing. However, small firms are understandably reluctant to blame themselves for all of the managerial problems they face: thus only 14 per cent of growth firms in the recent West Lothian study (and 7 per cent of stable firms) highlighted lack of managerial skills as a constraint on their expansion (Turok and Richardson 1989). Curran (1986) summarises the literature as showing that there is a tendency for owner–managers who have survived this risky start-up period 'to opt for a "steady state" existence, managing their firms cautiously and rarely either taking risks or adopting established management techniques for optimising the enterprise's performance'.

Market failure through lack of managerial competence might be offset if firms make use of supplementary sources of management expertise, such as those which are available through management consultancy services.

There has, however, been surprisingly little research into the levels of usage of consultancy and other information and advice services by SMEs in the UK. An unpublished survey carried out for the DTI by Industrial Market Research Limited in 1983 involved a sample of 415 manufacturing and service-sector firms in selected regions of England. The results indicated that 32 per cent of firms with fewer than 500 employees had made use of consultancy services in the previous three years (Industrial and Market Research 1984). However, the variation was wide: over 50 per cent of firms with more than 200 employees had used consultants and over 50 per cent of firms involved in professional and computer services had used consultancy services, whilst only 15 per cent of firms with under 10 employees had done so.

No previous surveys give such a comprehensive overall perspective. However, some other partial studies help to complement these findings. In surveying business needs Coopers and Lybrand (1990) report that the need for more or better business information and advice was mentioned by only 17 per cent of all firms (although it was mentioned by 23 per cent of firms with under 10 employees). On the other hand, the early evaluation of the Consultancy Initiatives carried out for the DTI showed that 53 per cent of firms which were assisted under the first phase of the scheme (early 1988) had used consultants previously (Segal, Quince, Wicksteed Ltd 1989). Of course, early applicants for assistance were especially likely to include firms which were favourably disposed towards the use of consultants. (Indeed, this study concluded that 22 per cent of these firms would have undertaken the same consultancy even without the DTI assistance.)

Since 1988, MORI has been commissioned by the DTI to track the use of consultants by SMEs. Their earliest estimates suggested that 37 per cent of firms had used consultants previously (MORI 1988), rising to around half by 1991; however, these tracking surveys were based on a sample frame believed to under-represent the smallest size bands of firms (Aston Business School 1992).

None of these previous surveys has been constructed in such a way as to allow exploration of the underlying level of market failure in managerial competence and the contribution of consultancy services to alleviating these market failures.

The widespread use of management consultancy is, however, ambiguous in that it could either signal widespread market failure, partially recognised and responded to by the firms concerned, or it could mean the virtual elimination of market failure through the firms concerned making the appropriate response. What is required, therefore, is some research into the extent to which consultancy studies have failed to equip firms to deal with their own managerial problems or have given them such a sound trading position that they can afford to buy in required managerial expertise (for example, specialist marketing or financial advice) in the future when the need arises. Only the study reported later in this chapter has given detailed examination to such issues.

Constraints on the availability of finance

The Bolton Committee (1971) concluded that there was no institutional deficiency in the finance market for small firms and that, while there were some differences in the bases on which small and large firms could raise money, these were mostly functions of inherent cost and scale differences and did not justify government intervention in either the availability of finance or the cost of finance to small firms.

This conclusion was based on the view that the 'Macmillan Gap', which had been a feature of small firms' finance from the 1930s, had been filled in the 1960s by the development of new types of financial institutions, and that consequently finance could not be provided on a commercial basis more cheaply than it was already in 1971.

The research studies carried out for the Bolton Committee failed to find a significant number of clearly deserving firms which were unable to raise finance on reasonable terms. The Economists Advisory Group (1971) carried out a sample survey of small firms which had made unsuccessful approaches to financial institutions. They found only one or two firms in their sample of 50 which needed finance, deserved it, had made serious efforts to get it and had been turned down. (They were also surprised to find that some firms which they considered uncreditworthy had been able to obtain outside finance.) The Economists Advisory Group therefore suggested in summary that there was some slight evidence that the 'market mechanism is sometimes deficient in spotting the winners among infant (as opposed to simply small) firms, whose immediate past performance has been unimpressive, but which, if they could achieve a 'take-off' in their growth, would become the successful small or medium-sized firms of the future'. Their main conclusion, in accord with that reached by the Bolton Committee, was that there was 'no single major defect in financial facilities for small firms that calls for radical action'.

The Bolton research studies pointed up very forcibly, however, that many small firms were prevented, by lack of information and by prejudice against borrowing, from making use of the full range of financial facilities available to them. Thus the 'finance gap' was in fact an 'information gap' plus an 'availability of funds gap'. The Economists Advisory Group (1971) concluded that most of the firms which they considered unfortunate not to have obtained finance had been insufficiently informed or poorly advised about the appropriate sources of finance or had failed to make out a good enough case to the supplying institutions which they had approached. This analysis has proved very powerful – this 'information gap' has since provided the rationale for many of the activities of enterprise agencies and small-firms advisory services which have sought to provide firms with comprehensive information on funding sources and the means for accessing these.

The Wilson Committee (1979) concluded that financial institutions were cautious about lending to small firms and that there were far more financial avenues open to large firms than to small ones. It was not able to find, however, a general shortage of funding to small firms. Rather it suggested that there were funding gaps for small start-up firms (projects requiring up to £10,000) and for development funds (from £15,000 to £150,000) in some specific cases, particularly in areas where there was not a significant tradition of small firms. Its recommendations on small firms included the introduction of a Loan Guarantee Scheme.

Writing ten years after the Bolton Report, Greenhow (1982) concluded that the growth of a multiplicity of financial assistance methods and schemes from the banks meant that the conclusions of the Bolton and Wilson Committees on the adequacy of small firms' sources of finance were even more justified by the early 1980s. These same conclusions were reached by a number of other studies during the 1980s. The CBI (1983) report on Smaller Firms in the Economy quoted its Industrial Trends Surveys of 1982 to show that only a small percentage of firms regarded shortage of external finance as a constraint on capital expenditure, and this was equally the case for small and large firms. Woodcock (1986) carried out an extensive survey of the range of financial sources available and concluded that they were sufficient for the needs of small firms although there was an 'information gap', mainly because of the lack of awareness about finance sources in small businesses. Curran (1986), in reviewing small-business research, agreed that it had yet to be established that there was a shortage of finance for either the typical or high-flying small enterprise.

However, Turok and Richardson's study of 196 new and recently started firms in West Lothian found that lack of finance was considered the major constraint on expansion by 65 of the firms and a secondary constraint by a further 8: a total of 45 per cent mentioning this factor (Turok and Richardson 1989). This was by far the biggest factor given by small firms: only 16 per cent of firms mentioned lack of premises and 10 per cent mentioned lack of workforce skills. Moreover, this sample included firms which were not actively seeking to grow (indeed 21 per cent said that they had no desire to expand), so that the financial constraint was rather higher for the subsample of growth-oriented firms. For the 22 fast-growth firms identified in this study, lack of finance was considered the main constraint on expansion by 55 per cent of the firms. (None of the firms in this study had experienced such rates of growth as would have qualified as 'fast-growth' firms under the definition in Storey et al. (1989).)

It is also significant that the Coopers and Lybrand survey of 244 businesses in England (Coopers and Lybrand 1990), including 120 firms with up to 50 employees, found that 26 per cent specified direct financial assistance as their main need from business support agencies (and 30 per cent of the small firms specified this). This was substantially more important than any other form of assistance mentioned. The survey identified high-street banks as the main sources of financial assistance (although this assistance was meant to be quite general and not only for expansion purposes), with 66 per cent of respondents quoting this as the main source. The most important sources of financial assistance after the banks were the DTI Enterprise Initiative (22 per cent), merchant banks (21 per cent), local authorities (20 per cent), Small Firms Service (6 per cent), Local Enterprise Agencies (5 per cent) and universities and polytechnics (3 per cent).

A survey undertaken by the Forum of Private Business in 1987 showed that small firms had a number of serious criticisms of their banks: particularly that banks tended not to understand their industry or their markets and used the 'carcass' method of asset valuation for security purposes (that is, value in prospective open-market sale) with a consequent magnification of the problems of collateral (Binks et al. 1988). However, the study did not pursue the issue of how many of these dissatisfied firms were unable to find finance on more favourable terms from a bank other than their own.

A study of the practices of banks and venture-capital sources, commissioned in 1989 by the Department of Trade and Industry, concluded that some evidence could be found of market failure for the funding of particular types of projects and of particular categories of firms, though it did not find evidence of a funding gap at any particular level of funding (Cousins Stephens Associates 1991). Specifically, interviews with suppliers of capital finance suggested that funding in the £50,000 to £100,000 range tended to pose problems when the amount of equity available internally to firms was insufficient to support the borrowing. Furthermore, innovation generally was more difficult to fund both because of risk and because of the need for funding institutions to take a long-term view of returns. Similarly, small firms with a weak asset base were most likely to encounter difficulties in securing development funding.

Nevertheless, in spite of these three studies which indicate some potential problems in the supply of finance for small firms, a summary of the recent major programme of research into small businesses in Britain has concluded that a large percentage of small firms are satisfied rather than dissatisfied with the assistance offered to them by the banks (ESRC 1993).

It has often been suggested that a finance gap for small firms is more likely to be a difficulty in peripheral and remote rural areas (Davies and Yeboah 1990). However, very few empirical studies in industrialised countries have thrown direct light on this issue and the evidence is by no means clear-cut. On the one hand, Perry (1988) finds no pattern of rural disadvantage for small firms in New Zealand and Keeble et al. (1992) reported that in the UK 'there appears to be no overall difference in access to capital between rural and urban businesses, taken as a whole'. On the other hand, while Schaeffer and Pulver (1985) found that rural areas in Wisconsin, USA were not generally disadvantaged in terms of their access to capital, they did find that firms more than 30 miles from towns of over 30,000 population and in sparsely settled areas encountered some problems and Weber (1993) reported special difficulties in capital access for small firms in the rural areas of northern Bavaria.

Constraints arising from the cost of finance

The Bolton Committee (1971) did not consider that the higher rates of interest which small firms in general had to pay for some types of finance constituted discrimination against them. Though unfortunate, these differences were rather rooted in the economies of scale which existed in most forms of financing and did not result from imperfections in the supply of finance.

In similar vein, the CBI (1983) reported from its Industrial Trends Survey of 1982 that only a small percentage of larger (over 200 employees) firms found cost of finance to be a constraint on capital expenditure but this rose to about 8 per cent in the case of smaller firms. The cost of finance was not mentioned explicitly as a constraint on expansion by the firms interviewed in the surveys reported in Turok and Richardson (1989) and Coopers and Lybrand (1990).

However, during 1991 UK clearing banks received widespread and intensive media criticism for their treatment of small businesses, particular attention being paid to the high rates of interest and wide margins applied to small-firm lending – which was unjustifiable, the critics alleged, in terms of the levels and spread of risk involved, and artificially sustained by the banks' cartel and market power (Keasey and Watson 1993b). Accusations of collusion amongst the clearing banks were not supported by the inquiries carried out by the Treasury and Bank of England in 1991; and the charges that banks had failed to pass on interest-rate cuts were refuted by a Bank of England report and Treasury Select Committee inquiry in 1992 (Bradford 1993). Recent evidence from surveys of small-business owners (Cowling et al. 1991; Binks et al. 1992) has been summarised as indicating 'that most small firms pay interest rates only some two to four per cent above base rate and that bank margins on lending to small firms increased only marginally as the recession deepened' (Keasey and Watson 1993b: p. 35).

Financial constraints on fast-growth small firms

A very different view has been put forward by Storey et al. (1989) based on their study of 40 fast-growth small businesses in North East England. They report relatively low levels of satisfaction expressed by fast-growth firms with provision of loan and overdraft facilities by local branches of the clearing banks. They imply that previous findings on the 'funding gap' have given insufficient attention to the problems of fast-growth firms. They hypothesise that 'if the entrepreneur requires modest loan and overdraft facilities and has plans for moderate rates of expansion of the business, especially where the loan can be secured by corporate or personal assets, then he is unlikely to experience significant difficulty ... [and] is likely to be quite satisfied by the service which he receives from the bank. Yet for the fast-growth firm frustrations appear to abound precisely because they are so unusual.'

Storey and his colleagues argue that bank managers have in the past avoided taking the risk of fully funding rapid-growth firms (perhaps because of the performance criteria on which their own career progression depends); these risks are perceived to be especially high because of the typically high gearing of such firms, the exceptional rates of growth which are projected and which seem suspiciously optimistic, the tight operational planning which is dependent on all aspects of the business plan working, the high dependence on new products for which demand is uncertain, and the low knowledge of the bankers of the actual business about which they are making a decision.

The Storey team conclude that, in North East England, there is a strikingly large number of firms exhibiting the rates of asset and profitability growth demanded by venture capitalists and that there are potential opportunities for venture capitalists to make a number of satisfactory investments in the region. By implication, the banking and venture-capital markets are failing to identify and support these potentially high-growth firms at the moment.

The ACOST (1990) report on barriers to growth in highly innovative small firms took up this theme. It proceeded from the assumption that 'bank finance was not appropriate because it required the security of marketable assets which risky innovative activities cannot supply' (ACOST 1990: p. 19) and therefore considered equity financing and government schemes as the only proper sources for developing the technology base in such small firms. It attempted to deal with the problems of 'picking the winners' by proposing that all government schemes be highly competitive in nature: either through awarding a quota of all government R & D contracts to small firms through a competitive tendering process; or through giving grants (not loans) to winners of a twice-yearly competition (open to all firms with between 50 and 500 employees) for projects 'involving major strategic transitions'.

THE ASTON BUSINESS SCHOOL SURVEYS

Given the rather indirect evidence on market failure in the markets for finance and business services for small firms which is reported above, there is a clear need for more direct evidence to be gathered from specifically designed studies. The opportunity to gather such evidence arose when Aston Business School was commissioned in 1989 jointly by the Department of Trade and Industry, the Scottish Office and the Welsh Office to carry out a study into constraints on the growth of small firms in Great Britain. From the outset, this study was intended to investigate the extent of market failure in the provision of finance for small firms. Subsequently, a further research study commissioned by the Department of Trade and Industry into the demonstration effect of the Consultancy Initiatives (part of the Enterprise Initiative) allowed a detailed exploration of the use of business services by small and medium-sized enterprises and the possible extent of market failure in these services also.

Survey of the constraints on the growth of small firms

The first survey (Aston Business School 1991) involved 1,095 detailed telephone interviews with stratified random samples of small firms (defined as independent businesses, or groups of businesses, employing up to 50 people in total, measured as full-time equivalents) from the main UK policy areas (Development Areas, Intermediate Areas, Urban Programme Areas, Task Force Areas) as well as possible European Commission policy areas and a control group of firms outside these areas. Businesses were excluded if they were in sectors not eligible for Regional Enterprise Grant – mainly agriculture, forestry, fishing, construction, retailing, consumer services or utilities.

The random samples were drawn from British Telecom's 'Connections in Business' database. The overall sample matched very closely the DTI estimates for the distribution of firms in the appropriate areas of Great Britain. An analysis of SIC class was undertaken for the achieved samples to check that they matched the populations defined by the 'Connections in Business' database as a whole and in each case the match was very close. As it was not possible to ascertain what stage a firm had reached in the product life-cycle until contact had been established, a screening procedure had to be incorporated into the survey. This consisted of three main components:

- an initial series of questions to check that the firm fell within the scope of the survey;
- a series of questions concerning the extent to which small businesses were considering, or had in the previous three years considered, introducing new products, new processes or some other major investment;
- follow-on questions designed to explore in depth the levels and types of constraints experienced by those businesses which were considering or had considered such innovations or expansion, the reasons for these constraints, and how businesses had responded to these constraints.

The survey was carried out between October 1989 and February 1990, a period characterised by historically high interest rates and a slowing down of industrial output growth from its high rate of the previous several years.

Of the 2,189 firms actually contacted, only 506 (23 per cent) refused to be interviewed, which is very low for a survey of this nature and is sufficiently small to be unlikely to introduce bias into the results. A further 588 firms proved, after the initial screening, to be too large, in an ineligible SIC activity code or to have moved into a different policy area. Therefore, a total of 1,095 full interviews were carried out with eligible firms. Of these, 780 'in-depth' interviews were carried out with firms which were either planning developments in the next three years or had actually undertaken such developments in the previous three years.

Survey of the use of consultancy services by small and medium-sized enterprises

This study was commissioned by the Department of Trade and Industry with the overall purpose of assessing the extent to which the Consultancy Initiatives (started in 1988 as part of the DTI's Enterprise Initiative) had encouraged the spread of best practice by increasing the awareness amongst non-assisted small and medium-sized enterprises (SMEs) of the cost-effectiveness of consultancy services and encouraging them to emulate those firms which had successfully improved their management strategies. In this study, SMEs were defined to be independent businesses, or overall groups of businesses, which employed up to 499 people in total, measured in full-time equivalents.

The achieved sample consisted of 526 firms which, though potentially eligible for assistance under the Consultancy Initiatives, had not applied for assistance, and 207 firms which had been offered assistance but had not taken up this offer. The interviews were carried out during August and September 1991.

The sample of businesses which had not applied for assistance was drawn at random from within each of the size categories of British Telecom's 'Connections in Business' database, after excluding businesses in SICs which were ineligible for assistance under the consultancy initiatives (essentially the sectors of agriculture, horticulture, forestry, fishing, primary extraction of coal, oil and gas, and electricity generation, but also all firms which are franchisees, nationalised industries, public utilities or are otherwise primarily grant-aided by public or charitable organisations). All firms which had in fact been assisted under the scheme were excluded from the subsequent analysis.

The sample of businesses which had not taken up an offer of assistance under the Consultancy Initiatives was drawn from the

DTI's database of all firms which had participated in some way in the initiative.

Findings on the constraints on the growth of small firms

Of the 1,095 firms interviewed, 10 per cent were new or had been established for less than two years. Over 56 per cent indicated that they wished to carry out an innovation or an investment during the next three years; they were categorised as 'future growth-oriented' firms. A further 9 per cent indicated that they had carried out a major innovation or investment in the last three years, but had no plans to do so in the near future; these firms were categorised as 'recent growth-oriented' firms. Thus, a third of these small firms, at maximum, were 'non-growth-oriented', a much smaller proportion than has been traditionally assumed: Hakim (1989), for example, estimated that this proportion was 50 per cent. It seems that overestimates from previous studies may have paid too little attention to the effects of constraints upon growth intentions and to the stage which firms have reached in the cycle of growth and consolidation.

The main problems experienced by firms considering growth was the recruitment of skilled labour. About half of all 'future growth-oriented' firms indicated that this was a problem and 17 per cent also quoted unskilled labour availability as a problem.

About half of firms believed that their innovation or investment proposal would entail a change or expansion of premises; 43 per cent of firms in this category believed that they would face problems making these changes to their premises.

Only 19 per cent of 'future growth-oriented' firms reported that obtaining finance had been or was expected to be a problem, although another 6 per cent were unsure. Over a third of these 'future growth-oriented' firms had already approached at least one source of finance and 83 per cent of these had already received at least one offer of funding; only 14 per cent of the remaining firms anticipated that they might experience problems when they made an approach for external funding. There was no significant tendency for firms with highly innovative products (that is, new to their country, to Great Britain, or entirely new) to experience financial constraints, and firms with highly innovative processes were actually less likely to experience financial constraints than firms with less innovative processes.

By comparison, 78 per cent of all 'recent growth-oriented' firms reported no problem at all in the innovation or investment project which they had undertaken in the previous three years; and only about one in ten had experienced a problem in raising finance.

Evidence of market failure in financing small-firm expansion

The existence of difficulties in raising market finance was not taken as, in itself, indicating market failure. The survey probed the reasons for turning down funding applications which had been given by those funding sources which had been approached.

Only 18 per cent of 'future growth-oriented' firms which had already made an approach for external finance had been unable to find it on terms which were agreeable to them and only 3 per cent had experienced complete market failure in the sense that they had not been offered any finance and the reasons given were unconnected with the viability of the proposed projects.

In summary, only a very small number from our overall sample of 609 'future growth-oriented' firms seemed likely to be unable to raise external funding for market-failure reasons. Fewer than 10 were able to be identified as already having suffered market-failure reasons for not getting a loan, and some of these had subsequently found funding from another external source, generated the funds internally or indicated that they did not expect the problems encountered in obtaining finance to delay the project. In some instances firms encountering problems showed evidence of poor-quality project development: characterised, for example, by the absence of a business plan.

A further 15 firms had turned down funding offers received for reasons which might possibly have indicated market failure: for example, because of unacceptably high interest rates. However, this figure is almost certainly a substantial over-estimate of the level of market failure for these reasons, both because other survey findings suggest that many of these firms are likely eventually to receive more favourable offers from another funding source, and because, in some cases, their decisions disguised a reluctance to invest at all until general interest rates fell.

These patterns of low levels of market failure were found consistently across all policy areas, sizes of firms, industrial sectors and types of project. While a number of firms did not give sufficiently detailed answers for a full picture of their funding position to be established, it seems highly unlikely that as many as 50 small firms could have been experiencing severe market failure in obtaining finance, even using the very wide-ranging definition of market failure adopted in this research. A maximum of 30 firms would be a more likely estimate. This is under 3 per cent of the total sample of 1,095 firms and less than 5 per cent of the sample of 'future growth-oriented' firms.

Since 'future growth-oriented' firms are precisely those firms which might be expected to form the pool of firms likely to apply for government assistance, these results suggest that government intervention to reduce market failure in financing small-firm expansion would be justified in the case of only about 5 per cent of all such firms. The clear implication is that such intervention would be unlikely to succeed, since it would be very hard to target such a tiny number of firms. Indeed, 'free-riders' on the policy would be much more likely to get the money.

Is market failure in finance caused by or combated by SME use of consultancy services?

Even if the small-firm finance market does not fail totally, significant transactions costs in accessing finance make it inefficient. Efficient market operation would entail firms knowing exactly how to find the available funds for their type of project and how best to appeal to a potential funder by means of an attractive project design and case presentation. This shifts attention to the 'information gap' and away from the 'funding gap'. It is, therefore, important to consider whether the market for small-firm finance also has an appropriate level of provision of information and whether it is complemented by use of appropriate business advice services such as management consultancy services.

The use of management consultants has grown rapidly in recent years: total UK employment in the 'other business services' sector (SIC 8395) more than doubled over 1981–87 (Keeble 1990). Yet the Aston Business School survey in 1991 indicated that only 24 per cent of SMEs had used outside consultants or experts to help improve or change the way they managed aspects of their business. This demonstrates how misleading is the common image of the universal use of consultancies. Unsurprisingly, rates of usage of consultancy services increased sharply with firm size: only 16 per cent of firms employing fewer than 5 employees had used consultancy, as compared to 35 per cent for firms with 10–24 employees, and two-thirds of firms with 100–499 employees. The most common types of consultancy which had been commissioned were business planning, financial and management information systems, marketing and design.

The Aston Business School survey did not find evidence of substantial supply-side market failure in consultancy services. The vast majority (88 per cent) of firms which had already used consultants at full cost indicated that it had been reasonably easy to find suitable consultants. Moreover, 68 per cent of businesses which had considered using outside consultants or advisers, but had not yet done so, were aware of consultants offering advice in relevant areas. However, awareness was rather lower amongst smaller firms and there had also been some difficulties in finding suitable specialised consultants: this was a major reason for not taking up an offer of DTI assistance.

The evidence for demand-side failure in the general market for consultancy services is rather fragmentary. The level of inertia of small-firm managers was illustrated in the earlier survey on the constraints on growth of small firms; this showed that perhaps as many as two-thirds of growth-oriented firms which expected to experience problems, including financial problems, had not yet sought information or advice on how to solve them.

The specific survey on the use of consultancy services explored other possible causes of market failure. Of firms which had previously used (or considered using) consultants, around two-thirds expressed interest in having better information on what consultancy services were available. Far fewer firms which had not considered using consultants in the past wanted such information – only one-third of them. This illustrates the imperfect information available even to experienced firms, but also suggests a more serious market failure related to asymmetries in the knowledge base of firms. Thus, whereas firms 'in the know' about the value of consultancy services recognise how little they know, those firms which do not realise the value of such services also place little value on the opportunity to find out.

Further evidence for this interpretation comes from the sample of firms which turned down the DTI's offer of a consultancy grant. Firms which had never before used or considered using consultants were particularly likely to suggest that an advisory service and/or better information would encourage them to use consultants in the future; indeed, they were twice as likely to respond in this way compared with those firms which actually had already used or considered using consultants. Given that these very positive responses came from firms which had turned down their first ever consultancy, at a highly subsidised rate, this would appear to confirm the hypothesis that getting involved in the design and appraisal of a consultancy project reveals to firms how little they know of the potential for this kind of activity.

Taken as a whole, the results of this survey provide clear evidence that for the larger SMEs (those with between 100 and 499 employees) a self-sustaining market in full-cost consultancy services has emerged. In contrast, firms in the smaller size bands are far more price-sensitive and may still underestimate the potential benefits of consultancy services, so that there may remain a need for some subsidy of consultancy services in order to tempt firms by giving them a first taste of the potential benefits.

CONCLUSIONS

The Aston Business School surveys suggest that the extent of market failure in the market for SME finance is small. This confirms the findings of most major studies during the past 25 years.

If market failure in funding SME growth is a small-scale phenomenon, should it simply be ignored? Government intervention in this area preceded the Bolton Committee, rose after the Wilson Report and has continued into the present. Clearly, it has been unacceptable in policy terms to ignore the financial constraints experienced by small firms, particularly in depressed regions, even though the proportion experiencing such constraints may be low and the consequent market failure may be minimal.

Yet the likelihood that public-sector schemes could 'pick winners' is very small. Recent data indicate that of the UK's 1.66 million VAT-registered firms, only 4,000 have a turnover of more than £1 million and are growing at a rate of 15 per cent or more per annum; perhaps another 750 firms are joining these 'high flyers' annually (Bannock 1991b). Such small numbers constitute a hard target to hit; it is even more difficult to guess which firms are likely to be joining this select band in the medium term. The difficulty is also greatly compounded by the likelihood that government support will induce exaggeration of the future prospects and plans of marginal applicants, or will induce applications from firms which would have been fully viable in the absence of any support.

A key market response to reduce market failure consists of the provision of information and advice, often in the form of consultancy, by which firms can maximise their chances of designing profitable projects, finding available funding and making a convincing case to the funders. The Aston Business School survey shows that there is a flourishing, self-sustaining market in such consultancies for firms at the larger end of the SME scale. However, the market for consultancies suffers from demand-side market failure on the part of the smaller firms, particularly those with under 50 employees.

Therefore, there is a strong case that government assistance to small firms with financing problems would be much more cost-effective if it abandoned grant and loan schemes and concentrated instead on ensuring that firms at the lower end of the spectrum of firm size got proper information, advice and consultancy, particularly on how to organise their projects in a way likely to be attractive to potential funders.

3

BANK FINANCE FOR GROWING SMALL BUSINESSES

Martin R. Binks and Christine T. Ennew

INTRODUCTION

The role and significance of small businesses in economic development has attracted considerable attention from both academics and policy makers. Within political circles and, perhaps to a lesser extent, academic circles, the small-business sector is viewed as having a significant contribution to make to the economy and to the development of an enterprise culture. Furthermore, it is generally assumed that the more small businesses can grow, the greater the benefits to the economy as a whole. Growing small firms can generate employment (Storey and Johnson 1987), promote competition (Bolton 1971; Wilson 1979), and facilitate economic restructuring (Binks and Vale 1990). The growth potential of small businesses is generally thought to be related to their operating flexibility and their ability (if unconstrained) to respond to and benefit from changing market conditions (Binks and Coyne 1983). In practice, however, not all firms wish to grow and not all firms are able to grow. For example, Hakim (1989) suggests that only a small proportion (around 10 per cent) of UK firms wish to grow rapidly and this may be attributable to the owner–managers being reluctant to expand beyond a size which they can continue to control personally. A recent survey (Binks et al. 1990) suggests that as many as 85 per cent of firms may resist external equity holders due to the potential loss of control, while Cowling et al. (1991) suggested a figure of 61 per cent. Of greater significance from a policy perspective is the fact that of those owner–managers who wish to grow their business only 10 per cent will actually do so.

There are a number of barriers to growth among small firms including the availability of skilled labour, management skills (Hay 1992), access to markets (Mayes and Moir 1989), and finance. As we have seen in Chapter 1, it has long been argued that small size may preclude firms from access to certain sectors of the capital markets, resulting in finance gaps (Macmillan 1931). However, it is also suggested that finance gaps may arise not because of size *per se*, but because of imperfections in information flows. Where finance gaps exist, potential viable growth may be forgone.

An overview of barriers to growth among small businesses is provided by Barber et al. (1989) and by Bovaird et al. in Chapter 2. This chapter considers specifically the issues relating to the provision of the sources of finance available to small businesses before going on to examine theoretical and conceptual issues relating to the financing of growing businesses. This is followed by an empirical analysis of bank finance for growing businesses. Finally we present conclusions and implications.

THE PROVISION OF BANK FINANCE TO SMALL BUSINESSES

External finance to small businesses is dominated by debt finance from the banking sector, while debt is the most common type of external finance used by small businesses. A recent survey (Binks et al. 1993) notes that 75 per cent of firms have overdrafts and 31 per cent have fixed-term loans. According to Keasey and Watson (1992), bank debt represents around 31 per cent of business liabilities and is equally as important as directors' equity and trade credit as a source of business finance. This study also indicated an increased reliance on short-term bank finance during the late 1980s. The recession of the early 1990s placed issues about the availability of debt finance to small businesses firmly in the political spotlight (Keasey and Watson 1993a). The issue that attracted most political attention related to the withdrawal of debt finance by the banking sector and the implications of this for the rate of failure among small businesses. However, in more general terms, where small businesses experience difficulties in obtaining debt finance, potential viable growth may be forgone.

Difficulties in obtaining debt finance do not refer simply to the fact that some firms cannot obtain funds through the banking system. Indeed, we should not expect that all projects would automatically be financed. In providing debt finance, a bank is making an investment in a business and needs to be confident that this investment will be realised at an appropriate future date. Thus, only proposals (business and/or projects) which offer realistic opportunities for repayment can expect to obtain bank debt. The provision of finance acts as a constraint on growth only in situations in which a project which is profitable at prevailing interest rates is not undertaken (or is restricted) because the firm is unable to obtain adequate funding.

The extent to which viable projects may fail to obtain funding is difficult, if not impossible, to measure. Even from a theoretical standpoint there is some debate as to the extent and even existence of forms of credit rationing by banks. The provision of finance to any business can be treated as a simple contract in which the bank may be regarded as the principal and the small firm as the agent. In effect, the bank is requiring the firm to undertake an investment project and generate a return on behalf of the bank. In order to enter into this contract the bank will require certain information. In particular the bank must be sure that the project is an appropriate one, that the firm is capable of undertaking it, and that once the contract has been written, the firm will do what was agreed, to the best of its abilities. Under conditions of perfect and costlessly available information, with no uncertainties regarding the state of the world which will prevail, these information requirements should not present any particular problem. In practice, information is not perfect and is often expensive to obtain. The particular problem is that the distribution of information between the parties to the contract is asymmetric. That is to say, there are certain pieces of information, having a material effect on the contract, which are available to one party but not to the other.

Information asymmetry poses two problems for the provision of debt finance. First, the bank cannot observe *ex ante* certain information which is relevant to the decision to enter into the contract, typically the actual abilities of the individuals applying for finance and the qualities of the project. Second, there is the risk that the small business will not perform in a manner consistent with the contract, necessitating some form of *ex post* monitoring procedure. Arguably, information could be collected regarding these attributes of the firm and the project, although the cost is likely to be prohibitively high. However, even if it were available, the bank is likely to encounter difficulties in processing that information, thus limiting its practical usefulness.

The implications of these information asymmetries for the provision of debt finance have been evaluated from a theoretical standpoint in a number of studies. Thus, for example, in examining capital market failure, Stiglitz and Weiss (1981) identify debt gaps as a result of both adverse selection and moral hazard problems. The adverse selection effect is analogous to that observed in insurance markets and arises because borrowers have different degrees of risk attached to their projects. As interest rates rise low-risk borrowers (although having viable projects) drop out, leaving only high-risk borrowers. This is reinforced by the moral hazard problem associated with the lender's inability to monitor the project undertaken; again it is shown that as interest rates rise the higher-risk projects will be substituted for the lower-risk projects, and there will be equilibrium credit rationing (see also Bester and Hellwig 1989). A contrary view is expressed by de Meza and Webb (1987) who identify adverse selection in the presence of different (but unobservable) entrepreneurial abilities as leading to an oversupply of credit rather than a debt gap.

While there is a need for further work to reconcile these views, in practice they may not be mutually exclusive. Information asymmetries will in some situations lead to low-quality projects being funded (oversupply of credit), and in others to high-quality projects being denied funding (credit rationing). In particular, this result may be related to the role of collateral in bonding debt finance. Indeed, from a theoretical perspective it has been shown that the availability of sufficient collateral can counteract these problems; the low-risk borrowers who leave the market in the Stiglitz–Weiss model can signal their status by their willingness to offer appropriate levels of collateral, and the taking of collateral by the banks can provide an incentive to ensure that the firm will perform to the best of its abilities in undertaking the project (Bester 1987). However, if collateral is in limited supply, debt gaps may still exist.

The extent of such debt gaps may be exacerbated by the presence of further information problems which may arise in relation to less costly and more objective information regarding the firm and its project. In addition to the information requirements described above, the bank's willingness to enter into a contract to provide debt finance will be affected by the information it can collect regarding technical aspects of the project, the financial and managerial strengths of the business, and the prospects for the industry and the market. Information regarding the managerial strengths of the business and its track record may be of particular significance since it may help to reduce the extent of the adverse selection and moral hazard problems. Information of this nature can be important in improving the process of load evaluation and finance provision, but there are costs associated with the collection of such information and these costs are typically higher when dealing with smaller businesses. Even with more objective information, the problems of processing and interpretation are not eliminated, although they are likely to be less extensive than is the case with highly subjective information. In the absence of information regarding the prospects for the firm, its industry and its markets, the risks associated with the provision of debt finance can be significantly reduced by the application of a simple capital-gearing approach to loan evaluation.

LOAN EVALUATION

The approach taken by the banks when assessing applications for loans will tend to fall somewhere along a continuum for which the limiting cases are income gearing at one end and capital gearing at the other. Income gearing focuses upon the income stream which is anticipated from the enterprise to be financed and the extent to which it is able to cover the servicing of the debt used to finance that enterprise. In this case, therefore, the critical factors refer to the profit stream, interest rate and capital-repayment schedule. This approach emphasises the prospects of the enterprise in determining whether or not it is funded. The extent to which security is taken to underwrite the loan is, in principle, separate as an issue from the consideration of whether the enterprise should be funded. A capital-gearing approach to loan evaluation emphasises the value of the security or collateral which is to be provided. This value is then considered against the size of the loan requested and, if the bank is confident that in the event of default it would be able to recover both the loan and the costs of recovery, then the loan may be forthcoming.

Clearly in-between these two approaches lie many permutations. Banks will tend to consider both the prospects of the enterprise to be funded and the value and realisation prospects of the collateral which is being put forward as security. The points made above with respect to asymmetric information are relevant here. Given the information costs required to assess loan applications, it is possible that banks will risk adverse selection and also moral hazard. There is the potential for unprofitable projects to be funded with debt finance if sufficient collateral is made available and the information costs of evaluating the project prohibit a full analysis. Conversely in the absence of sufficient collateral it is possible for credit rationing to occur when a bank is unwilling to provide debt finance for viable projects. In such situations the reluctance to provide debt occurs partly because of the inherent riskiness of the project, but also because there is no guarantee that the bank's stake could be recovered in the event of default.

Banks must place a valuation on the collateral offered that reflects the realistic price that could be gained in the event of default. The collateral taken is essentially of two types, business and personal. It is the manner in which business collateral is valued which may introduce a higher probability of credit rationing. In the event of default, business assets could be sold off in order to cover the value of debt outstanding. The assets concerned will therefore be valued as if the business were no longer trading. This means that such assets will be assumed to have, for security purposes, carcass value only. For some assets this does not constitute a problem in that they may be saleable at a price which reflects their value as part of a going concern. Until recently, land and property would have been included among such assets. For other items such as plant and equipment, however, the carcass valuation process means that their value for security purposes is much smaller than that associated with them in the context of the going concern. If it is assumed that new plant and equipment would be sold off at auction in the event of default then it might also be estimated that the value achieved could be as low as 10 per cent of the face value of the plant and the equipment.

Indeed, Keasey and Watson (1992) take this argument a stage further and argue that the quality of formal financial information available from small firms is poor, that owner–managers have the opportunity to dilute creditor claims and that consequently, for an outside investor, tangible business or personal assets are the best indicator of the investor's security. They also reiterate the importance of collateral as a device to allow small businesses to self-select. In effect this phenomenon may be illuminated by earlier work by Marsh (1982) who found within very much larger quoted UK firms that debt incurred was related to balance-sheet values of tangible assets. More recent research into much smaller UK newly quoted firms by Buckland and Davis (1989) strongly supports the hypothesis that asset composition, leading to differentials in available security for borrowing, is crucial in gearing decisions.

The typical solution to such problems is the employment of personal collateral, either instead of or as well as business collateral. However, a low-quality project may be able to obtain funding where the bank is insufficiently well informed to judge its viability but is unwilling to refuse finance to a customer who offers more than adequate security. Clearly small firms can experience a loan gap because they have insufficient collateral. Alternatively, they may gain access to loan finance, but only at the cost of providing personal collateral in the form of a guarantee or house deeds. Where this refers to companies, there is a direct erosion of limited-liability status and the protection it provides. This would be expected to discourage investment at the margin, given the additional personal risk it implies.

The extent to which the financing of expansion in small businesses is problematic depends upon the traditions and background which underpin the banks' approach to loan evaluation. There is evidence to suggest that conditions vary considerably between different countries (Bannock and Doran 1991; Binks et al. 1992; Yao-Su Hu 1984). In particular it is suggested that countries such as Germany and Japan may have a banking system which adopts a more income-gearing, prospects-based approach to loan evaluation than is the case in the UK (Charkham 1989). It is argued that they are able to do this for a number of reasons. First, there are many more banks in Germany and many of them are locally based. The quality of relationship between the bank manager and small businesses may be much higher in the context of a small regional bank than in the branch of a large national bank. Bank managers in Germany may be more highly qualified than their British counterparts and also they have more experience of industrial lending. In Britain there has been considerable pressure for the main clearing banks to change their approach to financing small businesses. Regular surveys of the membership of the Forum of Private Business (Binks et al. 1988, 1990, 1992) have demonstrated that change is occurring. Banks which had been revealed as having an uncanny similarity in the perceptions of their customers in 1988 were becoming increasing differentiable by 1992, adopting different strategies in their attempts to maximise their returns from lending in the small-business market.

FINANCE FOR GROWING FIRMS: GENERAL CRITERIA

The specific financial requirements of a growing small business will vary according to the nature of the business, its profitability, the rate of growth to be obtained and the financial condition of the owner–managers. Where profitability is high or the owner–managers have access to accumulated capital, then growth may be financed from internal equity. In many cases, firms are unable to finance their growth from retained profits and their owner–managers do not have access to accumulated capital of sufficient quantity. In these cases the financial requirements characteristic of firms which are growing from a small base need to be considered.

Firms which grow rapidly may find it more difficult to borrow because their acquisition of plant and equipment may grow faster than the value of assets which can be provided as collateral due to the impact of carcass-valuation procedures. This vulnerability will be increased further in cases where firms suffer delayed payment from customers but, due to their small size and limited market power, cannot obtain the same terms from their suppliers. There is thus a time lag between production costs and sales revenues for a given cohort of output. The faster the rate of growth the larger the amount of working capital required to cover the lag. Funding this through increased access to overdraft finance may increase the probability of a loan gap if available collateral is fully committed. Small, rapid-growth firms may therefore have a higher probability of experiencing a loan gap because their earnings potential is not considered in a capital-geared approach to loan requirements.

It is not possible to measure the viable growth which is lost due to finance gaps, but where they exist they will tend to have the greatest impact on small firms with growth potential, in part because it is here that a close relationship with suppliers of finance and a good flow of information are particularly important in order to incorporate future income prospects in the investment decision. A closer relationship, and consequently more accurate information exchange, would *ceteris paribus* increase the income-gearing element of project evaluation and reduce the loan gap. This is not a smooth process, however, since the collection of information over and above simple descriptive statistics causes a discrete and disproportionately large rise in costs to the financial institution concerned: because the assessment of more qualitative aspects such as management skills is more time-consuming to perform and requires a much higher level of investment in the training of those undertaking the evaluation.

For many small businesses the growth process involves discrete rather than smooth increases in the capital base of the firm. For example, the movement from one machine to two requires a 100 per cent increase in the volume of plant and equipment. The more such indivisibilities are pronounced, the greater the impact upon the firm's financial requirements for expansion. The smaller the firm the larger the impact will be. Aside from supply-side considerations there are also demand-side characteristics which may augment the process described above.

In some cases demand may also grow in discrete steps rather than on a continuous basis. Where smaller businesses are becoming established in new markets, it is quite possible that having ascertained the consistency of the product quality, customers may increase orders by a multiple of the initial order placed with the firm. Firms may be required to meet such increases in demand or lose the customer entirely. The impact of this kind of expansion path on the capital-base requirements of the company are further magnified as a result of the indivisibilities referred to above. The financing of such expansion would therefore require funding in amounts which are often a multiple of the asset value of the business concerned, particularly where it is growing from a small base. Given the points on carcass valuation made above, the provision of collateral from business assets alone would clearly be problematic.

As a result of the valuation principles described in the previous section, there are significant implications if business assets are to be the main source of collateral for debt-financed expansion. The faster the growth rate, the more rapidly the firm will be required to expand in terms of new plant and equipment. Higher rates of growth mean that the gap between the cost to the firm of new plant and equipment and the addition which such plant and equipment makes to business assets for collateral purposes will grow larger. Each additional purchase of plant and equipment adds significantly more to the costs of the firm than it does to the capital base for security purposes. It would be expected, therefore, that the more rapid the growth rate of the firm, the more likely it is that the managers concerned will be asked for personal as well as business collateral. In the case of incorporated businesses it would be expected that the higher the rate of growth the more likely it is that the protection of limited-liability status will be eroded in order to gain access to the debt finance required to fund the expansion.

FINANCING GROWING FIRMS: SOME EMPIRICAL EVIDENCE

The previous sections have highlighted the types of problem experienced by small businesses in gaining access to adequate finance with a particular focus on the problems which might be experienced by faster-growth firms. This analysis has been undertaken largely from a theoretical perspective, and although there are a number of studies which provide empirical evidence in relation to the equity gap (see for example Harrison and Mason 1990, 1993b), studies which address problems relating to the provision of debt finance are limited. The most recent survey of the membership of the Forum of Private Business (Binks et al. 1993) does shed some light on these issues. This survey was conducted in late spring 1992. Approximately 16,000 questionnaires were administered and over 6,000 responses were received from the FPB membership. Although there are some minor regional and sectoral biases in the sample, the coverage can nevertheless be considered to be reasonably representative of small businesses in Britain.

The sample can be divided up into three categories: declining firms (negative growth rates in the previous year); slow-growth firms (growth of 0–10 per cent in the previous year); and fast-growth firms (growth in excess of 10 per cent in the previous year). The fast-growth firms represent about 17 per cent of the entire sample. These firms tend to be younger, with around 44 per cent being less than five years of age (compared with 23 per cent for the sample as a whole) and are slightly more prevalent in the manufacturing sector (24 per cent compared with 20 per cent in the sample as a whole) and the services sector (34 per cent compared with 29 per cent in the sample as a whole). In relation to profitability and size, the fast-growth firms do not appear to be significantly different from the sample as a whole. A large proportion (53 per cent) of these fast-growth firms anticipate similarly fast rates of growth in the future.

Respondents to the survey were asked to assess the extent to which they perceived their business to be constrained by current bank policies and practices. The pattern of responses (based on mean scores) is given in Table 3.1. This suggests that there are some areas

Table 3.1 Average constraint ratings by size of firm
(1 = no constraint to 5 = serious constraint)

Constraint	*Decline (D)*	*Average (A)*	*Fast (F)*	*Significant differences*[a]
Collateral	2.78	2.55	2.88	D, F against A
Interest rate	3.30	3.08	3.02	D against A, F
Availability of credit	2.71	2.46	2.81	D, F against A
Charges	3.34	3.17	3.03	D against A, F
				D against A
Manager's competence	2.28	2.15	2.25	D against A
Speed of service	2.17	2.03	2.12	D against A
Term of loan	2.69	2.44	2.58	D, F against A

[a] Based on Tukey HSD test from a one-way analysis of variance. This provides a robust test for differences in the means, on the basis of multiple comparisons across the groups.

in which fast-growth firms are significantly more constrained than other firms. In particular, fast-growth firms appear to experience significant constraints in relation to collateral, availability of credit and term of loan, although there is no evidence to suggest that fast-growth firms see interest rates or charges as more of a constraint than do other types of firm.

THE NATURE OF FINANCIAL CONSTRAINTS

A more detailed analysis of the factors influencing perceptions of the degree of constraint suggests that the most important influences are the quality of the relationship with the bank manager and assessments of the quality of service. Indeed, when these factors are accounted for, there is less evidence of significant constraints between growing and non-growing firms (Ennew and Binks 1993).

More specific details about the sources and uses of funds for different types of firm in the survey are contained in Tables 3.2 and 3.3. In the case of overdrafts there is no evidence of any significant difference in the pattern of use, with working capital being the most common use. Interestingly, however, the slow-growth firms do appear to be more inclined to use overdrafts to fund a mixture of working capital and fixed assets as opposed to working capital only. There is little evidence of differences in the take-up of fixed-term loans, as Table 3.3 shows, but there is evidence of significant

Table 3.2 Overdraft take-up and use

Growth rate	*% with overdraft*	*% using for working capital*	*% using for fixed assets*	*% using for both*
Decline	76	80.3	2.2	17.5
Average	74	78.1	2.3	19.5
Fast	76	79	3.3	17.8

Table 3.3 Fixed-term loan take-up and use

Growth rate	*% with loan*	*% using for working capital*	*% using for fixed assets*	*% using for both*
Decline	39	23.7	59.5	16.8
Average	44	21.3	61.5	17.2
Fast	43	19.6	56.4	24

Notes: Chi-squared = 13.67, $p = 0.008$

differences in the pattern of usage. Rapid-growth firms are more inclined to use loans for a mixture of working capital and fixed assets and less inclined to use these solely for working capital. This use of term funding for short-term liquidity provision may imply a shortage of more appropriate sources of finance.

The type of collateral required varies according to growth rate, with a greater requirement for personal collateral, as shown in Table 3.4. A similar pattern is evident for fixed-term loans. Rapid-growth firms are required to give more personal collateral and less business collateral, and the differences are statistically significant.

Table 3.4 Overdraft collateral requirements by growth rate of firm

	% of firms reporting overdrafts which were required to provide			
Growth rate	*Personal*	*Business*	*Both*	*Any collateral*
Decline	35	32	33	92
Average	33	33	34	92
Fast	39	24	37	89

Notes: Chi-squared = 24.15, $p = 0.0005$

In addition, more of them are required to give a mixture of business and personal collateral.

Collateral was identified earlier as a constraint by fast-growth firms, but an examination of collateral ratios in Table 3.5 suggests that growing firms are generally required to give lower ratios (the difference between fast-growth and declining firms is statistically significant). This suggests that the reason for the constraint may lie with the type of collateral rather than the amount. There are fewer significant differences in relation to collateral requirements on loans. It is interesting to note that fast-growth firms also face slightly higher interest charges on overdrafts relative to average-growth firms, although the analysis of constraints suggested that this was not a problem. Both declining and fast-growth firms are rather more likely to experience financial difficulties whilst slow-growth firms are significantly less likely to do so, but despite these difficulties there is again no clear evidence that the attitude of their respective bank managers is either more or less supportive.

Finally, a more general overview of the position of growing firms can be obtained by examining their assessments of the relative importance of attributes of bank services and their assessments of the relative quality of provision of these services. This information can be presented in summary form using a series of weighted average scores which measure assessments of the importance (*demand*), quality of provision (*supply*), and extent to which there is a match between the two (*attainment*). The derivation of these measures is explained in detail in Ennew et al. (1993). The *attainment* scores shown in Figure 3.1 are generally lowest for the declining firms. This is primarily a consequence of a poor perceived quality of provision, although in the case of the knowledge-based characteristics, the poor

Table 3.5 Collateral ratios and interest rates by growth rate of firm

Growth rate	*Collateral ratio on overdraft limit*[a]	*Collateral ratio on fixed-term loan*[a]	*Percentage over base rate on overdraft*	*Percentage over base rate on loan*
Decline	4.75	2.74	2.91	2.68
Average	4.32	3.01	2.78	2.49
Fast	3.29	2.02	2.95	2.53

[a] Corrected for possible double counting

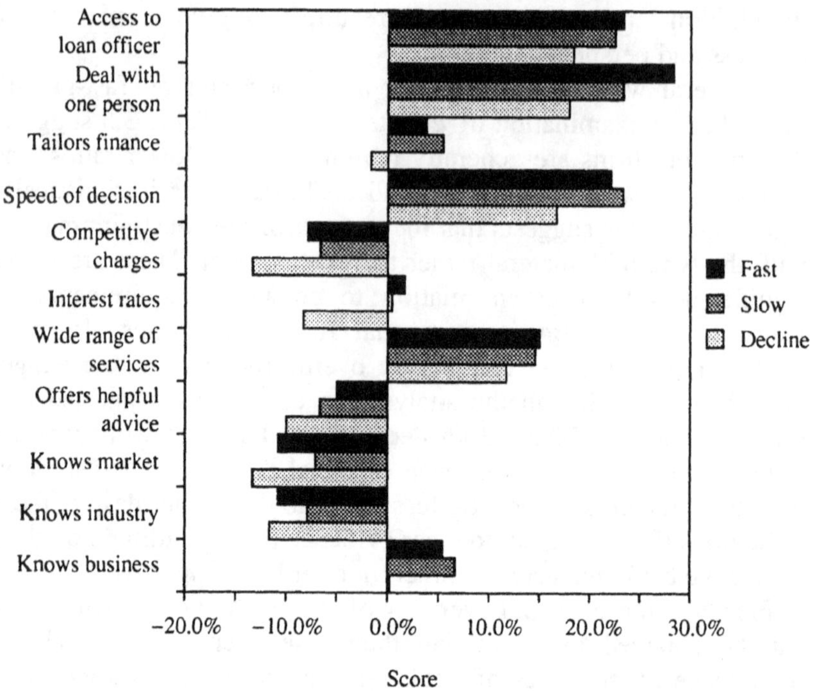

Figure 3.1 Variations in the attainment score by growth rate

attainment scores can be attributed to the fact that declining firms consider the provision of these characteristics to be quite important. Given the difficulties being experienced by firms with falling turnover, it is perhaps not surprising that a premium is attached to the banks' knowledge and understanding of the business and the industry and markets in which they operate. It is interesting to note that the rapid-growth firms also attach a high degree of importance to the provision of knowledge-based characteristics and this may reflect their dependence on a high degree of flexibility on the part of the banks due to the rapidly changing needs of such businesses. Declining firms are also particularly dissatisfied with the banks in relation to charges and interest rates, although, in the economic climate at the time of the survey, dissatisfaction in these areas was to be expected.

CONCLUSIONS

In this chapter we have explained why smaller firms may confront finance gaps when seeking external funding. We have also explained why the severity of these gaps may be positively related to the rate of growth of the firm. Our arguments focus particular attention on the role of collateral in the capital-gearing approach to loan assessment which typifies most bank lending to small businesses in the UK. We then provide evidence based on the responses of over 6,000 firms in the largest study of its kind undertaken in the UK, which tends to substantiate many of the arguments raised in the theoretical approach taken in the first parts of the chapter. Both theory and available evidence indicate quite strongly that many rapidly-growing firms will confront problems when attempting to obtain external finance to underpin that growth.There is clearly the potential for viable growth to be lost in such businesses although the extent of the loss is difficult to estimate.

Since growing firms are relatively more attractive to banks as customers than stable or declining firms because of the increase in the use of bank services which their growth implies, it would be expected that banks would attempt to overcome the problems outlined earlier in the chapter in order to attract this particular kind of customer. Similarly it might be expected that government would attempt to close the gaps identified, since the firms most affected would appear to be those best placed to generate wealth and employment. There is evidence that many of the banks are beginning to adopt strategies that will place more emphasis upon a prospects-based income-gearing approach to loan evaluation. This is not a trivial process, however, since it involves considerable retraining costs and runs counter to the traditional approaches taken by banks in the UK. This process of change is also problematic because the evidence provided by firms as to their future prospects is extremely difficult to interpret and the banks themselves have been involved in considerable bad debts in recent years. Although change in this direction is occurring it is unlikely to have a significant effect in the short run.

4

SMALL FIRMS AND BANK BORROWING IN THE UK

Issues and evidence

Kevin Keasey and Robert Watson

INTRODUCTION

In the UK both the adequacy of the supply of debt finance to small firms and the contractual conditions attaching to it have often been criticised by small-business pressure groups, researchers, government agencies and the mass media (see Keasey and Watson (1992) for a review). In spite of the fact that the main UK clearing banks provide around 90 per cent of all small-firm lending (Batchelor 1989b), they have been criticised for being too 'risk-averse' and as being responsible for creating the so-called 'finance gap' (for example, see Bolton 1971; Wilson 1979), particularly in relation to the financial needs of rapidly-growing small firms. As we indicate later in the chapter, even if it could be unambiguously shown that substantial numbers of small firms with viable and highly profitable projects have been denied bank finance, it is far from clear that

(a) an economically important gap with respect to debt finance actually exists, or,
(b) that the lending behaviour of the banks is unreasonable in this regard.

Analysis of the theoretical and empirical literatures suggests that the perception of a finance gap and other contractual conflicts between banks and small firms can be more adequately explained in terms of the differences in the economic functions, relative risks, payoffs and, therefore, the economic interests of the suppliers of equity and debt finance.

More recently, since the start of the UK recession in 1990, the main clearing banks' post-contractual behaviour towards their small-business customers has become the focus of criticism. Much of the mass-media coverage of these conflicts has been based on the premise (and has therefore inevitably concluded) that the banks act as a profiteering cartel, intent simply upon stripping small firms of profits via high bank charges and then forcing many into receivership by the sudden and unwarranted withdrawal of overdraft facilities. The underlying economic logic of such behaviour is, however, far from obvious: the banks do not profit from losing customers or from forcing solvent firms into liquidation.

As with the analysis of the debt finance gap, once the nature of the debt contract and the other contractual difficulties associated with small-firm financing are highlighted, the plausibility of such claims become extremely doubtful. Indeed, from this perspective, the perception of a finance gap and the *ex post* contractual conflicts with debt suppliers are simply opposite sides of the same coin. Though each can be expected to surface at different stages of the trade cycle, both problems are manifestations of the same inherent economic tensions. In this chapter, we examine the economic basis of these conflicts between banks and small firms by focusing on the nature of the debt contract and the characteristics of small-firm equity ownership and management. An empirical analysis of the financial structures and returns to debt and equity suppliers for a sample of small firms in the UK is also undertaken.

The remainder of the chapter is structured as follows. In the next section we examine the economic changes, policy initiatives and regulatory developments of the 1980s that had a significant impact upon the bank/small-firm relationship. This section also contains a discussion of the differences between debt and equity finance and the characteristics of small firms that create an inherent conflict of interest with a debt supplier. In the third section we empirically investigate the financing of small firms via an analysis of the published accounts of a sample of 110 UK small firms over the period 1986 to 1990. More specifically we examine how the capital structures and relative returns to equity and debt changed over the five-year period. The fourth section explores the basis of the *ex post* conflicts associated with debt financing, especially those that surface during an economic downturn. In particular, we discuss the main difficulties faced by banks in accurately assessing their exposure to risk when small-firm owner–managers have both the motive and opportunity to take *ex post* actions which increase the banks' exposure to uncompensated risk. The final section presents some concluding remarks.

THE ECONOMIC BACKGROUND

The UK banking sector

Since 1980, the UK banking sector has faced increased domestic and international competition due to several public-policy initiatives that have significantly altered the economic and regulatory environment within which they operate. For example, the abolition of exchange controls has opened up the UK domestic market to international competition, whilst legislation on financial deregulation has allowed other financial institutions (such as building societies) to offer a full range of banking facilities, including the provision of current accounts. As a consequence the UK banks have discovered that they can no longer rely upon an uncompetitive domestic market to supply them with a cheap source of funds from non-interest-bearing current accounts. This, along with the 1987 Basle Agreement, which increased the minimum capital adequacy ratios of banks, has significantly increased the costs of making loans.

As profit margins on lending have been squeezed, the banks have competed more vigorously in terms of the prices of their other services. This has led to the elimination of implicit cross-subsidisation and to the passing on to the customer of the costs of supplying specific services. Hence, while those customers with deposits have gained from a more competitive rate of interest, charges for many other services have had to be introduced and/or be increased to reflect the marginal cost of supplying these services. This, as might be expected, has made banks unpopular with customers who previously obtained these services free or at a subsidised rate. As Chrystal (1992: p. 54) has noted, 'it is ironic that banks have been criticized, often by politicians, for responding in the only way possible to new regulatory requirements imposed by the political authorities themselves'.

The growth of small firms in the UK

Over the past 10 to 15 years, small firms have been perceived to be an increasingly important part of the UK economy (see Stanworth and

Gray (1991) for a review of the evidence), with all the main political parties preaching the economic benefits of developing a more vigorous and internationally competitive small-firm sector, so much so that even by 1982 over 100 policy measures designed to help existing small firms and/or encourage the creation of new firms were in operation. Although many of these policy initiatives have met with limited success (Keasey and Watson 1993a), particularly in terms of the small size and limited economic potential of many of the new enterprises created (Storey and Strange 1992), the numbers of both UK small firms and the self-employed increased dramatically over the 1980s. Despite the economic marginality of much of the greatly enlarged UK small-firm sector, by the late 1980s there was much talk of the small firm having an important role to play in reconstructing not just the economy but also the national psyche via the creation of an 'enterprise culture' (Bagguley 1991).

The vulnerability to an economic downturn of many of the new enterprises created during the expansionary late 1980s became evident in 1990 when failure rates increased dramatically (see Keasey and Watson 1993b). Even so, the political rhetoric that small enterprises were somehow necessarily more 'flexible', entrepreneurial, innovative and competitive than were large 'rigid', 'bureaucratic' organisations did not help the banks in putting across their case when their conflicts with small firms, created largely by the economic downturn, surfaced in late 1990.

Small-firm debt and equity finance

An important consequence of the growth in the numbers of micro-enterprises over the 1980s has been the increase in the level and a change in the distribution of risk in the economy. The empirical evidence presented in the next section indicates that the banks played a large role in financing the expansion of our sample of UK small firms over the six-year period up to 1990. However, in addition to debt finance, firms also need to obtain equity finance. This is because the main economic function of equity is to provide long-term risk capital, where the return is contingent upon the success of the enterprise. Since debt suppliers contract to receive a fixed return irrespective of how well or badly the firm is performing, equity acts as the financial buffer that enables the firm to absorb the inevitable uncertainties of business life.

Typically, however, the owner–manager's personal sources of equity finance are quickly exhausted, particularly for those with new and/or growing firms. The lack of financial and other managerial expertise within the small firm, the high fixed costs of acquiring and accessing information of adequate quality on a timely basis and the volatile economic performance of many businesses frequently means that outside equity investors experience problems in effectively monitoring the actions of owner–managers. The problems associated with exiting, due to the lack of a public market for their shares, compound these difficulties and outside equity finance may often be unavailable if the above problems are not satisfactorily overcome. Any unwillingness to seek, or difficulties experienced in obtaining, equity finance may result in too heavy a dependence upon debt finance, particularly short-term bank loans and overdrafts. Short-term debt finance is obviously a highly uncertain means by which to finance long-term investment, since there is always the possibility that the finance will not be renewed. It is also clearly an unsuitable substitute for long-term risk capital for firms with volatile cash flows or low equity bases: features characteristic of many young, small firms. Such highly levered enterprises will be exposed to considerable additional financial risk whenever current cash flows prove to be insufficient to meet prior debt obligations. Of course, as debt-repayment obligations are independent of firm performance, the converse is also true – namely, that when the firm is performing well all increases in value above that required for debt servicing belong to the equity holders.

A lack of sufficient equity finance can therefore be expected to lead to difficulties in obtaining even very short-term debt finance. As debtholders do not participate in upside gains, they will be generally unwilling to bear business risks that potential equity investors refuse to accept. Indeed, because of the typically small margins on bank lending, it takes a comparatively large number of good loans to cover the losses of just one bad loan. Moreover, debtholders will be wary of providing too high a proportion of a firm's finance due to the fact that the return distribution of equity for incorporated businesses is truncated on the downward side which makes the equity of a levered firm analogous to a call option (see Brealey and Myers 1991: p. 485). Because of the presence of limited liability in a two-period formulation, the payoff function to a risk-neutral owner–manager will be $\max[P - (1 + i)D, 0]$, where P is the net cash flow accruing to the firm, D is the debt and i is the interest rate on the debt. As Stiglitz and Weiss (1981) originally noted, this is a convex function which, because of the restricted downside potential, motivates the owner–manager to act in a more risk-preferring manner. Quite simply, in the event of failure (that is, when $P-(1+i)D<0$), part of the cost of failure (that is, $(1+i)D-P$) will be borne by the debtholder. This provides the owner–manager with incentives for undertaking actions which expose debtholders to greater risk or which otherwise reduce the value of their financial claims.

In addition, the incentives and opportunities for the owner–manager to gamble with outside investors' claims are, as will be discussed later, greatly enhanced when the firm becomes financially distressed. The 1986 Directors' Disqualification Act, which allows for the disqualification of directors who have gambled excessively with creditors' funds, is clearly an attempt to mitigate this problem. However, as the courts have recognised, the vast majority of small-firm failures occur because of managerial inadequacies and unexpected economic downturns rather than as a result of deliberate attempts to cheat creditors. Hence this legislation, even if its main provisions were known and understood by owner–managers, is unlikely to have much of an impact on their behaviour (see Keasey and Watson (1994) for a review).

The most common contractual solution adopted by the banks to reduce their exposure to risk is to offer primarily short-term, frequently reviewed loans and overdrafts and to secure these on the personal assets of the small-firm owner–manager. This effectively ensures that owner–managers continue to personally bear all the business risks associated with their actions without the banks needing to engage in costly monitoring activities. However, it is precisely these aspects of the debt contract which have become the focus of recent criticisms.

THE BANK FINANCING OF SMALL FIRMS: SOME RECENT UK EVIDENCE

The sample and data

To assess the relative position of the bank financing of small firms across the late 1980s, we analyse the published accounts of a sample of UK small firms. The data on small-firm accounts was provided by local bank branches. This will form a backcloth against which to judge both the extent of bank financing and the recent conflicts between the banks and small firms.

The sample consists of 110 small firms[1] based in the Yorkshire region of the UK. Evidence from other UK studies (Bradford 1993) indicates that the financial and sectoral characteristics of the sample are generally representative of UK small firms and that the sample does not appear to display any obvious regional biases. The following statistics describe the basic features of the sample for the period 1985 to 1990:

Turnover – the sample has a mean of £308,140 and ranges from a minimum of £17,240 to a maximum of £822,730 in 1985; for 1990 the mean is £446,481, minimum £78,786 and maximum £1,443,980.

Sectors – the number of firms in Services is 27; Construction, Chemicals and Extractive Industries is 18; Metal Goods, Engineering and Other Manufacturing is 34 and Distribution, Transport and Communication is 31.

Company Age – the firms range in age from a minimum of 3 years to a maximum of 224 years. The median of the distribution is 13 years, whilst the mean, which is unduly influenced by the few extreme values for firms which claimed to be of very old vintage, is 20 years. Thus the sample consists of a mix of reasonably well-established and young firms.

Number and Type of Directors – the median number of company directors is two and the range is from one to six. Not surprisingly, the sample of firms contains many family businesses, with some 41.8 per cent of the sample having at least one other member of the family as a director. Interestingly, 24.5 per cent of the sample have husband and wife teams as directors. Furthermore, the average age of the board of directors is 46 years, with a minimum age of 30 years and a maximum of 64 years. In terms of gender, 74.8 per cent of the 270 directors in the sample are male.

Number and Type of Loans – the mean number of loans per firm is 1.64 with 88 per cent of the sample having two loans or less. Only 8.2 per cent of the sample did not have some form of debt finance. Of the loans in the sample, 91 per cent of the loans came from banks, with the mean level of bank loans equalling £22,656, overdrafts equalling £48,022 and other loans equalling £3,168. Thus, for loans in total, the mean amount equals £73,847.

Loan Security – only 7.3 per cent of the overall sample did not have to provide some form of security. In fact, of those with loans only two cases did not have to provide some form of security. Of the firms with loans (101 cases), 47 per cent had to provide unlimited personal guarantees, whilst 25 per cent provided no personal guarantees but instead secured the loans solely on the business assets. In terms of the amount of security, the mean level of security for the sample is £115,710 and the average security ratio is 2.95. These figures may be an underestimate of the security provided because they do not allow for cases of unlimited security on personal and business assets. However, it also needs to be realised that the provision of security is often 'lumpy' due to the fact that the assets (often the personal home of one or more of the directors) providing the security are indivisible. Thus when a loan of £50,000 is secured on the property of the owner, the property may be valued at £100,000 – the non-divisibility of this asset implies that the security ratio is 2 : 1. Hence, the security ratio may simply reflect the lumpiness of the owner's assets, rather than being indicative of any 'excessive' concern with security by the banks towards the granting of small-firm loans.

Loan Status – most of the loans (89 per cent) were classified as sound by the bank branches. Only 8.2 per cent of firms were (or had been) under scrutiny during the study period and only one firm (0.9 per cent) was in the recovery department. Finally, only 2 firms (1.8 per cent) in the sample had failed – one being a creditor's voluntary liquidation and the other currently in administrative receivership.

Descriptive analysis of the financial information

The purpose of this section is to describe the broad asset and financial structures of the sample. This will allow the relative position of bank financing to be assessed. Tables 4.1 and 4.2 show the financial summaries in terms of nominal £000's, whereas

Table 4.1 Summary of raw accounts data 1986–90

	Mean values in £000's[a]				
Balance sheet	*1986* *N = 72*	*1987* *N = 90*	*1988* *N = 102*	*1989* *N = 102*	*1990* *N = 91*
A Fixed assets					
Land and buildings – Freehold	15.3	19.1	19.2	31.0	35.3
– Leasehold (over 21 years)	6.4	7.0	8.5	9.9	13.7
Plant and machinery	13.7	15.0	17.1	20.6	21.1
Fixtures, fittings, tools and equipment	5.0	5.2	7.0	7.4	9.9
Motor vehicles	18.7	23.1	23.7	31.7	40.6
Leased assets	0.6	0.6	0.6	0.7	0.9
Fixed assets (Total)	59.7	70.0	76.1	101.3	121.6
B Investments	0.7	0.9	0.9	1.4	1.4
C Current assets					
Stocks – Raw materials	12.9	10.7	11.5	12.0	12.2
– Work in progress	8.4	10.9	12.5	14.7	13.9
– Finished goods	16.8	17.8	15.7	16.0	19.2
Debtors – Trade	57.3	57.6	62.4	69.6	72.4
– Others	2.6	2.3	4.3	3.9	5.6
– Pre-payments	2.0	2.1	2.0	2.4	3.0
Listed investments	0.0	2.3	2.2	3.7	2.8
Cash at bank and in hand	7.9	6.8	7.8	10.2	8.8
Other current assets	1.8	1.6	1.3	3.3	2.7
Current assets (Total)	109.8	111.8	119.7	135.8	140.6
D Current liabilities – due within 1 year					
Owing to banks	29.6	27.3	27.2	39.5	46.6
Creditors – Trade	37.9	39.4	44.1	43.9	45.5
– Others	8.7	9.9	10.1	12.3	11.5
– Preferential	7.1	7.1	7.4	8.3	8.8
Taxation – Current	6.2	5.8	6.1	7.1	6.9
Hire purchase/leasing agreements	4.5	5.7	6.7	7.2	8.6
Other short-term liabilities	8.7	9.6	8.7	12.2	15.9
Current liabilities (Total)	102.6	104.6	110.4	130.7	143.9
E Net current assets (liabilities)	7.2	7.3	9.3	5.1	–3.2
F Amounts due after 1 year					
Owing to banks	6.1	7.7	8.3	15.6	18.0
Mortgages/secured loans – Up to 5 years	0.5	0.8	0.6	3.4	3.0
– 5 years or more	1.2	0.7	1.5	1.8	2.8
Unsecured loans	4.7	7.6	10.6	10.4	11.7
Amounts due after 1 year (Total)	12.5	16.8	21.0	31.2	35.5

Table 4.1 (continued)

Balance sheet	Mean values in £000's[a]				
	1986 N = 72	*1987 N = 90*	*1988 N = 102*	*1989 N = 102*	*1990 N = 91*
G Other liabilities/provisions					
Directors' loans	7.8	10.5	11.5	11.4	11.3
Taxation – Future	0.2	0.0	0.0	0.2	0.3
– Deferred	3.2	2.4	1.6	2.1	2.5
Specific provisions other than tax/dividends	0.8	0.9	1.2	1.6	2.1
Other liabilities/provisions (Total)	12.0	13.8	14.3	15.3	16.2
H Net assets (A + B + C – D – F – G = H)	43.2	47.5	51.0	61.3	68.1
J Capital and reserves					
Called up share capital	5.2	5.7	6.9	7.3	8.1
Reserves	2.8	4.6	5.3	9.0	12.2
Profit and loss account (adverse)	37.0	38.6	40.8	47.4	50.9
Less intangibles	1.9	1.3	2.1	2.1	3.0
Surplus resources	43.2	47.5	51.0	61.3	68.1

[a] Arithmetic mean of sample firms' accounts items

Tables 4.3 and 4.4 report the financial data in terms of common size statements where all profit-and-loss account items are expressed as a percentage of turnover and all balance-sheet items are expressed as a percentage of total assets.[2]

Balance sheets

Consideration will be first directed to the summaries of the raw accounts (Table 4.1). Average fixed assets increased in nominal terms by over 100 per cent for the period 1986 to 1990. Not surprisingly, given the high levels of activity in the property and vehicle markets in the late 1980s, land, buildings and motor vehicles seem to account for a major part of the increase in fixed assets. However, it is clear that land and buildings account for the largest proportionate increase and that motor vehicles actually formed a marginally declining proportion of fixed assets. Given the inflation in the property sector during the late 1980s and the option provided by UK Company Law of revaluing freehold land and buildings,[3] it is unclear whether there has been any real increase in the fixed-asset base of the sample. Current assets showed a far

Table 4.2 Summary of profitability and returns, 1986–90

	Mean values in £000s[a]				
	1986	*1987*	*1988*	*1989*	*1990*
Profit and loss account	12 months	12 months	12 months	12 months	12 months
Turnover(less returns)	308.1	341.6	360.4	398.9	446.5
Cost of goods sold (if available)	209.8	241.0	245.0	267.7	292.5
Gross profit/(loss)	98.3	100.6	115.4	131.2	154.0
Depreciation	9.5	10.5	12.3	15.1	15.8
Repairs/renewals	3.8	2.4	3.0	3.5	4.4
Directors' withdrawals/remuneration	24.4	26.1	26.3	31.7	32.6
Interest paid – Bank	4.3	4.2	4.6	7.0	9.2
– Hire purchase	0.9	1.0	1.1	1.8	1.9
– Leasing charges	0.6	2.9	0.9	0.3	1.3
– Other	0.5	0.4	0.3	0.5	1.7
Other items	0.1	0.5	3.6	3.6	–0.4
Net profit before tax (NPBT)	11.2	11.3	14.5	13.2	18.3
Non-recurring items	0.1	0.6	0.3	–0.3	–0.2
Taxation – Current	3.5	2.4	3.4	4.1	4.9
– Future/deferred	0.5	0.4	0.2	0.3	0.3
Dividend – Paid and proposed	0.6	2.1	2.0	3.8	5.2
Balance added to Profit and loss account	6.5	6.2	8.6	5.2	7.9

[a] Arithmetic mean of sample firms' accounts items

lower nominal increase than fixed assets (only 28 per cent) and are dominated by trade debtors (approximately 50 per cent of the current assets for 1990); stocks and work-in-progress of various kinds account for most of the remaining balance.

Across the whole period, current liabilities stayed roughly in balance with current assets. In terms of the nominal figures, bank overdrafts accounted for the largest absolute increase, with trade creditors showing the next largest absolute increase. In 1990 bank overdrafts and trade credit each provided approximately 32 per cent of the current liabilities of the firms in the sample. Longer-term loans are on average small relative to these short-term sources of finance. Thus in terms of debt finance the sample is similar to other studies, which have invariably found that short-term bank finance and trade credit are the major sources of finance. However,

Table 4.3 Accounts data: common size statements[a]

		Mean values (per cent)			
Balance sheet	*1986* *N* = 72	*1987* *N* = 90	*1988* *N* = 102	*1989* *N* = 102	*1990* *N* = 91
A Fixed assets					
Land and building – Freehold	5.3	6.9	6.7	10.4	10.1
– Leasehold (over 21 years)	2.7	3.0	3.4	3.1	4.2
Plant and machinery	6.7	6.9	7.7	6.9	6.5
Fixtures, fittings, tools and equipment	3.4	3.6	4.7	4.5	4.9
Motor vehicles	13.0	11.8	10.5	11.0	12.0
Leased assets	0.4	0.3	0.3	0.2	0.4
Fixed assets (Total)	31.5	32.5	33.3	36.1	38.1
B Investments	0.3	0.3	0.3	0.6	0.5
C Current assets					
Stocks – Raw materials	7.0	5.4	5.6	4.9	4.9
– Work in progress	6.9	6.9	6.9	6.9	6.3
– Finished goods	8.6	9.8	8.6	7.7	7.7
Debtors – Trade	35.6	34.6	34.7	33.5	31.6
– Others	1.5	1.6	2.7	1.7	2.7
– Pre-payments	1.1	1.2	1.1	1.1	1.3
Listed investments	0.0	1.2	1.4	1.4	1.2
Cash at bank and in hand	6.8	5.6	5.0	4.8	4.6
Other current assets	0.6	0.8	0.7	1.4	1.2
Current assets (Total)	68.2	67.2	66.4	63.3	61.4
D Current liabilities – due within 1 year					
Owing to banks	14.6	14.7	14.0	18.3	18.3
Creditors – Trade	25.0	23.6	23.6	21.3	21.7
– Others	8.0	6.0	6.1	6.3	6.1
– Preferential	3.9	4.1	4.4	3.8	4.3
Taxation – Current	3.6	3.7	3.5	3.6	2.9
Hire purchase/leasing agreements	3.5	3.1	2.8	2.7	2.8
Other short-term liabilities	6.3	6.0	4.7	4.4	5.6
Current liabilities (Total)	64.9	61.6	59.1	60.2	61.7
E Net current assets (liabilities)	3.3	6.1	7.3	3.1	-0.3
F Amounts due after 1 year					
Owing to banks	3.2	3.7	4.2	6.1	5.9
Mortgages/secured loans – Up to 5 years	1.0	0.9	0.3	0.9	0.8
– 5 years or more	0.4	0.2	0.3	0.4	0.9
Unsecured loans	3.4	4.1	4.8	4.0	3.4
Amounts due after 1 year (Total)	8.0	8.9	9.6	11.4	11.0

Table 4.3 (continued)

	Mean values (per cent)				
Balance sheet	*1986* *N = 72*	*1987* *N = 90*	*1988* *N = 102*	*1989* *N = 102*	*1990* *N = 91*
G Other liabilities/provisions					
Directors' loans	9.3	9.2	7.8	6.2	5.5
Taxation – Future	0.1	0.0	0.0	0.1	0.1
– Deferred	1.3	0.9	0.6	0.6	0.6
Specific provisions other than tax/dividends	0.7	0.3	0.6	0.5	0.8
Other liabilities/provisions (Total)	11.4	10.4	9.0	7.4	7.0
H Net assets (A + B + C – D – F – G = H)	15.7	19.1	22.3	21.0	20.3
J Capital and reserves					
Called up share capital	3.2	3.2	3.9	3.5	4.2
Reserves	0.8	1.4	1.6	2.1	2.5
Profit and loss account (adverse)	13.0	15.3	17.9	16.6	15.1
Less intangibles	1.3	0.8	1.1	1.2	1.4
Surplus resources	15.7	19.1	22.3	21.0	20.4

[a] Average of items, as converted into percentages of total assets of sample firms

although longer-term loan finance is somewhat less than either trade credit or overdrafts, it did show a remarkable increase across the period (the mean level increasing from £12,500 in 1986 to £35,500 in 1990). If total bank finance (defined as all secured and unsecured loans owed to banks, both short- and long-term) is considered, the sample showed an increase in the mean level from £42,100 in 1986 to £82,100 in 1990. Thus, in nominal terms, the banks almost doubled their finance to small firms across the period.

In comparison to the increases in bank finance, the pattern of equity finance looks decidedly different. Defining equity finance as consisting of directors' loans, called-up share capital, (unrealised revaluation) reserves and retained profits, the total for 1986 was £52,800. Thus, in 1986, equity finance was approximately 25 per cent greater than bank finance. In 1990, equity finance (inclusive of unrealised holding gains) equalled £82,500 and was only providing, on average, marginally more finance (£400) than the banks.

The common-size balance sheet displayed in Table 4.3 confirms the above picture of the financing of small firms. It shows that the only short-term finance category to show an increase in relative position is bank finance. Thus, as suggested above, short-term bank

Table 4.4 Profitability: common size statements[a]

	Mean values (per cent)[a]				
	1986	*1987*	*1988*	*1989*	*1990*
Profit and loss account	12 months	12 months	12 months	12 months	12 months
Turnover(less returns)	100.0	100.0	100.0	100.0	100.0
Cost of goods sold (if available)	63.1	66.1	63.2	63.3	61.7
Gross profit/(loss)	36.9	33.9	36.8	36.7	38.3
Depreciation	3.0	3.4	3.7	4.1	3.9
Repairs/renewals	0.9	0.6	0.9	0.9	1.1
Directors' withdrawals/remuneration	9.6	8.8	8.8	9.8	9.6
Interest paid – Bank	1.5	1.4	1.4	2.0	2.5
– Hire purchase	0.3	0.4	0.4	0.4	0.5
– Leasing charges	0.3	0.2	0.2	0.1	0.2
– Other	0.3	0.2	0.1	0.2	–0.4
Other items	1.2	0.9	1.1	0.4	–0.4
Net profit before tax (NPBT)	4.4	4.3	4.2	2.7	2.8
Non-recurring items	0.1	0.0	0.1	–0.1	0.0
Taxation – Current	0.0	0.8	0.9	1.1	0.9
– Future/deferred	0.3	0.2	0.1	0.0	0.0
Dividend – Paid and proposed	0.2	0.8	0.5	1.1	1.0
Balance added to Profit and loss account	2.8	2.7	2.6	0.6	0.7
Ratios					
– Current assets/ Current liabilities	1.2	1.2	1.2	1.2	1.2
– Stock/Turnover × Number of days	43.4	41.8	40.4	41.0	41.2
– Debtors/Turnover × Number of days	68.5	61.5	63.0	67.5	60.7
– Creditors/Turnover × Number of days	43.5	41.9	43.3	40.8	37.4
– Gross profit/Turnover × 100	36.9%	33.9%	36.8%	36.7%	38.3%
– Net profit before tax/ Turnover × 100	4.4%	4.3%	4.2%	2.7%	2.8%

[a] Averages of items, expressed as percentage of turnover; and arithmetic averages of ratios for sample firms

finance became an increasingly important source of funding for small firms over the late 1980s. Interestingly, the relative gain by short-term bank finance offsets the reducing share of trade credit. In other words, it appears that short-term bank finance is being substituted for trade credit. The increase in the relative position of short-term bank finance is supported by the increase in the relative position of longer-term bank finance. In general, the banks' share of the funding side of the balance sheet increases from 22.6 per cent in 1986 to 29.3 per cent in 1990. In comparison, the equity financing position increases from 24 per cent in 1986 to 25.9 per cent in 1990.

Thus over the late 1980s it is evident that the banks played a major role in funding the growth of small firms. By 1990 their stake in funding small firms was almost equal to that of equity finance. However, this gearing-up by firms over the period meant that, when the economic downturn occurred in late 1990, many firms were financially vulnerable and rapidly became distressed when earnings began to decline.

Profitability and relative returns

The average profitability of the sample was consistently high over the six-year period. For instance, in 1990 the average profits before interest payments and directors' fees as a percentage of turnover was approximately 16 per cent, and as a percentage of total assets this equated with a return of some 46 per cent. However, in each year directors' fees were approximately 70 per cent of total operating profits. Since this represents funds withdrawn from the business, it is clear that typically only a small proportion of the firm's earnings will be directly available for satisfying creditor claims. Attention will, therefore, be directed towards the relative returns to bank and equity finance. To analyse the gross returns to each party, interest payments relative to the book value of debt are compared to directors' remuneration and dividends as a percentage of the book value of equity.[4]

Table 4.2 indicates that in 1986 the payments to equity finance equalled £25,000. This is approximately a 48 per cent return on the average invested capital of £52,000. In comparison, interest payments equalled £4,300 in 1986 and this gives an approximate return of 10 per cent on the bank finance of £42,100. This difference in the returns to the two types of finance is marginally diminished when 1990 is considered. Equity finance received £37,800 on an average invested capital of £82,500 and thus obtained a 46 per cent return. In contrast, interest payments were £9,200 on bank finance of £82,100 and, therefore, the return equalled approximately 11 per cent. Although the differences between the returns slightly diminished over the late 1980s, it needs to be remembered that both types of finance provided approximately equal funding in 1990. Furthermore, in payment for providing approximately equal funding, the banks received roughly a quarter of the returns paid to equity finance. The 'fairness' or otherwise of these large differences in the relative returns to equity and debt finance is not an issue addressed in this chapter. Nevertheless, this pattern of returns is exactly what one would expect given that, unlike equity holders, banks do not contract to bear business risk or to receive any of the upside gains from the enterprise. In short, debtholders contract to receive a low but certain return.

The financing of small firms

The above statistics indicate that bank finance and owners' equity provided almost equal proportions (about 31 per cent each) of the overall funding of small firms in 1990. The 31 per cent of funding provided by banks consisted of 17 per cent short-term (overdraft) finance and 14 per cent longer-term loans. Furthermore, 55 per cent of the total funding of small firms was short-term, with the banks providing roughly a third of this short-term finance. Of the longer-term bank finance, approximately a third was unsecured. The majority of both the bank overdrafts and longer-term loans were secured on either just the directors' personal assets or a combination of business and personal assets. The average security ratio of assets to loans was slightly under 3, which is remarkably similar to the figures reported by both Cowling et al. (1991) and Binks et al. (1992). The statistics also indicate an increased reliance upon short-term debt relative to equity over the expansionary period to 1990 and this certainly increased the vulnerability of firms to the subsequent economic downturn.

DEBT FINANCE, RISK ASSESSMENT AND *EX POST* CONFLICTS

As noted in the introduction to this chapter, a perennial theme of small-business representatives and government enquiries has been the notion of a 'finance gap' in relation to small-firm financing. While we accept that such a perception is widespread, it is far from clear from the above and other published evidence that this perception has any firm grounding in reality. A number of studies have certainly indicated that many small businesses often experience difficulties in obtaining finance and/or are dissatisfied with the terms and conditions attaching to it (see Binks et al. 1988; Storey et al. 1987; Cowling et al. 1991). These studies have, however, also indicated that a significant proportion of owner–managers are highly reluctant to seek external-equity finance and have never attempted to obtain debt finance from sources other than the bank. Interestingly, the study by Cowling et al. found that 70 per cent of their sample of small-firm owners had never considered external equity from banks as a source of long-term finance and, furthermore, 61 per cent said that they would object to banks having an equity stake in their firms. Thus, although the banks have been criticised for not providing equity finance (only partly true, since the largest venture-capital organisation in the UK, 3i, is actually owned by the main clearing banks) it is the small-firm owners themselves who seem to be most opposed to equity finance.

Even in the best of times, the small-firm sector is characterised by high business risks and enterprise failure due to their low degree of product and/or market diversification, reliance upon relatively few customers and/or suppliers and dependence upon the continued good health, energies, business acumen and financial probity of the owner–manager. Moreover, the closely held ownership and management structures of small firms provides owner–managers with opportunities to take actions which dilute creditor claims. Any action by the bank which attempts to prevent any such wealth transfers will, therefore, bring it into conflict with the owner–manager. Indeed, conflicts between banks and their small-firm customers seem to be inevitable given the relative payoffs to debt and equity holders and the vagaries of the business environment within which contractual rights and obligations are negotiated.

This suggests that the earnings of small firms (either actual or anticipated) will generally be a poor indication of a bank's security. The more relaxed financial reporting regulations, the scope for manipulation and the endemic uncertainty associated with small-business operations render the quality, reliability or timeliness of the financial information produced by small firms insufficient to provide reliable risk assessments (see Keasey and Watson (1991) for a review). The bank's security will, therefore, have to be closely related to the realisable value of the firm's tangible assets, plus any sums recoverable from the personal wealth of the owner–manager if the finance has been partly secured by personal guarantees. Only these funds (net of any realisation costs) will typically be available for distribution to creditors if the firm is liquidated.

The basic problem for the bank is that, as the owner–manager obtains private benefits from the firm as a going concern, he or she cannot be relied upon to act in the best interests of other investors when the value of the firm as a going concern falls below the liquidation value of the firm's assets. Consequently, debt contracts usually allow control to be transferred to the debt supplier whenever the going-concern value falls below the liquidation value. This could, in principle, be achieved by setting the debt level equal to the (net) liquidation value – since this would ensure that the debtholder only bears risks to the extent that future liquidation valuations are uncertain.

Of course, in practice, future liquidation values are usually far from being certain *ex ante* because they can be radically affected by the actions of the firm's management and *ex post* changes in the level of economic activity. Thus, once the contracting parties have agreed to the design of the financial contract, an *ex post* conflict arises, particularly if the probability of financial distress increases significantly due to some exogenous event.

With this form of contractual arrangement, conflicts can arise from differing perceptions of firm value and prospects by the two parties. In situations approaching financial distress, differences in perceived value (and hence appropriate courses of action) will be particularly likely. As analyses of the differences in the Official Receiver's and owner's perceptions regarding the causes of failure demonstrate (see Storey (1982) for a review), owners are generally more 'optimistic' in this regard and their forecasts are, therefore, unlikely to provide a reasonable basis for debtholder decision-making.

Economic recessions will increase the business risk of small firms at the same time as their assets are providing decreased security for the banks. The differences in perception are a function of the fact that each party is primarily concerned with different aspects of the return distribution. The owner–manager, because he or she obtains the full benefits of any upside gains, is naturally primarily concerned with the upper tail of any return distribution but will only be interested in downside risk up to the point when the current value of his/her investment falls to zero. In contrast, the bank does not share in any upside gains and may lose up to 100 per cent of its investment if the firm defaults. Thus the recent conflicts may be largely due to different perceptions of the consequences of exogenous shifts in the macro-economy.

Other conflicts may arise because of the incentives for the owner–manager to act in a manner which results (by accident or design) in a shift in the distribution of business risk onto the bank. These incentives are greatest when the owner–manager has a relatively low equity position. For example, an owner–manager with a low equity position (inclusive of personal guarantees) has a clear incentive to take excessively risky decisions using creditors' funds. Banks are acutely aware of this possibility and may, therefore, view liquidation as the preferred course of action if they perceive that continuation will result in increased exposure to risk without any corresponding increase in expected returns. Thus, what from the owner–manager's viewpoint may seem to be an economically irrational liquidation decision may, from a bank's perspective, be prudent banking and the only way of reducing its over-exposure in a depressed market.

Another source of potential conflict is the ability of the owner–manager to reduce the cash base, and thereby diminish the security of the debt prior to the bank being able to take action. From the owner–manager's perspective it is often desirable to remove equity from the business, say in the form of increased managerial remuneration, if the firm looks to be in financial difficulties. Indeed, because the bank's cash can be used to pay off other creditors, it is particularly vulnerable in this regard when a firm becomes financially distressed.

Given the above, the ever-present need for banks to cheaply monitor and to protect the security of their investments requires them to impose a range of contractual safeguards which creates potential conflicts between themselves and their small-business customers. Perhaps such conflicts could be reduced were there a more plentiful supply of equity finance to small firms. However, as we have indicated, small-firm owners are often unable and/or unwilling to have the involvement of external equity partners. Indeed, it may be that the apparent finance gap exists precisely because, first, small-firm owners are unwilling to bind themselves to agreements that require them to share control and upside gains with equity partners. Second, since the debt contract does not allow banks to share in these upside benefits, their preference for agreements which allow them to take protective action against uncompensated business risks is unsurprising.

A lack of appreciation by small-firm owners of the crucial difference between the relative risks and returns accruing to debt- and equity-holders would seem to be one of the chief reasons why small-firm–bank relations are often strained. During 1991 the main UK clearing banks received a lot of criticism from small businesses, particularly those experiencing financial difficulties. The criticisms were wide-ranging and included claims of insensitivity over the handling of small-firm accounts, of over-charging in terms of interest payments, of applying bank charges without informing the customer, of being overly eager in calling in their loans, and of demanding too high a level of security. The media and small-business pressure groups were not slow to take up these issues and even the 'quality' newspapers devoted several pages to the 'horror stories' recounted by small-business owners. Now that the media interest in the issue has diminished, it has become obvious that the main cause of the large increases in small-business failures was the recessionary impact of the then government's high-interest-rate monetary policy, and that many of the most serious complaints were based upon a few heavily cited, and unrepresentative, cases. Although the Cowling et al. (1991) and Binks et al. (1992) studies were critical of the banks on some counts, both reached similar conclusions: namely, that the reporting of the mid-1991 conflicts between banks and small firms was largely 'hysterical' and that the popular horror stories represented an unrepresentative minority and were certainly not the norm. This conclusion is supported by the Treasury and Bank of England inquiry reported in the *Financial Times*, 18 July 1991 and the report by the Director General of Fair Trading reported in the *Financial Times*, 28 June 1991, which both found there was no evidence of an organised cartel or collusion between banks in their dealings with small firms.

In reply to the accusation of abusing their monopoly power by increasing their margins on small-firm lending precisely when firms were most financially vulnerable, the banks have argued that this simply reflects their increased monitoring costs and greater exposure to business risk in economic downturns. The published evidence from the Cowling et al. (1991) and Binks et al. (1992) surveys indicate that most small firms pay interest rates only some 2 to 4 per cent above base rates and that bank margins on small-firm lending have increased only marginally as the recession deepened.

Perhaps the major source of recent concern has been the perception that a significant number of small firms have failed because the banks were too ready to call in the receivers whenever any hint of financial problems came to light. These concerns were inevitably fuelled during 1991 and 1992 by the downturn in macroeconomic activity because, as Chrystal (1992) has noted:

> Money lenders have had a bad press in recessions ever since Biblical times. In this regard, banks do not cause the problem – rather it is the inevitable outcome of a business downturn. The bank simply conveys the news that negative cash flow cannot go on for ever.

The banks' concern with protecting the security of their investments merely reflects the nature of the debt contract – lenders do not share in upside potential and, therefore, do not expect to bear any uncompensated downside risks.

CONCLUDING REMARKS

This chapter has examined the often strained relationships between banks and small firms by focusing upon the nature of the debt contract and the ownership and management characteristics of small firms, which create problems for both parties in accurately assessing their exposure to business risk. Given the potential business risks involved, the empirical evidence presented regarding the extent of bank financing over the boom period of the late 1980s does not suggest that firms were in general being denied bank finance. The arguments and analysis indicate that the more recent *ex post* contractual conflicts between banks and small firms can be largely seen as being due to a combination of economic factors not of the banks' making. Briefly, changes in the banks' competitive and regulatory environment and the public-policy emphasis upon encouraging new start-ups had, by the late 1980s, led to the creation of many economically marginal, inadequately managed and financially vulnerable small firms. When these factors are coupled with a heavy reliance upon debt finance and the difficulties associated with monitoring and controlling the actions of the small-firm owner–manager, then conflicts between banks and small businesses became an ever-present possibility. With the onset of the deepest UK post-war recession in late 1990 conflict became inevitable. The impact of the downturn upon the commercial property and private housing sectors seriously undermined the main source of the banks' security for small-firm loans and the banks had to take actions which reduced their exposure to increased levels of uncompensated risk.

We conclude that understanding of these issues is a prerequisite for reducing tensions and for improving the relationships between banks and small businesses in the future. In economic recovery this will be crucial, as many firms will need substantial amounts of additional working capital to expand production. However, because of the not unreasonable perception of the banks that small businesses are likely to be particularly high-risk propositions, the availability of this finance will be vitally dependent upon small firms and banks working in a more cooperative manner in sharing information and assessing risks.

NOTES

1 The sample and data used in this study are discussed in more detail in Keasey and Watson (1992). The actual number of firms in the sample varies from year to year to avoid 'survivorship bias'.

2 Figures in the common-size statements are 'equally weighted' averages of the individual ratios computed for each firm in the sample. For example, the equity to total assets ratio in the common-size statement was calculated as follows:

$$\frac{1}{n}\sum_{i=1}^{n}(\text{Equity}_i/\text{Total assets}) \times 100.$$

Because larger firms are given more weight in value-weighted ratios, computed in Tables 4.1 and 4.2, these do not equate exactly with the figures shown in the common-size statements of Tables 4.3 and 4.4.

3 Non-profit-and-loss account reserves represent revaluations of freehold land and buildings. Increases in these reserves are 'unrealised gains' and do not represent any actual increase in the business equity funds.

4 This comparison understates the total return to equity by ignoring the additional implied return represented by the undistributed earnings. Moreover, by focusing on the bank's gross returns (that is, ignoring all the bank's costs), we necessarily overstate the actual profitability of small-firm lending. However, the comparisons indicate the relative size of the firm's cash flows that are appropriated by each of the two main suppliers of finance.

5

THE ROLE OF INFORMAL VENTURE CAPITAL IN FINANCING THE GROWING FIRM

Richard T. Harrison and Colin M. Mason

INTRODUCTION

This chapter continues the reappraisal of the UK's equity 'finance gap'. Despite the introduction from the early 1970s onwards of a number of measures to promote small businesses in the UK (Beesley and Wilson 1982; Burns and Dewhurst 1983), subsequent reports have continued to identify the constraining effects of a finance gap, particularly for relatively small amounts of money (Wilson 1979; Robson Rhodes 1984; NEDC 1986a). Although some commentators have argued that policy initiatives such as the Loan Guarantee Scheme and the Business Expansion Scheme (BES) have closed the external finance gap for small business (e.g. Burns 1987), this has been disputed on both empirical and theoretical grounds (Harrison and Mason 1986; Mason et al. 1988; Binks and Vale 1990).

Against this background, this chapter examines the role of *informal* venture capital in the financing of small firms. Informal venture capital is defined as equity and near-equity risk finance invested by private individuals directly in unquoted businesses without the use of formal intermediaries (Gaston 1989). This chapter has five objectives. First, it summarises the evidence for the existence of a finance gap in the UK, particularly as it affects the supply of institutional or formal sources of equity finance. Second, it considers from a theoretical standpoint the role of informal venture capital in filling this gap and explanations for its existence. Third, it reviews the empirical evidence on the role of informal investors – or 'business angels' as they are often termed – in the financing of small firms in the United States. Fourth, it uses a variety of published and unpublished sources to assess, for the first time, the significance of informal investors in the United Kingdom, and presents some results from the first systematic study of informal investors in the UK. Finally, it reviews some strategies that can be adopted by policy makers for increasing the flow of informal venture capital into unquoted businesses in the UK.

FINANCE AND THE SMALL FIRM

Recent discussions of the finance gap in the UK have increasingly seen the problem in terms of a shortage of start-up and early-stage equity capital from either institutional or private sources. For example, an evaluation of the operation of the Loan Guarantee Scheme concluded that 'there is still a gap in the market for long-term funds (whether equity or loan) for businesses which need to raise relatively small amounts of money'. (Robson Rhodes 1984: p. 39). This view is corroborated by the experience of small-firm assistance agencies (Batchelor 1987). As a consequence, many small businesses are undercapitalised, their capital structure is heavily dependent upon short-term funds, including creditor financing, and there is limited reliance on long-term debt and equity finance (Burns and Dewhurst 1983). This is particularly true of businesses in the early stages of their development, where the founder's own resources and, later, bank debt dominate (Mason 1989; Peterson and Shulman 1987; Walker 1989; Storey and Strange 1992). More recently, the ACOST report on barriers to growth in small firms re-emphasised the continuation of an equity gap, particularly for seed capital and for technology-based ventures, and, for the first time in the UK, identified the potential role of the informal venture-capital market in closing that gap (ACOST 1990; see also Bannock 1991b).

The problems experienced by small firms in gaining access to equity finance in particular reflect both demand and supply factors. On the demand side, small-business owner–managers often do not fully appreciate the advantages of equity finance. Consequently they are reluctant to surrender equity to outsiders because of the perceived loss of independence, control and freedom of action, the dilution of earnings, and the cost in terms of fees to professional advisers and in terms of the restrictions placed on managerial actions justifiably demanded by outside investors (Day et al. 1985).

For such businesses, bank debt is preferred to equity as a source of capital, and other financing options such as venture capital and private equity will only be explored – if at all – at a much later stage of development (Peterson and Shulman 1987). Indeed, many businesses regard long-term external-equity investment as financing of the last resort (Walker 1989; Myers 1984; Robson Rhodes 1984).

However, for small businesses which are actively seeking external-equity finance the supply is limited. Equity investment in small businesses is unattractive to institutional investors because the risks are not commensurate with the potential returns (Table 5.1). Small, especially new, businesses have a high failure rate and, more importantly, their growth potential is highly uncertain. Furthermore, a large number of small investments creates severe portfolio management problems for the institutional investor and imposes considerable additional evaluation and monitoring costs, and there may also be difficulties in finding an exit route for the investment (Harrison and Mason 1988).

Although venture-capital funds (including 3i plc) invested over £1.1 billion in over 1,200 companies in the UK in 1990, compared with £530 million in 1,100 companies in 1986 (BVCA 1990), this has only a limited impact on the availability of equity capital (Mason and Harrison 1991b). First, venture-capital funds have very restrictive investment criteria, often looking for returns of 30 per cent per annum, and hence are reported to accept only between one in thirty and one in sixty proposals (NEDC 1986a); second, the average size of venture-capital investments has risen sharply, from £450,000 in 1986 to £910,000 in 1990, and funds have increasingly moved away from providing investments of under £250,000 (Mason and Harrison 1991b); third, venture-capital investments are

Table 5.1 Risks/rewards at various investment stages

Investment stage	*Risk level*	*Time scale to exit (years)*	*IRR target (%pa)*
Seed capital	Extreme	7–10	>60
Start-up	High	5–10	>50
Expansion	Medium	1–3	25–40
Management buy-out	Medium/low	1–5	25–40

Source: Murray 1992b

increasingly favouring management buy-outs (MBOs) and buy-ins (MBIs) which have lower risks and quicker exit routes than start-ups: in 1987 over 60 per cent of UK venture-capital investments were accounted for by MBOs (Martin 1989; Murray 1991).

Following the amendment of the BES in April 1988 to include investments in private rented housing, it has largely ceased to be a source of small-business finance (Mason et al. 1988). Of the £631 million raised in the first two years of this extension of the remit of the BES, 84 per cent has been invested in housing projects (Inland Revenue 1991). Moreover, even before this change to the scheme, the average size of investments had risen from £183,000 in 1983–84 to £245,000 in 1987–88 (Inland Revenue 1991), which is approximately the upper threshold of the supposed equity gap. The Chancellor of the Exchequer announced in his 1992 Budget the end of BES in 1993.

Attitudes to equity finance among small-firm owners

This difficulty in raising equity finance is compounded by the general patrimonial attitude of most small-business owners which leads to high levels of equity aversion, where external equity is regarded as financing of last resort (Vickery 1989; Walker 1989). This is in turn reflected in survey evidence which suggests that, in the UK at least, high-growth and high-growth-potential firms are still likely to rely primarily on retained earnings and bank finance, rather than equity finance, to fund growth (Mason and Harrison 1992b, 1993a; Nash 1993).

Credit rationing, firm size and the economic cycle

There is, however, evidence to suggest that, on the supply side, these conventional funding mechanisms may become less attractive and more restricted in availability. Of particular interest in this context is the concern expressed over the emergence of a 'credit squeeze' as the banks reconsider their lending policies in the small-firm sector. This concern emerged first in 1991:

> The instruction from head office may be mild and judicious, but the message between the lines is stark: the easiest way to wreck your career prospects is to be caught with bad loans on your books. Hence the loan facilities for small companies ...

> and hence, too, the efforts to call in loans which are effectively the core capital of perfectly sound business ... This apparently rational, but in fact largely self-defeating behaviour is what most businessmen mean when they talk about a credit crunch. Everybody knows it is happening – except, it seems, the Bank of England, and the academic economists in the City who are paid to think like the Bank.
>
> (*Financial Times*, 2 April 1991, p. 18)

A month later, the point was reiterated:

> The CBI small firms survey confirms that there is indeed a credit crunch – if you are too small to borrow outside the banking system. It is small companies who complain that credit is sometimes difficult and always expensive ... The Bank of England calls that a fall in credit demand, the victims call it a squeeze, and all too often a fatal one.
>
> (*Financial Times*, 14 May 1991, p. 20)

By the middle of 1992, the emergence of what amounted to a dual capital market for business lending was being discussed as a real possibility:

> We are seeing a reversal of important trends that became evident when the deregulated lenders were left to run riot in the 1980s. It was, after all, the decade of the small business sector – which the banks made into their own territory ... Now the credit taps have been mostly shut off. Local bank managers tell their clients that they have been ordered by head office to stop lending ... the small business sector is in for some tough years. Big companies, on the other hand, have direct access to the still buoyant capital markets ... But most companies are too small for this to be a solution, and many ... would fail the required tests of financial health.
>
> (Riley 1992: p. 1)

The emergence of a credit crunch which affects those businesses that do not have access to public markets is not confined to the United Kingdom, nor is it restricted to the pages of the financial press (Syron 1991; Bernanke and Lown 1991; Peek and Rosengren 1992): there is sufficient emerging research and case-study evidence to confirm that many entrepreneurial firms, and not just conventional small low-potential businesses, are finding it harder to acquire new loans, and are encountering more difficulties in the application/review process, reporting requirements and collateral requirements (Goodman and Allen 1992; Vyakarnam and Jacobs 1991).

These recent credit-crunch problems have been compounded by the restructuring of the equity-capital markets and the strategic repositioning of the major players in the institutional venture-capital industry (Murray 1991a). This has led the CBI, for example, to call for major changes in the way small businesses in the UK are financed, involving both a revision of bank lending practices and a revitalisation of the venture-capital market, BES and USM (Hamilton-Fazey 1993). However, in all this debate over the problems faced by small firms in the UK in accessing external-equity finance, the informal venture-capital market has received virtually no attention, with the notable exception of ACOST (1990) and Harrison and Mason (1993b). In the remainder of this chapter, therefore, we review the nature, operation and relevance of this source of finance in the United States, where it has long been recognised as important (Wetzel 1983; Gaston 1989), and in the United Kingdom, and draw out some implications for extending the supply of equity finance to growing and growth-potential businesses in the UK.

INFORMAL VENTURE CAPITAL AND THE EQUITY GAP

One of the features of research in small-firm financing is the general lack of a theoretical framework to provide a context for empirical research (Pettit and Singer 1985). There is, however, an emerging consensus that agency theory provides a useful context for such research, if not yet a fully worked theoretical framework for the understanding of the small-firm financing situation (Landstrom 1991). Eisenhardt (1989), for example, has identified small firms as one research topic which provides a theory-relevant context for agency theory research. This rests on the argument that agency theory is relevant to those situations in which contracting problems are difficult, such as where there is substantial goal conflict between principals and agents, outcome uncertainty and unprogrammed jobs in which evaluation of behaviour is difficult.

In general, small-business finance choices are strongly influenced by cost factors. The most important of these are *agency costs* – the monitoring and information costs that outside providers of debt or equity finance incur to ensure proper use of their assets. The recipient business also incurs additional expenses because of the need to reconcile the divergent interests of the lender/investor, the loss of independence in using business assets, costs of generating and communicating information to outsiders, risk of disclosing business secrets to competitors, and other restrictions on the small-business owner–manager's ability to conduct business. Both debt and equity can be obtained from internal sources, informal external sources, financial intermediaries and public markets. Agency costs increase when financing moves from internal to external sources, from debt to equity, from secured to unsecured debt, from short-term to long-term and from private placement to public markets (Day et al. 1985; Barnea et al. 1981; US Small Business Administration 1987).

Monitoring costs arise from the needs of the lender/investor to establish (often complex) financial arrangements to monitor a business operation, to prevent the borrower's misuse of assets due to conflict of interests. In small and young firms in particular, these costs are likely to be high because of the inherent difficulty of clearly differentiating between the owner's personal finances and those of the business. This difficulty is often increased by the lack of formal financial controls. Both the lender/investor and the borrower/investee incur these costs. Lender/investors also incur costs in drawing up contracts with special covenants, in enforcing these restrictions and in constantly reviewing the performance of the business. Borrowers incur both audit and compliance costs when their freedom of action is restricted and when additional efforts are required to generate information or special reports that facilitate monitoring.

Information costs arise from the information asymmetry (differences in information available to the entrepreneur's outside investors) in a transaction involving a small business which is highly dependent on its owner. The higher the information asymmetry, the easier it is for the owner–entrepreneur to take actions detrimental to the interests of others, and this is likely to be more pronounced because of the lower control exercised by the managerial labour market on information about small-firm managers acting in this manner (Pettit and Singer 1985). Information asymmetry is particularly pronounced for small and young businesses in dynamic industrial sectors. Owners of small businesses have much greater knowledge of their business than external lenders/investors and may not easily be able to communicate this knowledge to outsiders. Moreover, much of this knowledge and expertise is intangible and, therefore, hard to quantify, thus reducing the equity value of the firm and thereby diluting the original equity holder's value. In the small firm these dilution costs will be larger due to the concentration of ownership and management relative to larger businesses (Myers and Majluf 1984). The small-business owner–manager is more knowledgeable of the market for the firm's product or service than are outsiders, including potential investors, and is reluctant to disclose this information for fear that the key features may be appropriated by competitors. Lender/investors also incur costs in acquiring the information needed to understand and place a value on the potential of the business (Pettit and Singer 1985).

Agency cost considerations are a major factor in a small firm's choice of financing. The agency costs of equity capital are higher than for debt finance: for the investor, a firm's profit potential is harder to monitor and evaluate than its debt-paying potential, equity investment requires that all aspects of a business operation be monitored, and the investment is long-term with little scope for renegotiation. For the small-business owner, the information costs of equity capital are higher because of the need to reveal more information about the business and costs of locating suitable investors. To minimise agency costs a small firm will first turn to internal capital. As it grows and the demand for capital increases, the owner may raise debt capital from friends and relatives and commercial banks. Reliance on banks will increase over time as monitoring costs decline with repeated borrowing. Most small firms will only seek external equity capital when the gearing/leverage becomes unacceptable to the banks. The equity gap arises because most small firms find that raising equity capital from the public market is too expensive (Walker 1989; US Small Business Administration (USSBA) 1987; Jensen and Meckling 1976).

The use of private informal equity investment provides an appropriate resolution for the new/small business equity gap because it has lower agency costs than are incurred in borrowing from external sources and less likelihood of owner-equity value dilution. In particular, it is possible that informal equity investment may involve lower information and monitoring costs for a small business than unsecured loans from financial intermediaries, due to the need to prepare detailed credit reviews and collect information for formal reviews of the progress of the loan. Most informal investors develop prior knowledge of the industry, the business and its owners. Moreover, the asymmetric-information problem is reduced by information disclosure to investors in private negotiation rather than public documentation (Pettit and Singer 1985).

INFORMAL VENTURE CAPITAL IN THE USA

In the United States informal investors (that is, excluding investments by professionally managed venture-capital funds, other institutional investors and the public stock market) play a significant role in filling the equity gap. Informal investors – often known as 'business angels' – are private investors who provide risk capital directly to new and growing businesses. Informal venture capital has a number of advantages over alternative sources of external equity finance. First, it is easier to obtain small amounts of finance from business angels than from institutional providers of venture capital, as informal investors generally operate at the lower end of the investment size range (see below). Second, raising equity capital from informal investors does not involve the high fees (which may range from £100,000 to £300,000 depending on the source of the finance used) that are incurred when financial institutions provide finance. Third, business angels are frequently 'hands-on' investors, contributing their own management skills to the businesses in which they invest (Harrison and Mason 1992a). Fourth, the private investor does not apply the same criteria to the investment decision as the venture capitalist. Fifth, informal risk capital is regarded as 'patient money' because the informal investor may be prepared to take a longer-term view of the investment than the venture capitalist. Sixth, according to Gaston (1989), business angels live virtually everywhere and – unlike venture-capital firms – are not restricted to major financial centres and large urban areas. Finally, raising capital from business angels at least partially overcomes the problem of agency costs and asymmetric information which underlie the existence of the equity gap (Pettit and Singer 1985; Harrison and Mason 1988).

Business angels are a long-established source of risk capital: indeed, Henry Ford raised $41,500 from five informal investors to start his automobile business (Gaston 1989). However, it is only very recently that their major role in the financing of small businesses has been recognised: for example, it has been claimed that angels represent the largest pool of risk capital in the US and finance as many as twenty times the number of firms financed by institutional venture capitalists, while the aggregate amount they invest is perhaps twice as big (Wetzel 1986a, 1986b). Gaston (1989) similarly concludes that informal capital is the single largest source of external equity capital for new and growing small businesses in the United States, and almost exceeds all other sources combined: 'their commitments add up to over $32 billion in equity financing per year ... By contrast professional venture capitalists supply only about $3 to $8 billion per year, and small business public stock issues are not even in the same league'. He goes on to note that angels provide capital to over forty times the number of firms receiving investments from professional venture-capital funds.

There is now a substantial volume of research in the US on the informal venture capital market. Much of this literature comprises studies of informal investors in various states and regions (Wetzel 1981; Wetzel and Seymour 1981; Haar et al. 1988; Myers and Moline 1988; Neiswander 1985; Schell 1984; Tymes and Krasner 1983; Postma and Sullivan 1990; Sullivan and Miller 1990). The US Small Business Administration has also sponsored studies of the informal risk capital market in various regions (Aram Research Associates 1987; Gaston and Bell 1986, 1988). Other studies have examined the role of business angels in the financing of high-technology and high-growth firms (Freear and Wetzel 1988; Wetzel and Wilson 1985). Recent research from Canada has also demonstrated that informal venture-capital represents the most important source of external equity capital for small businesses (Riding and Short 1987a, 1987b; Short and Riding 1989; Government of Ontario 1990).

Characteristics of business angels

As a result of this research the main characteristics of business angels in the US are now fairly clear (Table 5.2). Business angels are predominantly white males in the 35–55 age group and are highly educated, generally in business or engineering disciplines. Most informal investors are business owners with entrepreneurial experience. Contrary to popular belief, relatively few doctors, lawyers, dentists and other professionals are business angels: in Gaston's (1989) study this group comprised just 8 per cent of all

Table 5.2 The US informal risk capital market: a composite profile

Angel personal characteristics

- Business owner/manager is a principal occupation (69 per cent)
- Has personal entrepreneurial experience (83 per cent)
- 47 years old (median)
- White male (84 per cent)
- College degree (72 per cent) in Business (44 per cent) or Engineering (19 per cent)
- \$90,000 annual income (median)
- \$750,000 net worth (median)

Angel investment behaviour

- Friends and associates are primary information source
- Accepts three out of ten investment opportunities (median)
- Rejects deals mostly due to insufficient growth potential
- Invests about every 18 months (median) and has 3.5 firms in portfolio
- \$131,000 informal equity invested in portfolio (median)
- \$75,000 more via loans/guarantees to portfolio firms (median)
- Two other co-investors per deal (median)

Angel investment preferences

- Prefers investing in services or finance, insurance and real-estate firms (35 per cent)
- Minimum ROI target is 22 per cent per year
- Active as consultant, board member or employee (81 per cent)
- Does not seek voting control (85 per cent)

Firms raising informal risk capital

- Firm obtains \$176,700 in total angel financing (median) (\$112,000 in equity and \$64,200 in loans/loan guarantees)
- Investor group comprises three angels (median)
- Firms are at start-up or infant stage of growth (69 per cent)
- Firms have between zero and nine employees and sales of under \$350,000 per year at time of investment (74 per cent)
- Firm is 50 miles or less from angels' homes or offices (72 per cent)

Investment deal structure

- \$37,500 in equity per investor (median; mean = \$67,800)
- \$21,400 in loans/loan guarantees per investment (median; mean = \$65,000)
- Minority voting power to angel in 73 per cent of deals, with median angel equity share of 37 per cent
- 30 per cent risk of substantial capital loss expected by angel
- 25 per cent rate of return per year anticipated by angel (median)
- Investment holding period of four years anticipated (median; 5.1 years mean)
- Investor becomes active in firm as employee (39 per cent), consultant (29 per cent) or board member (15 per cent)

Source: Gaston 1989: Profiles 1.1, 2.1, 3.1 (amended)

informal investors. Informal investors have relatively high incomes and net worth, although (dollar) millionaires are in a minority. They tend to be experienced investors, with many having previously invested in stocks, bonds and even formal venture-capital funds. Informal venture-capital investments make up a significant minority of their total personal assets. They are motivated by the opportunities for high rates of return and for capital appreciation; conversely, few business angels make investments for tax-shelter purposes (Tymes and Krasner 1983; Haar et al. 1988).

Angels generally learn of investment opportunities through their friends and business associates. They typically make one or two deals over a three-year period. Investments by individual angels can range from less than $10,000 to over $500,000, but amounts of under $50,000 are most common. With an average portfolio of 3.5 investments, the typical angel may have invested well over $100,000 of informal equity, plus additional loans and loan guarantees. Angels generally invest with others (two or three co-investors is the norm), hence a typical deal may involve a firm raising over $100,000 of equity, plus loans and loan guarantees, which is well below the minimum size of investment made by most professional venture capitalists.

For every investment made, the typical angel will also consider and reject two or three other investment opportunities. The most common reasons for rejecting investment proposals are inadequate growth potential, a lack of confidence in the management, unsatisfactory risk/reward ratio, and the investor's unfamiliarity with the firm's principals and management, or with its product, process or market.

The industry preferences of business angels in Gaston's study were, in rank order, finance, insurance and real estate, manufacturing, retail and construction (Gaston 1989). However, in a number of other studies informal investors have expressed a preference for manufacturing industry, particularly high-technology sectors (Wetzel 1983; Tymes and Krasner 1989; Haar et al. 1988). In practice, angels make investments in every sector: no single industry group has attracted more than one in five informal investments in the regional studies to date. The majority of informal investments are concentrated at the start-up and infant stages; thus, firms are typically small in terms of both numbers of employees and sales. Business angels and professionally managed venture-capital firms thus play complementary rather than competing roles in the financing of small firms in terms of both size and stage of investment. This is illustrated by a study of new technology-based firms in New England which found that informal investors were dominant in financial rounds of under $500,000 but that their role diminishes quite rapidly, relative to venture capitalists, in financing rounds of over $500,000. The study also noted that in terms of the stage of financing, informal investors were the largest source of seed funds but their role declined in subsequent stages (Freear and Wetzel 1988, 1989). Similar results have been reported in surveys of high-growth firms in New Hampshire and of firms receiving equity financing from venture-capital funds (Wetzel and Wilson 1985; Freear and Wetzel 1989).

Business angels generally have fairly modest annual rate-of-return expectations relative to those of the institutional venture capitalist, normally within the 15 per cent to 30 per cent range. In many cases angels are motivated in part by non-financial rewards (Mason et al. 1991): these may include forms of psychic income (or so-called 'hot buttons'), the desire to contribute to social objectives, and personal satisfaction from assisting entrepreneurs to build successful ventures.

Informal risk capital is 'patient money'. Approximately half of all angels anticipate a holding period of at least five years. The majority of investors expect to play an active role in the businesses which they finance, generally either in an informal consulting role, serving on a working board of directors or as an employee. However, only a minority of business angels either wish for, or achieve, majority voting control (Wetzel 1983; Gaston 1989).

Informal investments are characterised by a high level of geographical localisation, with over half of all such investments typically made in firms located within 50 miles of the investor's home or office. This reflects the close working contract between investors and the ventures which they finance. However, it also stems, in part, from the absence of systematic channels of communication between investors and entrepreneurs: the distance decay that is inherent in information flows means that the likelihood of an investment opportunity coming to the attention of the investor increases exponentially with the inverse of the distance between the two parties (Wetzel 1983; see also Mason et al. 1991).

Evidence from two studies in Canada – a national survey (Venture Economics 1991) and a local study in the Ottawa– Carleton region (Short and Riding 1989; Riding and Short 1987a, 1987b) – indicates that characteristics and investment behaviour of informal investors in Canada are similar in most respects to those of their counterparts in the USA. The average age was about 50 years; approximately three-quarters had university degrees and the majority had experience of founding a business venture. As in the USA, business associates and friends were the most useful and frequent sources of information concerning investment opportunities although most angels already knew the management before making the investment. Other similarities in investment preferences and behaviour included the syndication of most deals between informal investors and a strong tendency to investment in companies located close to the angel's home. However, Canadian angels tend to invest rather more often than their US counterparts (once a year on average), commit a higher amount per investment, and are more likely than US investors to become a member of the board of directors of the firms in which they invest. However, they are less likely to work in the business. Riding and Short (1987a, 1987b) also found that Canadian business angels take similar factors into account in the acceptance/rejection decision to those of US informal investors but have a higher rejection rate. This may be related to the higher rate of return expectations of Canadian

Table 5.3 Special types of US business angel

Devils	Angels who gain control of the company
Godfathers	Successful, semi-retired consultants/mentors
Peers	Active business-owners helping new entrepreneurs, with vested interest in the market, industry or individual entrepreneur
Cousin Randy	A family-only investor
Dr Kildare	Professionals such as MDs, CPAs, lawyers and others
Corporate Achievers	Business professionals with some success in large corporate organisations but who want to be more entrepreneurial and in top-management roles
Daddy Warbucks	The minority of angels who are rich as all angels are commonly – and incorrectly – believed to be
High-tech Angels	Investors who invest only in firms manufacturing high-technology products
The Stockholder	An angel who does not participate in the firm's operations
Very Hungry Angels	Angels who want to invest over 100 per cent more than deal flow permits

Source: Gaston 1989: p. 10

informal investors – 26 per cent and 32 per cent in the Venture Economics Canada (1990) and Riding and Short (1987a) studies. The concentration of investments in high-technology manufacturing firms (70 per cent) also contrasts with the pattern in the USA, but may be explained in part by the fact that the Ottawa area contains the largest concentration of high-technology industry in Canada (Steed and De Genova 1983).

This discussion of angel 'profiles' and 'typical' investment behaviour should not obscure the fact that there is considerable heterogeneity within the population of informal investors. Gaston (1989) has identified ten special types of angel who differ in various important respects from the 'composite' informal investor (Table 5.3). A comparison of the various regional studies in the US also reveals geographical differences in certain investor characteristics, investment preferences and investment behaviour: an analysis of the characteristics of the informal risk-capital market in each of the USSBA's ten regions reveals a number of differences in angel characteristics, investment preferences and deal structures, with New England and the South East exhibiting the greatest deviations from the national pattern (Gaston 1989).

THE INFORMAL VENTURE-CAPITAL MARKET IN THE UK

In contrast to this North American research, the role of business angels in financing small businesses in the UK has been substantially ignored, until recently, by small-business researchers. The informal venture-capital market received virtually no attention in the three NEDC studies on finance for small firms which were published in 1986 (NEDC 1986a, 1986b, 1986c): coverage was almost exclusively limited to institutional sources of finance, although the more recent ACOST (1990) report did acknowledge the potential importance of the informal venture-capital market in the UK. Similarly, studies of new and small firms rarely, if ever, differentiate the various sources of finance in sufficient detail to enable the contribution of informal investors to be identified. Indeed, until very recently, the business angel was widely assumed to be extinct in the UK. For example, the Wilson Committee (1979) highlighted the decline in the availability of equity capital for small businesses from private investors – the so-called 'Aunt Agatha' figure, or what Bolton (1971) termed the 'rich uncle' – namely wealthy relatives and family friends and local businessmen, accountants, lawyers and other professionals. The committee's interim report commented that:

> In the past, it was not unusual for businessmen and other individuals to make investments in local businesses known to them or in those of relatives. Such investments were often made on flexible terms, were often more like equity in the servicing and repayment obligations they carried, even when nominally in the form of loans, and were not always motivated entirely by hopes of a quick, or substantial return on capital. They are now becoming increasingly rare.
>
> (Wilson 1979: pp. 12–13)

However, sufficient anecdotal and circumstantial evidence has emerged in recent years to conclude with some confidence that informal investors have reappeared on the small-business scene in the UK. The Business Expansion Scheme, which offered substantial tax breaks to private individuals who invested in unquoted companies, was one indication that many people are willing to provide equity capital to small businesses. Admittedly, much of the investment under the BES was made through intermediaries – fund managers and sponsors – and therefore cannot be regarded as informal investment; however, private placing – which can be regarded as informal investment – was the most significant form of BES investments in numerical terms (Mason et al. 1988). The recent creation of 'marriage bureaux' or business introduction services by some local enterprise agencies to introduce investors to small firms seeking risk capital, and the establishment of various informal-investor syndicates provide further evidence that there are individuals in the UK who are prepared to invest in small businesses (see, for example, Planning Exchange 1986; Small Business Research Trust 1989; Mason et al. 1991). Another indication of informal investment activity in the UK is the *Venture Capital Report*, a monthly publication providing subscribers with information on businesses seeking mainly seedcorn investment: private individuals account for about one-quarter of its subscribers and are the most frequent financial backers for the featured projects (Cary 1991).

Case-study material also highlights the existence of informal investors. For example, a private investor invested £4,000 in the Body Shop, in return for a half-share in the business, to finance the opening of a second shop following a bank refusal to make a loan available. When the company went public in 1984 this investment was worth several million pounds (McKay and Corke 1986). According to Body Shop founder Anita Roddick, 'Giving away half the business is considered by many as the biggest mistake I ever made, but I don't resent it. I needed the money, I needed it quickly, and Ian was the only one then who would give it to me. £4,000 was quite a sum in those days, and it was not unreasonable of him to expect something back in return – a 50 per cent stake in two small shops was hardly a fortune. I think he believed that if he eventually got eight grand back it would have been a terrific investment: in fact it was like entering the football pools over and over again' (Roddick 1992: p. 86). The financial press provides many examples of less well-known entrepreneurs and companies that either have raised or are seeking to raise finance from informal investors and also confirms that many private individuals are looking to invest in small businesses, leading Batchelor (1988) to conclude that 'private individuals are starting to emerge as an alternative source of finance in Britain for the small company which is unable to raise money from more conventional sources'.

The re-emergence of business angels in the UK during the 1980s (if indeed this is what it was) can largely be explained by two aspects of changing social, economic and fiscal circumstances. First, the highest-paid groups enjoyed the fastest increases in income during the 1980s, and recent tax changes have allowed such groups to accumulate more disposable capital rather than have this tied up, as previously, in their own businesses or as savings through tax-efficient institutional channels (ACOST 1990). In addition, a growing number of individuals have received large lump sums from such sources as 'golden handshakes', early retirements, intergenerational wealth transfer, and the sale of businesses; anecdotal evidence suggests that the small-business sector is often viewed as an attractive 'alternative' investment for some of this newly acquired capital (Cary 1991; Batchelor 1989a). The creation of the USM and high levels of acquisition activity by the corporate sector have turned many entrepreneurs into millionaires (some admittedly only on paper); if US trends are a guide, then some of these individuals will be the most prominent business angels in the UK (Conlin 1989). Second, private investors may now be more favourably inclined towards the small-company sector as a result of the Business Expansion Scheme and the superior performance of small companies on the stock market compared with their larger counterparts during much of the 1980s.

Identifying the significance of UK informal investors

Despite the plethora of studies which provide information on the sources of finance used by small businesses at various stages in their development, the contribution of informal investors is rarely identified or identifiable. Researchers have generally not recognised this source of financing in their classifications and so have failed to differentiate between different sources of equity finance in sufficient detail. Fortunately, there are three studies in which the role of informal investors can be identified and its significance assessed. First, Cross (1981) provides a detailed breakdown of sources of start-up finance by a sample of new manufacturing-firm formation in Scotland. Although some of his descriptions of sources are ambiguous, his categories of 'local businessmen' and 'shareholders' can be taken as business angels: these provided finance for 3.8 per cent and 2.5 per cent of firms respectively. A second study, of businesses on UK science parks, noted that 2 per cent of firms used private equity capital at start-up and 3 per cent had private investors as a current source of finance. This compares with 3 per cent of firms which had raised start-up finance from venture-capital funds and 8 per cent of firms whose current sources of finance included venture capital sources (Monck et al. 1988). A third study, of small plastics-manufacturing firms, observed that only 6 out of 117 firms (5.1 per cent) had shareholders who were not directors, members of directors' families or representing financial institutions (Peters 1989).

A follow-up questionnaire survey of entrepreneurs featured in the *Venture Capital Report* provides a second piece of evidence on the significance of informal investors (Cary 1991). About one-third of the thousand or so businesses featured in *VCR* since 1978 reported that they were successful in raising some or all of the finance that they sought (based on a 90 per cent response rate to the survey). The single more important sources of finance were private individuals, who backed 107 projects, and private companies which backed 71 projects. Less frequent providers of finance included the clearing banks (38), specialist venture-capital companies (19), public companies (23) and merchant banks (7) (Bannock 1991b; Harrison and Mason 1992b).

Another source of information on the significance of informal investors is provided by surveys conducted commercially by the market research firm MAS in its 'Business Line' survey for Barclays Bank. The survey, which is run as a monthly omnibus, consists of

2,000 interviews of 10 to 15 minutes' duration with the owner, director or other senior manager of a stratified random sample of establishments with a business telephone line and less than 50 full-time employees. British Telecom's Yellow Pages Business Telephone Directory provides another sampling frame (BT's computerised directory is updated monthly), and MAS has developed techniques for automatically grossing up survey results to national estimates (Hakim 1989). Questions on sources of equity capital were included in a survey that was undertaken for Barclays Bank in August 1988 (Table 5.4). This indicates that 2 per cent of firms raised equity from private investors; only family and friends (4 per cent) and banks, including their venture-capital subsidiaries (9 per cent), were more significant as sources of equity finance. Put another way, informal investors were the source of finance for about one in seven of the firms which raised equity capital. Firms which raised finance from informal investors were disproportionately concentrated in southern regions of England and Wales: 3 per cent of firms cited informal investors as a source of finance compared with less than 0.5 per cent in the Midlands and North. It would, therefore, appear that as with other sources of risk capital – notably venture capital and the

Table 5.4 Sources of equity capital: 1988 survey

Source	*Percentage of firms*[a]
Bank	9
Family/relative	4
Friends	2
Private investors	2
Other sources	2
Another company	1
3i	1
BES – direct investment	1
BES – fund investment	[b]
OTC	[b]
Venture-capital fund	—
USM/third market	—
None raised	85

[a] Multiple sources of finance were possible, so totals exceed 100%
[b] Less than 0.5%
Source: MAS 'Business Line' survey

Business Expansion Scheme (Martin 1989; Mason and Harrison 1989, 1991b) – there is a north–south divide in the availability of informal risk capital in the UK. A more recent survey undertaken by the Small Business Research Trust (1991) paints a similar picture (Table 5.5): after family and friends (10 per cent), other private individuals (3 per cent) were the most important external sources of equity finance, and were used over three times as frequently as the formal venture-capital industry. This growing evidence on the role of private individuals as an alternative source of finance in Britain for the small company which is unable to raise money from more conventional sources is reinforced by the initial findings from the first formal study of the informal venture-capital market in the UK (Mason et al. 1991; Harrison and Mason 1992b).

Summary of the characteristics of UK informal investors

From the recent research into the supply of informal venture capital in the UK it appears that UK informal investors share many of the characteristics of those in North America, in terms of demographics, investment behaviour and motivation (Table 5.6). They are almost exclusively male and most are 45 years old or over. The overwhelming majority have business backgrounds. Most informal investors are business owners, business managers, chief executives or business-related professionals (accountants, company secretaries, consultants). Moreover, most are also experienced entrepreneurs. Three-quarters

Table 5.5 Sources of equity capital in the UK: 1991 survey

Source	*No. of responses*[a]	*% of firms (n = 835) citing this source*
Personal sources	562	76.3
Retained earnings	341	40.8
Family and friends	85	10.2
Other private individuals	25	3.0
Venture capital	7	0.8
Trade investors	4	0.5
Other	5	0.6
No response	142	

[a] Multiple responses possible
Source: Small Business Research Trust

Table 5.6 Comparative analysis of 'typical' investor profiles

Characteristics	*Sunbelt Region USA*	*New England States USA*	*Ottawa–Carleton*	*Canada*	*United Kingdom*
Age	49 years	n/a	50 years	n/a	53 years
Sex	Male	n/a	Male	n/a	Male
Family income	$70,000 US	n/a	>$150,000 Can	$121,429 Can	£46,000
Net worth	$750,000 US	n/a	>$1,000,000 Can	$1,000,000	£312,000
No. of past investments	2 every 3 years	1 every 2 years	1 every year	1 every year	2 every 3 years
Average value of investments	$37,500 US	$50,000 US	$109,000 Can	$200,000 Can	£22,000 in total (£10,000 per venture)
Involvement with firm	Consulting help	Board of directors or consulting help	Board of directors	Board of directors or consulting help	Board of directors, informal consulting help
Voting control	50%	n/a	<10%	10%	10–24%
Geographic preferences	Within 50 miles	Within 50 miles	Within 300 miles	Within 10 miles of home	Within 50 miles
Business/industry	Manufacturing, Finance, Real Estate	High-tech Manufacturing	High-tech Manufacturing	Technology, Industrial Products, Consumer Products	Consumer Services, Distribution, High-tech Manufacturing, Finance
Rejected opportunities	2 per year	2–3 per year	6 per year	2 of these seriously considered (15 in total)	4 per year
Minimum required rate of return	20%	20%	32%	26%	31%
Liquidation expectations	3–4 years	5–7 years	5 years	5 years	3–5 years
Future investments	1 in next year	n/a	1 in next year	1 in next year	n/a
Primary source of opportunities	Friends, business associates	Business associates, friends	Business associates, friends	Already know management, friends and business associates	Business associates, friends
Previous start-up experience	<50%	75%	84%	75%	67%
Dissatisfaction with existing communication channels	33% dissatisfaction	65% dissatisfaction	33% dissatisfaction	n/a	47% dissatisfaction/ very dissatisfied
	$n = 158$	$n = 133$	$n = 25$	$n = 73$	$n = 86$

Sources: Harrison and Mason 1992b; Venture Economics Canada 1990

of informal investors have founded at least one business (in two-thirds of cases more than one business). Many of the entrepreneurs have subsequently sold these businesses. Informal investors are well off but certainly not 'rich': their average income is just under £50,000 and their net worth (excluding principal residence) exceeds £100,000. However, relatively few have very high incomes or are millionaires.

Angels make informal venture-capital investments primarily for financial reasons, notably because of the opportunity for high capital appreciation. However, non-financial motives, including the opportunity to play a role in the entrepreneurial process and the fun of making informal investments, are important secondary investment motives for a significant proportion of angels. The key factors that they take into account when evaluating investment opportunities are the entrepreneur and the management team and the growth potential of the market.

The typical business angel is a relatively infrequent investor, investing once every 18 months on average, although a small minority are more active investors. They generally inject small amounts of capital into the firms in which they invest: typically less than £10,000. Only a minority of angels commit more than £50,000 to a single investment. However, investments syndicated between a number of investors involve considerably larger amounts. The majority of business angels are minority shareholders in the companies in which they invest. Informal investors invest in virtually all industrial sectors and at all stages of company development. However, they have a strong preference for investing in companies located fairly close to where they live and work (typically within 100 miles). Most business angels are moderately patient investors and anticipate holding their investments for up to five years and in a significant minority of cases for longer. Sale to another company and stock-market flotation are the most commonly anticipated exit routes.

A particularly significant finding is that most business angels in the UK want to invest more but cannot find sufficient investment opportunities that meet their investment criteria. Nearly three-quarters of the investors in our survey would have invested more in the previous three years if they had come across a greater number of suitable investment opportunities. Indeed, on average informal investors have £50,000 available for investment, compared with the average of £22,000 that they had invested during the three years prior to the survey. In aggregate, the amount available for investment is three times the aggregate amount that they had invested during the previous three years. The informal venture-capital market is therefore a largely untapped source of funds for small businesses seeking venture capital.

There is as yet no evidence to indicate the size of the informal venture-capital pool in the UK or its significance as a source of equity capital. Extrapolating the proportions of small firms raising informal venture capital from the surveys summarised above, and the amounts invested and available for investment by informal investors to the population of unquoted companies in the UK suggests that the size of the informal capital pool in the UK may be in the order of £3 billion to £5 billion – a significant sum when set against the £1.1 billion invested in the UK by the venture-capital industry during 1990 (Mason and Harrison 1991b).

CONCLUSION

This chapter has attempted to provide the first overview of the role and potential of venture capital in closing the equity gap for new and small firms in the UK. Research in the United States suggests that this source of finance is more significant than formal venture capital, and by providing small tranches of seed or start-up capital as relatively patient money with moderate return on investment expectations in comparison with venture capital, complements rather than competes with institutional sources of venture capital. Preliminary, albeit impressionistic, estimates from information on informal venture capital in the UK suggest that the pool available for investment may be in the range of £3 billion to £5 billion.

The demonstration of the existence and importance of this market has considerable practical significance for central-government enterprise policy, local economic-development strategies, venture capitalists, financial intermediaries and small-business advisers (Harrison and Mason 1993a). First, increased knowledge and understanding of the informal venture-capital market in the UK can help to evaluate initiatives to link up investors with entrepreneurs seeking capital and, if appropriate, suggest more effective ways in which such introductions can be facilitated. Second, information on the characteristics and decision-making behaviour of informal investors can be used as a basis for developing strategies to reach the population of business angels and to stimulate greater investment activity. Third, detailed knowledge of the 'attributes profile' of active informal investors can help to define a target population of so-called virgin angels (Freear and Wetzel 1991), individuals who share the demographic and financial characteristics of informal investors but who have not yet made any informal investments.

From what is known already about the informal venture-capital market in both the US and the UK it is clear that this market is inefficient (Wetzel 1987). The key sources of this inefficiency are first, the invisibility of business angels; second, the fragmented nature of the market; and third, the imperfect channels of communication between bona fide entrepreneurs seeking risk capital and investors seeking investment opportunities. Thus, both the search by a business for an angel and the search by an angel for an investment opportunity 'can be ... expensive, time-consuming affair(s). The search is studded with pitfalls and dead ends that often result in failure and frustration' (Gaston 1989: p. 1). The outcome is a 'discouragement effect' (analogous to the discouraged-worker effect in labour markets) which discourages unsuccessful seekers of equity capital, would-be seekers of equity capital, would-be entrepreneurs and would-be business angels, to the detriment of the economic process.

A number of computerised matching services have been established in the USA and Canada in an attempt to overcome these sources of inefficiency in the informal risk-capital market by introducing informal investors to businesses seeking to raise capital that meet their screening criteria, and vice versa (Harrison and Mason 1993b). The first of these matching services – the Venture Capital Network (VCN) – was established by Wetzel in New England (Foss 1985; Wetzel 1992). There are at least 15 matching services in various parts of the USA and Canada, some of which are affiliated to VCN (Brown 1990). They all work in essentially the same manner. Angels and entrepreneurs pay a subscription fee to join. They complete a short questionnaire outlining their investment interests or business plan. Once the questionnaires are computerised a two-stage matching process takes place. First, the computer searches among its investor subscribers for angels whose investment preferences match the characteristics of the business seeking finance. When matches are found, a brief description of the business plan is sent to the matched-up angel. The angel can then request further information. Up to this stage names are not disclosed to either party. If the angel wishes to meet the entrepreneur the matching service will provide names and telephone numbers to each party. The role of the matching service ends at this point. What happens after direct contact is made is strictly a matter for the angels and entrepreneurs. Because of the operation of Securities and Exchange Commission guidelines, the involvement of matching services ends at the introduction stage, and it is therefore impossible to accurately assess the number of deals that they help to bring about. However, it is known that between 1984 and 1990 VCN generated approximately 35,000 computer matches which, in turn, resulted in around 3,500 requests by investors for introductions to entrepreneurs (Wetzel 1992).

A number of local enterprise agencies in the UK also operate financial 'marriage bureaux' which aim to bring investors and entrepreneurs together; however, many of these rely primarily on producing investment bulletins which provide details of companies seeking finance which are circulated to potential investors, backed up by meetings of investors to hear business-plan presentations by entrepreneurs, and so clearly lack the sophistication of US and Canadian computerised matching services (Mason and Harrison 1992a). LINC, the Local Investment Networking Company, was established in 1987 to integrate the local marriage bureaux operations of various local enterprise agencies into a nationwide business introduction service. In the three years 1987–89 LINC has facilitated the raising of over £3 million in private investment by 52 businesses in the UK (LINC 1990).

The research reported in this chapter has provided the first systematic account of the role of informal venture capital in SME financing in the United Kingdom. There is sufficient evidence to suggest that informal venture capital does play an important role in the UK, particularly for start-up and early-stage ventures, but that the informal venture-capital market in the UK is relatively underdeveloped in comparison with that in the US (Harrison and Mason 1992b). If the informal venture-capital market in the UK is to operate more effectively in improving the flow of equity finance into small and growing ventures, there is a need to improve the flow of information between investors and entrepreneurs. One such mechanism is to expand and improve the range and coverage of business introduction services on the model of those operating in the United States and Canada (Brown 1990; Wetzel 1992; Mason and Harrison 1992b). However, if this is to be effective there is in turn a need for more detailed and systematic research into the attitudes, behaviour and characteristics of informal investors in the United Kingdom as the basis for developing a wider understanding of the nature and functioning of the informal venture-capital market.

6

THIRD-PARTY EQUITY – THE ROLE OF THE UK VENTURE-CAPITAL INDUSTRY

Gordon Murray

The marked increase in insolvencies and liquidations among small and medium-sized firms (SMEs), as the United Kingdom entered into a protracted period of economic recession after 1989 (British Chamber of Commerce 1991), has added further import to the debate on the appropriate financial structure for small firms. The traditional predilection of SMEs to fund working capital and expansion via bank overdrafts materially increased their vulnerability as bank rates rose into the mid-teens and economic activity started to slow down. The funding environment of smaller firms, which are unable to access the diversity of financial instruments, including main and secondary (USM) capital markets available to larger firms (Buckland and Davis 1989), significantly worsened as UK clearing banks reduced or cancelled non-fixed-term lending facilities to commercial clients deemed an unacceptable commercial risk. This constraint in bank credit followed widespread clearing-bank losses, originating in part from the rapid expansion of small-business lending in the late 1980s (*Financial Times*, 26 April 1993, p. 16). In this hostile climate, the importance of adequate, long-term finance, that is equity, in buttressing the financial structure of the firm, was a lesson which was learned too late by many of the failing firms.

This chapter focuses on the specific role played by venture capitalists in financing the genesis and growth of new and young firms. It only looks at formal venture-capital provision although it recognises that informal private investors (often called 'business angels') have been shown to play a major role in the financing of new businesses in the United States (Wetzel 1986b) although there is less empirical evidence of them in the United Kingdom (Harrison and Mason, Chapter 5).

VENTURE CAPITAL DEFINITION

Two definitions by leading participants in the UK venture-capital industry illustrate the nature of this form of specialised investment activity:

> Venture capital in its widest sense is the investment in equity capital in unquoted companies to support their future developments and profitable growth.
>
> Dr Hugh de Quervain, Managing Director,
> Midland Montagu Ventures

> Venture capital is the investment in long term, risky equity finance where the primary reward for the providers is an eventual capital gain, rather than interest income or dividend yield.
>
> (The late) Tony Lorenz, Managing Director, ECI Ventures

Thus the venture-capital industry is characterised by a focus on primarily unquoted companies, possessing the potential to grow rapidly and to yield a level of return on capital that is commensurate with the additional risk and illiquidity of an investment which can seldom be traded during the lifetime of the investor's commitment to the enterprise. Particularly for start-up and other early-stage investments, annual returns (yield) on the investment are either absent or play a minor role in the total returns to the venture-capital investor. The venture capitalist's reward is primarily made on the capital gain at realisation or exit of his/her equity stake through the eventual sale, or, more rarely, the flotation of the business on either the main or the second-tier stock market.

The relevance of venture capital to a firm seeking additional finance is a source of frequent confusion. Depending on the degree of risk of the proposal, which may loosely be correlated with the maturity and track record of the investee company, the venture capitalist will usually demand annualised rates of return between 30 and 60 per cent over the period of their investment (Murray and Lott 1992). The ability of the majority of small firms to meet financing costs of this order is negligible. Thus, venture capital is a financing instrument which is only relevant to those fast-growth firms demonstrating the probability of achieving exceptional commercial returns, or which are in transition to different status, through which step changes in capitalisation can be realised by the equity investor. Storey et al. (1989) showed in their North of England study that these 'fast-track' firms only represented 4 per cent of the total sample of new firms investigated. That venture capitalists reject 95 per cent of the approximately 50,000 applications made to them each year (Bannock 1991b) is a reflection of their own views of the scarcity of such fast-growth firms. This situation led Bannock to argue that the limitation on venture capitalists investing more of their resources in early-stage investments is not fundamentally a supply or 'equity gap' issue concerning the availability of venture-capital funds, but rather a demand problem occasioned by the lack of attractive investee companies to venture capitalists. This view is supported by Dixon's (1989, 1991) findings.

A substantial element of the risk to the venture-capitalist investor is seen in his/her inability to exit quickly or costlessly from the investee firm in the event of its poor performance or failure. The shares of the investee firm are not traded and the investment is highly illiquid for the venture capitalist. Thus, potential future exit mechanisms are an important subject for negotiation during the initial structuring and negotiation of the deal. More importantly, considerable effort is placed on evaluating potential investments and undertaking all possible 'due diligence' in order to filter out poor investments in the pre-deal valuation process. This selection procedure remains more of an art than a science.

The venture capitalist can rarely be a remote or passive investor. The need to contain potential down side exposure obliges the investor to become closely associated with the operation and performance of the investee company's management team. In such a relationship, management has little autonomy to take material decisions without shareholder approval. Agency-cost problems of arm's-length financing contracts, considered in the Introduction (Chapter 1) and in other chapters are not relevant to investors of this nature. For example, venture-capital financing agreements are characterised by legalised control mechanisms which can, ultimately, be arranged to enable the venture capitalist to replace the original management team in the event of serious under-performance. The management of the venture capitalist and the owner–managers of the investee company are partners in an intimate alliance which can, on occasions, be fraught.

THE GENESIS OF VENTURE CAPITAL

While the rapid growth in current levels of formal venture capital in the UK and continental Europe are a phenomenon of the 1980s, the industry has had several antecedents. Hanna (1992) has noted that the clearing banks were making unsecured, equity investments to new industrial enterprises in the early part of the twentieth century. Earlier, the industrial revolution of the eighteenth and nineteenth centuries was in part funded by both rich individuals and financial institutions accepting the risks and rewards of common stock ownership in new manufacturing enterprises, such as the railways. Similarly, in the US in the 1930s, rich individuals and families were making speculative equity investments in promising new business opportunities.

The birth of the modern venture-capital firm is commonly attributed to the formation of American Research and Development by General Georges Doriot, a professor at Harvard Business School in 1946 (Bygrave and Timmons 1992). ARD's structure of a general partnership creating a management company which in turn seeks to raise term funds from financial institutions, that is the limited partners, in order to invest in entrepreneurs set the general blueprint for the subsequent industry. The attraction of this model was to grow so that by 1987, some 600 independent private US funds contributed $4.2 billion that year to a total pool of venture-capital funds under management of nearly $30 billion (NVCA 1992).

The UK, while heavily influenced by the US experience, did not establish a venture-capital industry proper until the late 1970s. In 1952, only Charterhouse and ICFC (the forerunner of 3i) were in existence. Twenty years later there were still only 16 firms, with the joint stock/clearing banks being the pioneering sponsors of mostly in-house or 'captive' venture-capital funds (Lorenz 1989). The dramatic growth in the number of UK venture-capital firms and the funds at their disposal started at the end of the 1970s.

When the British Venture Capital Association was formed in 1983, there were 36 founder members. As Figures 6.1 and 6.2 illustrate, membership was to peak six years later, in 1989, with 124 full members. In the same year, a record £1.42 billion was invested by BVCA members in 1,302 UK companies (BVCA 1992).

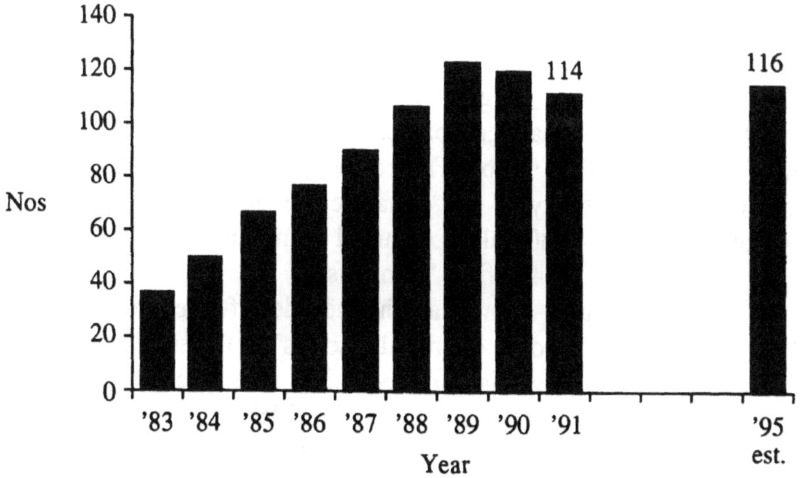

Figure 6.1 Actual and projected growth of BVCA full members, 1983–95
Source: Murray 1991a

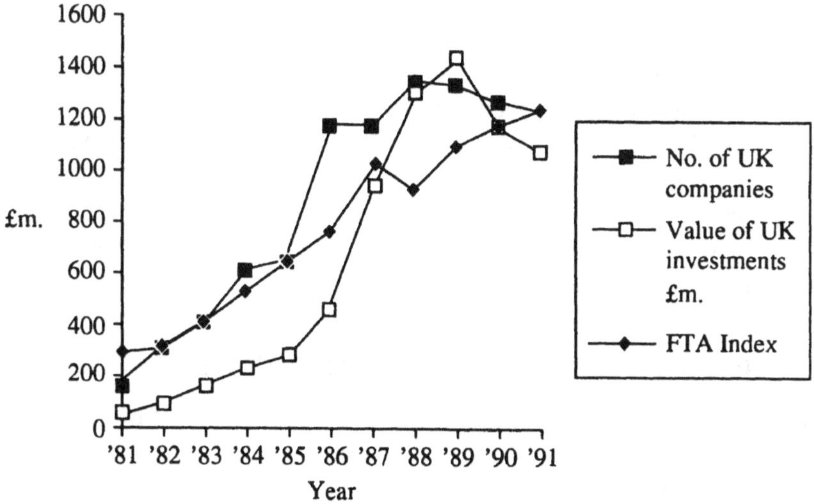

Figure 6.2 UK venture-capital activity and FTA index, 1981–91
Source: Murray 1991a

Several factors contributed to a compound annual growth rate in the value of UK venture-capital investments of 30 per cent over the ten years to 1989. Environmental 'push factors' included significant increases in unemployment as large firms restructured back to defensible core activities. The 1980s were to see unprecedented increases in the amount of new micro-firm formation (that is, with less than ten employees) an outcome which is often associated with high levels of unemployment. As larger firms restructured, there was some evidence that professional managers, in both the UK and other parts of Europe, began to take a more positive attitude to starting or joining small companies, including management buy-outs (Bannock 1987, 1991b). The corresponding growth of merger and acquisition activity in the dynamic UK market for corporate control in the mid-1980s also produced complementary opportunities for MBO creation and firm 'spin-offs'.

The 1980s became known as the decade of the entrepreneur. Government contributed its own 'pull factors' to the environment by a series of fiscal, financial and advisery incentives designed to encourage the formation and growth of SMEs. Entrepreneurs and small-business owners benefited from the decline in personal tax rates over the period, and from the creation of a plethora of small-business support programmes including the Business Expansion Scheme, the Enterprise Allowance, the Enterprise Initiative and, latterly, the Technology and Enterprise Centres. Above all, the existence in the 1980s of one of the longest 'bull' stock markets in the UK's post-war history gave both the commercial and psychological underpinning for an extraordinary period of entrepreneurial fervour.

The UK venture-capital industry, with its focus on and investment in entrepreneurship, new-firm formation, business growth, management buy-outs and buy-ins and in its exploitation of the relatively greater rise in small-firm stocks' value, both mirrored and exemplified the boom years of the 1980s.

UK VENTURE-CAPITAL INDUSTRY STATISTICS

The scale and scope of the industry may be referenced by both the finances raised by the industry from institutions attracted to venture-capital as an asset class, and by the subsequent financial disbursements by venture-capital firms to investee companies.

Funds raised

It is only possible to obtain details of those independent or semi-captive venture-capital firms which have raised funds from institutional investors on an open market. The statistics cited below do not include the funds available to 'captive' organisations, that is, those venture-capital firms which are wholly owned and financed by a parent organisation. Such organisations include the venture-capital subsidiaries and divisions of banks, insurance companies and pension funds. The funds available to captive venture-capital firms are determined by the views and policies of the parent companies, rather than a market assessment of a fund. In 1991, captive organisations were responsible for investing £240 million or 25 per cent of the total annual investment by BVCA full members (BVCA 1992).

As demonstrated in Table 6.1, finance into the UK venture-capital industry grew rapidly through the 1980s, peaking in 1989 at £1,684 million. The reduced level of funding over the next two years reflected the anxieties felt by many institutional investors as to the potential for attractive future returns from UK venture-capital activity. The figure for 1991 at £368 million was 78 per cent lower than the 1989 funds raised. In real terms, 1991 represented the lowest sum raised by the UK industry since 1984. Given that there is a two-to-three-year lag between creating a new fund and making material investments in investee companies, it is likely that this drop in new funds will be reflected directly in the reduced value of annual investments from 1994/95 onwards when the present uninvested funds under management are exhausted.

Table 6.1 Institutional sources of capital for UK independent funds, nominal and real values (1985 = 100)

	1983	*1984*	*1985*	*1986*	*1987*	*1988*	*1989*	*1990*	*1991*
Nominal £m	112	195	278	239	684	612	1684	830	368
Real £m	125	207	278	233	634	532	1360	621	260

Sources: Venture Economics Ltd 1991; BVCA *Directory 1992/93*

Funds invested

The industry categorises the use of funds by the 'stage of investment' of the recipients of venture capital. There are six discrete categories, although the first three are frequently aggregated as 'early-stage investments'. These categories broadly equate to the life-cycle of a firm from business concept, start-up, through expansion and maturity to restructuring of the established multi-enterprise, multi-product business:

Seed capital

Exploratory investment in assessing the viability of a concept/idea before commercial production or initial sales have been made.

Start-ups

Finance provided to companies for the use in product development and initial marketing. Companies may be in the process of being set up or may have been in business for a short time but have not sold their products commercially.

Other early stages

Finance provided to companies that have completed the product-development stage and require further funds to initiate commercial manufacture and sales. They may not yet be generating profit.

Expansion financing

Capital provided for the growth and expansion of an established company. Funds may be used to finance increased production capacity, market or product development and/or provide additional working capital. Capital for turnaround situations is also included in this category, as is the refinancing of a bank debt.

Management buy-outs/buy-ins (MBOs/MBIs)

Funds provided to enable current operating management (or in the case of an MBI, a manager or group of managers from outside the

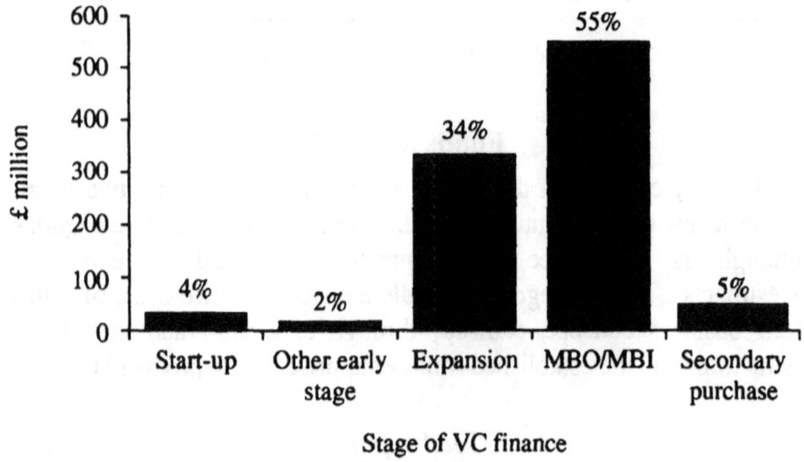

Figure 6.3 Percentage allocation of UK venture-capital investments by stage of investment, 1991

company) and investors to acquire an existing product line or business from a parent company.

Secondary purchase

Purchase of existing shares in a company from another venture-capital firm, or from another shareholder or shareholders.

As Figure 6.3 and Tables 6.2 and 6.3 illustrate, the investment activity of the UK venture-capital industry over the years 1988–91 was highly skewed towards investment in later-stage activities, particularly MBOs and MBIs. This dichotomy of venture-capital activity into early and later stage investment can also be defined as a separation into 'new' and 'replacement' equity, respectively (Murray 1991a). In the case of early-stage investment, new, third-party equity is being allocated to young firms. However, for

Table 6.2 Value of UK venture-capital investments by stage of investment, 1988–91

Nominal value £ million:	*1988*	*1989*	*1990*	*1991*
Seed capital	1.1	4	3	0.4
Start-ups	70	86	76	35
Other early stage	60	129	52	23
Expansion	402	319	343	333
MBO/MBI	733	867	582	544
Secondary purchase	33	19	53	54

Sources: BVCA *Annual Reports on Investment Activity* 1991, 1992

Table 6.3 Number of UK venture-capital financings by stage of investment, 1988–91

No. of financings:	*1988*	*1989*	*1990*	*1991*
Seed capital	13	30	42	18
Start-ups	202	177	199	158
Other early stage	182	344	141	115
Expansion	639	473	543	529
MBO/MBI	282	333	340	288
Secondary purchase	51	24	93	131

Sources: BVCA *Annual Reports on Investment Activity* 1991, 1992

MBOs/MBIs, secondary purchases and, to a certain extent, for expansion capital, the venture capitalist is acting as an alternative source of refinancing for the existing assets.

The long-term trend of the UK industry away from early-stage finance and, as some observers would argue, from the true venturing role of 'classic venture capital' (Bygrave and Timmons 1992) has occasioned much debate. The paucity of seed capital and start-up finance in particular was noted by the ACOST Committee (1990: p. 35) which argued: 'In short, the contribution of the venture capital industry to overcoming barriers to growth in small firms remains limited'. Pratt (1990) writing in the *Bank of England Quarterly Bulletin* expressed similar reservations about the role of venture capital in supporting new-business formation. Pratt also argued that the UK venture-capital industry could be seen as having an essentially short-term focus, thereby reducing its potential role as a secure form of long-term funding to SMEs.

However, venture capitalists are commercial financiers, not philanthropists or social investors. Faced with the choice of longer-term and highly speculative investments in young and unproven companies or refinancing activities in established enterprises with accessible track records, it is not surprising that the industry has elected to put the majority of its funds in the latter investment categories. In consequence, the industry is frequently criticised for the limited availability of small tranches of finance (under £100,000) for start-up companies. Less than one-fifth of the BVCA membership will seriously entertain such investments (BVCA *Directory 1992/93*).

The trend away from what are perceived by venture capitalists as very high-risk early-stage investments is also evidenced in statistics for continental European venture-capital industries. France, which has the biggest venture-capital industry in Europe after the UK, invested only 3.1 per cent of annual funds allocated of 6.9 billion FFr in seed and start-up funds in 1991, a decline to a quarter from the previous year (EVCA 1992). This trend in the UK and France is broadly replicated throughout Europe with the notable exceptions of Spain and Denmark, where start-up funds take approximately one-fifth of all investments by value. (While there are considerable reservations as to the accuracy of cross-European statistics, the underlying trend away from early-stage deals remains clear.)

It is only in the US where classic venture capital still has a major hold due to investors' interest in financing new-technology-based firms in such areas as California's Silicon Valley and Boston's Route 128. If comparisons are made between UK and US investments by value, seed, start-ups and other early-stage investments accounted for 32 per cent of 1991 disbursements in the US compared to 6 per cent in the UK (BVCA *Directory 1992/93*; NVCA 1992). There are similarly strong differences when the level of investments in technology-related enterprises are compared. If MBOs/MBIs are removed from the national figures to assist relevant comparisons, in the period 1986–91 the US venture-capital industry invested on average 84 per cent of total annual disbursements in technology-related projects. This is some two and a half times greater than the figure of 30 per cent for the UK over the same period (Murray and Lott 1992).

THE DOMINANCE OF MANAGEMENT BUY-OUTS AND BUY-INS

The single biggest product for the UK venture-capital industry throughout the 1980s has been the MBOs. Over the years 1979–91, the Centre for Management Buy-Out Research (CMBOR) at Nottingham University has recorded 3,506 MBOs with an aggregate deal value of £19.1 billion. There were also 994 management buy-ins (MBIs) worth £7.2 billion over the same period. Figure 6.4 illustrates that, while management buy-out/buy-in volumes reached a record high in 1990 at 594 deals, the value of annual transactions dropped from £7,501 million in the previous year to £3,110 million. This 58 per cent drop was, in large part, due to the decline in the largest deals (over £250 million). In 1989, there occurred twelve listed company buy-outs, valued in total at £3,780 million. In 1990, there were only four listed buy-outs totalling £170 million. MBO/MBI figures for 1991 show a continued decline in the total value of transactions since 1989. At £2,829 million, the aggregate value of MBOs/MBIs to the UK venture-capital industry can be evidenced if their value is removed from UK annual investment statistics. When excluded, annual venture-capital investment declined in nominal value terms over three years from £565 million in 1988 to £445 million in 1991.

In a survey of twenty leading UK venture capitalists in the autumn of 1990 (Murray 1991a), respondents estimated that MBOs would continue to be the single most important product in the UK venture-capital industry, still representing 51 per cent of the value

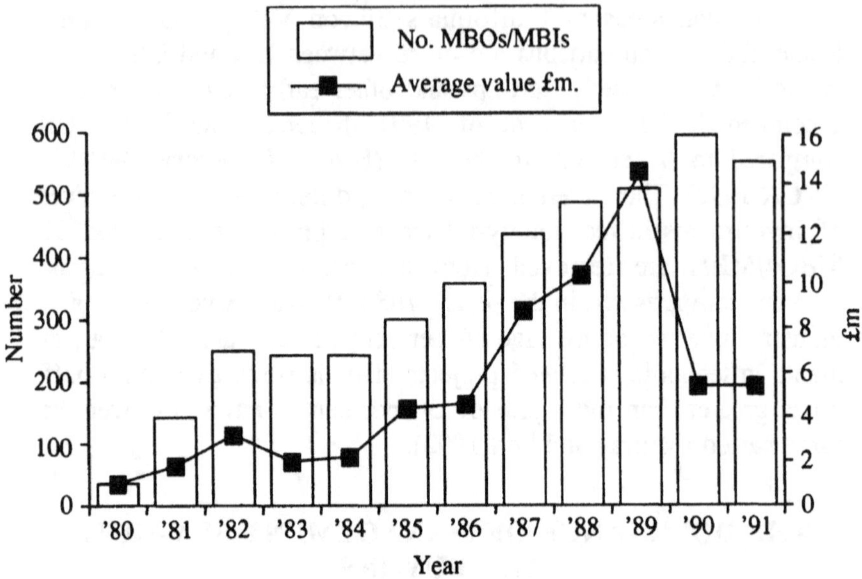

Figure 6.4 Growth of management buy-outs and buy-ins, 1980–91
Source: CMBOR 1992

of annual transactions in 1995. Respondents cited the necessary restructuring of the UK economy during the present recessionary period, coming after a period of historically high merger and acquisition activity in 1986–89, as an opportunity for continued MBO flow. The record number of MBOs in 1990, and the sustained level of 444 deals in 1991, supports this assertion. This restructuring would also give opportunities for management buy-ins but, with two exceptions of venture capitalists specialising in MBIs, the majority of respondents (77 per cent) believed the additional risks of MBIs would continue to constrain interest among venture-capital investors. MBIs were estimated to take 26 per cent of annual funds invested in MBOs/MBIs in 1995. In 1991, the percentage split in value terms between MBO and MBI venture-capital investments was 76 to 24.

Murray's respondents believed that while MBOs would continue to be the single largest product in value terms by 1995, a greater proportion of annual investment (estimated at 36 per cent, 1991 actual 34 per cent) would be applied to later-stage financing including development capital, secondary finance and, reflecting the problems of recession, rescue-type refinancing deals. The ability to provide capital for firms that remain basically sound but are financially constrained as traditional sources of borrowing and new equity become less available was seen as the single biggest contemporary opportunity, being mentioned by 59 per cent of respondents. Also in this context, UK venture capitalists have become increasingly interested in the novel activity of 'venture quoteds', that is, investing in smaller, quoted companies (see *UK Venture Capital Journal*, March/April 1991).

The continued resilience of MBOs/MBIs as a venture-capital mainstay, even in times of recession, is illustrated by the '1992 Report on Investment Activity' published by the BVCA (1993). The total value of MBO and MBI deals rose 48 per cent on 1991, nearly reaching the 1989 record of £867 million. At a total investment value of £807 million in 1992, this one investment category was responsible for 64 per cent of annual investment by BVCA members and represented just over a quarter of all financings in the year. Given that an increasing number of MBOs and MBIs were the result of rescue and receivership situations, this product has the additional attraction of appearing to be relatively less sensitive to recessionary factors.

THE VENTURE-CAPITAL INVESTMENT PROCESS

Tyebjee and Bruno's (1984) five-stage, decision-process model of venture-capital investment activity (Figure 6.5) accurately summarises the role played by the venture capitalist in identifying, appraising, investing in and subsequently advising the management of client investee firms. Interestingly the model does not include the deal realisation or exit from the venture capitalist's portfolio, a critical factor in the success of an individual investment. However, the authors do note the importance of 'cash-out potential' in their appraisal of venture capitalists' evaluation criteria.

The initial contact may be via an entrepreneur approaching the venture-capital firm directly. A number of major UK venture capitalists, particularly the largest UK firm, 3i plc, undertake substantial advertising activity to the business community. The venture capitalists also have a network of 'intermediary' organisations such as accountants, clearing and merchant banks, and commercial law firms, which will also direct potential investees to the equity providers. In addition, venture capitalists will syndicate the financing of deals with other venture capitalists, in part to offset risk but also for reasons of reciprocity in deal flow.

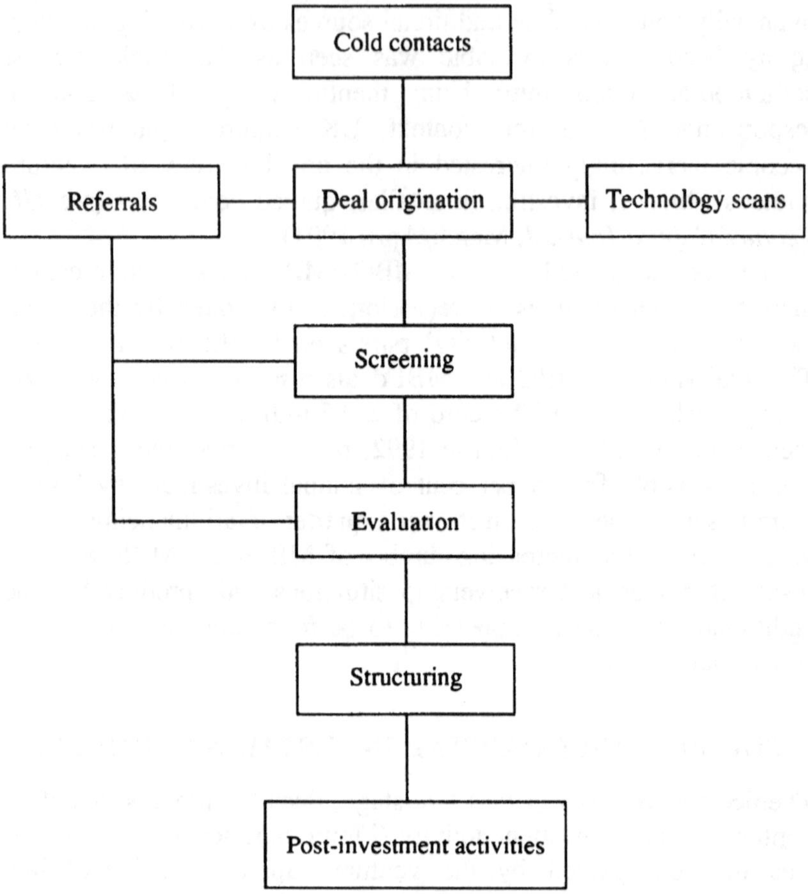

Figure 6.5 Tyebjee and Bruno's decision model of venture-capital activity

As Bannock (1991b) and Dixon (1989) note, venture capitalists receive vastly more applications than they could, or would wish to, finance. Initial screening, usually based on a brief appraisal of the business plan submitted with the original proposal, will invariably result in the rejection of approximately 80 per cent of all applications. The rejection may be for tangible reasons that the venture capitalist believes the deal is too small (or too large), is in a sector of activity which is unattractive to the fund, or where sufficient exposure to similar investments has already been achieved. The rejection may be for the more subjective reasons of the appraiser's initial personal reaction to the investment proposed. However, many investors are overwhelmed with applications, with entrepreneurs commonly making multiple applications to several venture-capital firms. Thus, this first 'cut' at the deal flow is invariably cursory.

It is for the remaining 20 per cent of applicants that the serious evaluative experience of the venture capitalist is largely employed. The business plan becomes the foundation document on which further product/market and financial investigations are conducted. These internal analyses are supported by external appraisals including accountants' reports and specialist evaluations by consultants experienced in the proposed area of activity. During this process, the entrepreneur and management team are invited to participate in repeated appraisals and reformulations of the proposed plan. Investigations will also encompass the personal and career histories of the entrepreneur and management team.

It is only after the venture capitalist has convinced him/herself of the merit, attractiveness and commercial feasibility of the project, including the capabilities of the management team, that the negotiations on the nature of the deal structure are seriously pursued. The allocation of potential rewards on the successful outcome of the investment is seen by the investee managers as a 'zero-sum game' and negotiations can be protracted and occasionally heated. For most management teams such negotiations are a 'once in a lifetime' exercise while for the venture capitalists they are their professional milieu. Managers who have gone through this experience repeatedly comment on the complexity and stress of what can be an extremely protracted exercise, often lasting over six months. The emotional tension during this process is raised on the occasions where an attractive proposal is being bid for by a number of competing venture-capital firms – a free-market situation that venture capitalists and other corporate financiers studiously strive to avoid.

Determining the decision criteria on which venture capitalists appraise investment proposals is one of the most popularly researched areas by academics (see Wells 1974; Pointdexter 1976; Tyebjee and Bruno 1984; MacMillan et al. 1985; Goslin and Barge 1986; Dubini 1989; Dixon 1989; and Murray and Francis 1992). The conformity of findings is high and can well be summarised by MacMillan et al.'s pithy conclusion (p. 140): 'There is no question that irrespective of the horse (product), horse race (market), or odds (financial criteria) it is the jockey (entrepreneur) who fundamentally determines whether the venture capitalist will place the bet at all.' Gorman and Salhman (1989) noted that, in their survey of venture capitalists, in 91 of 96 cases failures were in part ascribed to the 'shortcomings of senior management', and that this was the overriding factor in 62 of the cited cases.

Thus, despite the wealth of market and financial data available to the evaluators of project proposals, the final decision turns on both the venture capitalists' objective and subjective assessments of the quality of the entrepreneur and project management. While objective managerial track records may be available for later-stage deals and, particularly, MBOs/MBIs, in the case of seed-capital and start-up projects, the entrepreneur may well be a completely unknown quantity. As one venture capitalist ruefully noted to the author, 'You only know that you have invested in a maniac when he has cashed the cheque!'

The quality of the business plan and the rigour of the financial data included may well indicate the competence of the entrepreneur (or, possibly, the professional skills of his/her accountant or consultant adviser). However, Dixon (1989) has noted the limited use by venture capitalists of modern financial theory in choosing investments and constructing their portfolios to optimise risk/returns. Sampling 30 specialist UK venture-capital organisations, Dixon evinced surprise that none of his respondents explicitly classified projects into risk categories. Of his sample, 83 per cent evaluated risk on an individual project basis without reference to overall portfolio risk. In a related question, only 27 per cent of the sample attempted to mitigate risk through an actively diversified portfolio. Dixon attenuates his implicit criticism by noting the difficulties of information asymmetries between the investor and the prospective applicant for venture-capital finance.

In the absence of the employment of capital-asset pricing models, venture capitalists use a minimum-acceptable, annualised internal rate of return (IRR) threshold for individual-project financial assessment. The projected target IRR is primarily determined by the stage of investment, which becomes, in effect, the surrogate for risk (Murray 1991a).

If it is difficult to determine rigorously the competence of the management team prior to making an irreversible (in the short run) equity investment, the ability of the venture capitalist subsequently to advise and guide the management of the new enterprise increases in importance. Several venture capitalists argue that their financial resource is only one element of the value-added that they bring to the entrepreneur and his business. A 1992 study for the BVCA among recipients of venture capital found that, while price was the dominant factor in choosing a venture-capital partner, the respondents acknowledged that the advice and supportive relationship with their investors became, in retrospect, a more important selection criterion. In classifying the nature of the relationship between the venture capitalist and the management of the investee company, Sapienza and Timmons (1989) note that these functions are consistent with MacMillan et al.'s (1989) four categories of sounding board, financier, contact and management recruiter.

In Gorman and Sahlman's (1989) sample, the venture capitalists were allocating 80 hours on-site contact and a further 30 hours by telephone to each investee company annually. This advisery and support activity took up 60 per cent of the investment executives' work time. In order of priority, strategic analysis, managerial recruitment, operations planning and new customer and supplier contacts were the major contributions made by the venture capitalists. However, in Murray and Francis's (1992) review of European seed-capital activity, the seed capitalists were on average allocating 200 hours to each investee firm annually. This higher figure is to be expected, given the more limited commercial skills of new technology-based entrepreneurs. Sapienza (1992) also proposes that venture capitalists are more likely to add value for 'innovator' entrepreneurs who are seeking a longer-term partner.

The venture capitalists' belief that they can or cannot proffer useful advice on strategic product/market or operating issues differentiates the venture-capital firms into 'hands-on' and 'hands-off' investors. This spectrum of venture-capital/investee relationship is broadly analogous to what MacMillan et al. (1989) term 'close tracker to laissez faire'. Seed capitalists and technology investors are usually highly interventionist. This is an explicit recognition of the often imbalanced skills and absence of commercial management experience of new entrepreneurs coming from research laboratory and university backgrounds. Conversely, financial-institution-based venture-capital organisations (for example, 3i and the major bank captive funds) investing in a large and diversified portfolio of investee companies are almost invariably hands-off investors. Given the cost of a hands-on relationship, the managers of large portfolios have little economic choice. Their role becomes one of monitoring and only intervening where the situation deteriorates from agreed business targets. Their intervention may well be not to offer advice but to complement the existing management team with the recruitment of specialist staff. Their ultimate sanction is to replace the incumbent management team.

The later the stage of investment and the larger the deal size, the more likely the venture capitalists will restrict themselves to purely financial advice, including the search for an eventual exit by market flotation or trade sale. For example, in an MBO the management team purchasing the enterprise already knows the business and its product/market sector. They can usually demonstrate, objectively, the worth of their track record. In these circumstances, it is unlikely that the venture capitalists can offer skills of greater competence than those which already exist in the management team.

The venture capitalists' close involvement with their investee companies is predicated on the assumption that their efforts and interventions have a positive outcome on the success and value of the investee company, yet there is little robust empirical evidence to support this important assumption. Sapienza's study used the CEO's subjective appraisal of the value of the venture capitalists' involvement. While this is useful, it avoids the critical test of the commercial performance of the investments. Fredriksen et al. (1990) and MacMillan et al. (1989) both conclude in their respective studies of US and Swedish venture capitalists that there was no significant correlation between the venture capitalist's involvement and the venture's economic performance. Similarly, Cherin and Hergert (1988) found that the involvement of venture capitalists was not reflected in the enhanced performance of the price of stock in their ventures. It should perhaps be of concern to the venture-capital industry that this 'article of faith', which is the positive consequence of their intervention into investee firms, is not yet borne out by independent studies.

THE INVESTMENT PERFORMANCE OF VENTURE-CAPITAL FUNDS – THE FUNDAMENTAL QUESTION

A dearth of information

Since 1985, the UK venture-capital industry has seen an inflow of £7 billion of institutional investors' monies into this newest of asset classes. The majority of funds were raised in the mid-to-late 1980s and benefited from a market view of venture-capital opportunities which occasionally reached near-euphoria. The typical independent fund is structured on a 'closed end' basis, usually over a ten-year period. Thus, the investor in the fund will have no clear indication of the performance of that fund until the cycle of investee selection, investee nurturing and the sale and repatriation of returns (net of all management costs) to the private partners has been completed. During the period of the fund's life, performance information is frequently cursory and subjective. Interim performance details cannot reflect the consequences of future factors on the aggregate value of the portfolio and, at best, have limited value. The investors can have no references to price as the companies in which the fund invests are not quoted on any market. Reference to small-firm stock indices can only be of limited use given the often very 'thin' trade in smaller company stocks on the secondary market. The US, UK, and European venture-capital associations have all issued guidelines to members for the uniform valuation of portfolio companies. This is helpful but does not remove the generic ambiguity of interim valuations.

Thus, the highly peculiar situation exists whereby the investors, the fund management and the venture-capital industry at large have, at present, only the most limited information on the performance of the UK venture-capital industry over its first, dramatic decade of growth. This situation reflects in large part the immaturity of the UK industry. Problems of performance evaluation will similarly be evident in the continental European markets, the development of which have lagged behind the UK industry by between two and five years. However, it is not exclusively a problem defined by timing. Bygrave et al. (1989: p. 93) noted that 'published information on rates of return was skimpy and not very reliable' in the US, despite the organised venture-capital industry being over 40 years old. Chiampou and Kallett (1989: p. 2) also observe in their American study of the risk/return profile of venture capital that 'the lack of even working studies on this topic is remarkable'.

In both the US and the UK, the venture-capital community has been a relatively small and highly exclusive club. Until the start of the present decade, the apparent willingness of investors to subscribe to funds with necessarily limited track records has allowed the industry to shroud its activities and their material results in a pall of secrecy. The dramatically different and more hostile environment of the 1990s is already placing significantly greater burdens on the venture-capital fund managers to 'stand up and be counted' if they wish to secure continued institutional support for the financing of new and follow-on funds.

Investors' interests

If venture capital is to be treated as a distinct asset class, it must justify its peculiar advantages to the institutional investors (from the pension fund and insurance industries etc.). The majority of these investors' funds are allocated to equities and fixed-income securities. Neither of these investment categories allows the investor to tap into the market for smaller companies. However, studies comparing the performance of small companies' stocks against main market indices (FT Actuaries All-Share Index in the UK and Standard and Poors 500 in the US) over the 33 years 1955–87 show relative annual premiums of 4.8 per cent and 4.1 per cent respectively (Brakell 1988).

Until the late 1980s, the level of risk of venture-capital funds was no greater than that of small-to-medium-sized stock. Tracking a sample of 55 privately held venture-capital funds in the US over the years 1978–87, Chiampou and Kallett (1989) concluded that the dispersion of average returns for 35 mature (that is, over five years old) funds was no more risky than for SME stocks.

On a default risk basis, the mature subsample was only slightly riskier than S&P 500 stocks over the ten-year period. Yadzipour (1990), using the same time-frame with the results of fifteen US venture-capital companies, showed that the venture capitalists out-performed comparable high-growth mutual funds by nearly 10 per cent per annum while sharing the same level of risk (represented by beta values).

Venture capital can also assist the diversification needs of the institutional investor. Brakell (1988) calculated that an investor with £10 million to invest in venture capital can, by restricting his/her investment to a maximum of 10 per cent of any fund and assuming an average investment of £350,000 per investee, gain exposure to 285 companies. Given the diversity of venture-capital funds, the investor's commitment could also be balanced by stage of investment and sector.

In addition to straightforward portfolio optimisation issues, there is a more intangible attraction of venture capital. City institutions are regularly criticised for their short-termism and their lack of support for new firms, particularly in the risky but strategically imperative areas of new technologies. Whatever the intellectual merits of these accusations (see Marsh 1990, Murray and Lott 1992), public support for organisations investing directly in young companies can be politically highly attractive. This issue may be termed 'the Prince Charles factor' given his Highness's tendency to ask publicly of City leaders and the venture-capital industry, what exactly they are doing to help the nation's entrepreneurs.

Against these putative advantages of venture capital as an asset class, there are a number of limitations. Venture capital in a closed-end fund is, by definition, highly illiquid. Until the announcement by the small £60 million fund, Baronsmead, in March 1993, investors in an independent fund were irrevocably committed for the duration of the fund. Baronsmead, reflecting the increased difficulty of attracting investors, is offering to allow new investors to invest on a deal-by-deal basis and also to withdraw at any time (*Financial Times*, 30 March 1993: p. 16). Neither of these discretions has been generally available in the vast majority of fund agreements to date.

Vintage years – the critical influence of timing

Analyses undertaken by Venture Economic Inc., a US venture-capital research body, and supported by academic studies indicate that returns to venture capital in the US fell throughout the 1980s with the exception of the peak year of 1983. This was alarming for the venture-capital firms but a fact of economic life as less attractive projects are funded at the margin; the returns of this asset class were falling over the same period as the level of aggregate funds under management increased. It is highly probable that the US pattern was repeated in the UK over the 1980s.

Bygrave et al. (1989) evaluated performance data over the period 1979–85 on 131 venture-capital partnerships that were started over the period 1971–84. They showed that the returns to funds were significantly influenced by their date of starting. For example, when funds started in the period 1978–79 were three years old their compound annual IRRs averaged nearly 40 per cent. For funds starting in 1982, their returns by year three were less than 10 per cent. This study reinforced the findings of Pointdexter (1976) that the existence of 'hot' new-issue markets which occurred in the US in 1961, 1967–69, 1972, 1980 and 1983 had a significant effect on venture-capital-firm returns. During these 'feeding frenzies', as

Bygrave and Timmons (1992) have picturesquely termed them, venture capitalists can exit from investee companies at very high multiples of their original investment. Particular industries can also be the subject of periodic investor fashion. Bull markets existed for new bio-technology firms ('bio-mania') in the US in both 1980–83 and 1986–87, resulting in a flush of public offerings from venture-capital firms.

It is widely accepted in the industry that the performance of an entire fund is frequently conditional on the results of a few star performers. An often quoted rule of thumb in the industry is that, in a typical portfolio, one-third of investees will fail with the loss of all investment (the 'lemons'), one-third will neither lose nor make money (the 'living dead'), and, at best, one-third will earn significant multiples on the original investment (the 'plums'). A very high demand from external investors to purchase new shares at the initial public offering (IPO) of such a potential star company can completely skew the subsequent results of the fund. Conversely, if a fund does not have any companies ripe for harvesting at the time of a hot IPO market, then the whole portfolio has to

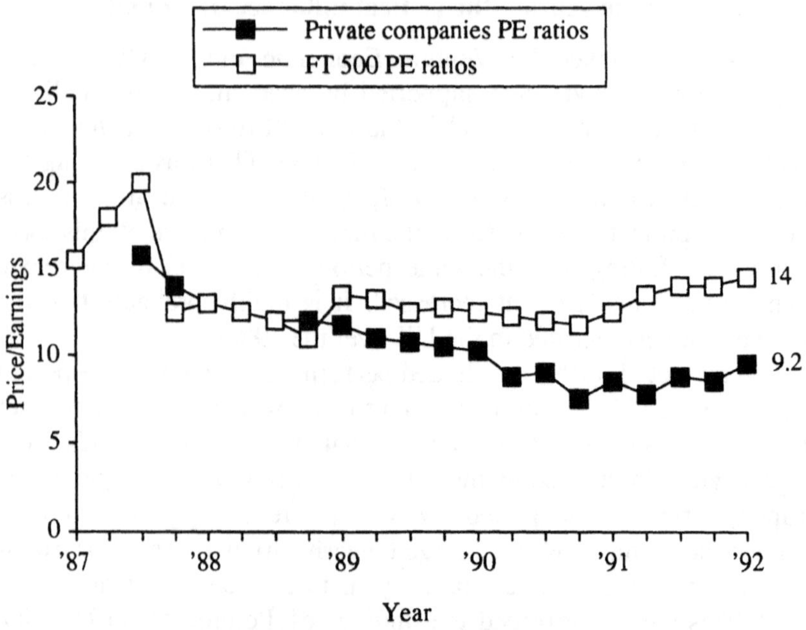

Figure 6.6 Comparison of private and quoted UK company price: earnings ratios, 1987–92
Source: *Acquisitions Monthly*, 1992, London: Stoy Hayward

achieve higher results to compensate for this absence of opportunity. During a recession, as witnessed in the UK from 1989, this places a considerable burden on the fund management team. The situation was made worse for UK funds, many of which had invested in companies during a period of exceptionally high price: earnings ratios in the mid-1980s (see Figure 6.6). Five to seven years later, when many of these investees would be expected to have exited at attractive premiums, Europe, North America, and Japan were facing severe economic downturns. These same economic forces had also severely eroded the performance of the investee companies themselves, further reducing their attractiveness and price to the now more limited numbers of potential purchasers.

The increasing power of investors as 'customers'

The mid-1980s can be seen in retrospect as the 'Klondike years' of UK venture capital. Each year saw an increasing amount of money invested in the industry and allocated by a growing number of venture capitalists in increasingly numerous and large deals. 'Black Monday' in October 1987 presaged the end. The onset of the UK recession in 1990 concluded the party. A number of large and excessively geared MBOs in the recession-sensitive retail markets collapsed spectacularly, occasioning widespread losses of (several tens of) millions of pounds. The 1990s heralded the start of the most difficult fund-raising environment in the brief history of the UK venture-capital industry.

Investors had become increasingly aware of the negative auguries for fund performance as small-firm stock values declined in relation to the main market, the level of flotations on the unlisted securities market dried to a trickle and SME failures and liquidations accelerated. Given the paramount importance of high exit values for portfolio companies to achieve fund-performance goals, the institutions became increasingly wary of venture-capital investment. Funds that had invested in the peak-price period of the mid-1980s and were coming again to the market to raise additional funds could not indicate satisfactory investment records or potential. Requests for additional funds from all but the most successful venture-capital management teams were met with an impenetrable wall of disinterest. Three-quarters of respondents in Murray's 1990 survey (Murray 1991a) acknowledged that venture capital had been 'oversold'. By 1991, the industry was reaping the consequences of this reality.

The changing bargaining power between the investors and the venture-capital management teams can be seen using Porter's (1979) 'five competitive forces model' (Murray 1991b). After 1988, the power relationships swung in favour of both investors and attractive investee companies and away from the venture-capital companies. Murray argued at the BVCA's Annual Conference in 1990 that the investors should properly be seen as 'customers' and not 'suppliers' (see also Lloyd 1989 and Salhman 1989). This view has also been increasingly forcibly expressed by senior institutional investors such as John Brakell, head of PosTel Investment Management Ltd. in the UK and Edwin Goodman, managing general partner of Hambros International Venture Fund in the US.

Investors are increasingly articulating their enhanced market power. Leading UK investors have formed the Venture Investors' Circle which reviews the changing nature of the industry and how the rights of investors should be pursued. At an individual level, investors are increasingly negotiating more demanding conditions aimed at reducing venture capitalists' rewards which are not linked directly to the funds' terminal economic performances. For those investors insufficiently informed of the performance of venture-capital funds, a breed of institutional adviser, the gatekeeper, has arisen (Murray 1991b). Gatekeepers evaluate competing venture-capital offerings and relative performance in order to inform the selection of the institutional investor. These trends represent a 'pincer movement' on the general partnership of the venture capitalists. They are seeing their rates and level of management incomes decline (Gregory 1991) at the same time as the funds under management at their disposal are also reducing. The effect of this will be to compel a number of weaker management companies to leave the industry as their existing funds are wound up and no new monies are forthcoming. As Murray (1991a, 1992a) has argued, UK venture capital is facing the classic symptoms of 'industry maturity'.

CONCLUDING COMMENTS

Venture capital represents a small but important part of the finance for new-firm formation and industrial restructuring in both the UK and continental Europe. From its antecedents in the United States after the Second World War, third-party equity investment has expanded both in the Western economies and, more recently, in the economies of the Pacific Rim and Eastern Europe. However, venture capital is a highly specific instrument and its relevance is confined to that narrow set of new and growing firms which can meet the substantial capital gain expectations of the investors. For early-stage technology-based firms with scarce collateral and assets primarily in the form of intellectual property, venture capital as a source of long-term risk equity is a more desirable alternative than debt. However, statistics for the UK and continental Europe indicate that early-stage deals, including technology-based enterprises, are becoming an increasingly minor element of the investment portfolio of the venture-capital industry. The earliest stage of finance, seed-capital, is particularly scarce and is a major concern for both governments and entrepreneurs. There still remains a fundamental question as to whether or not seed-capital investment can be seen as an economically viable investment activity. Contemporary experience in the UK, Holland and Germany would indicate that the high risk attendant on financing new technology-based firms is a major barrier to the commercial viability of specialist seed-capital funds.

UK venture-capital firms, operating across the full complement of stages of investment, have entered the present decade in a recessionary and increasingly hostile climate. The prognosis on the performance outcome of many closed-end funds which will terminate in the next five years is not encouraging. This has already resulted in a 'funds famine' for those venture-capital firms which cannot demonstrate to institutional investors attractive returns to this asset class subject to risk and illiquidity premiums. This curtailment of funding will produce a number of casualties among less successful venture-capital firms which will eventually be obliged to exit the industry as current portfolios are wound up. Small independent funds will be particularly at risk.

The UK venture-capital industry in the mid-1990s will consist of a smaller number of larger firms as industry concentration, similar to that which has already occurred in America, proceeds apace. The surviving firms will be more strategically aware of the industry/product sectors where they can add value to investee companies. They will also be strongly influenced by the more clearly articulated demands of their investors who will not be tolerant of unacceptable returns on their allocations to venture-capital funds. These changes now under way in the UK will also, over time, become the norm in continental Europe as European investors and fund managers learn rapidly from the UK and US experiences.

7

THE STOCK EXCHANGE AND THE UNLISTED SECURITIES MARKET

Edward W. Davis

INTRODUCTION

This chapter marks a transition point. Up to this point we have looked at the problems of the growing firm in its early development. We turn now to involve those that have obtained a stock exchange quotation. In that sense, therefore, these are companies whose growth strategies have been successfully realised. In other respects, however, many may continue to be relatively weak and vulnerable in the marketplace. The fact of a stock exchange quotation may not only be a testimony to emerging strength, but could as well reflect financial pressures which can only, ultimately, be alleviated by recourse to a larger source of external equity investors.

Of course the relevance of the Stock Exchange to smaller firms is that of a small fraction of that population seeking finance for growth or of the total capital supplied to such firms over any period. But the significance of its influence extends beyond the simple flows of funds involved in new quotation to the motivation provided to entrepreneurs and venture capitalists, whose investment strategy may ultimately be directed towards a stock exchange quotation as one form of exit mechanism. Examination of motives declared by firms themselves in coming to the Stock Exchange for the first time is revealing up to a point (see Buckland and Davis 1989), and ranges from 'passive' motives such as realising cash for shareholders or repaying bank loans to pro-active, more dynamic reasons implicit in capital-market access, whether for working capital generally or to fund acquisitions. A generally recognised measure by which the function of the new-issue market may be assessed is its role in raising new money for firms. Here one indication of the relative performance of the USM may be found in the relatively higher proportion of new money raised by USM entrants in the first half of the 1980s, involving an average of 44 per cent new money, compared to 34 per cent on the official list (Buckland and Davis 1989). By comparison, in Davis et al.'s (1974) study of new issues it was noted that issues in the late 1960s mainly comprised sales of existing 'old' shares, often induced by the need to make payments for death duties.

The new-issue market represents the apex of the pyramid of long-term capital provision, with prospects for higher equity value realisation than in a trade sale, alongside some retention of control, potentially greater than that generated by a trade sale. While the dynamism of the small-firm sector depends on real factors there is nevertheless a potentially important financial effect upon real performances deriving from an efficient equity market. So entrepreneurs, whether shareholders of previously unquoted firms, managers of subsidiaries of larger companies considering disinvestment or venture-capital intermediaries, will be encouraged towards resource investment in the sector if prospects for realisation can be seen to be more feasible through a stock exchange quotation. A successful role model for this process is regularly canvassed in the form of the US over-the-counter (OTC) market, whose experience was noted by the Wilson Committee when they advocated the formation within the UK of an unlisted securities market (Wilson 1980).

The remaining chapters in this book, therefore, deal with firms which have obtained a quotation but whose behaviour before and afterwards may reveal aspects both of firms themselves and also of the financial intermediaries involved with them.

In this chapter our principal concern is to examine the extent to which a stock exchange quotation is a feasible, cost-efficient means by which smaller firms obtain access to longer-term capital. The main focus of the chapter, therefore, lies with the efficiency of the market itself, and in particular the USM, in reducing entry barriers to quotation and the cost of access. The transactions costs involved in obtaining a stock exchange quotation may be considered part of agency costs incurred by virtue of the cost of compliance with Stock Exchange entry requirements, embodied, for example, in the standard of accounting information required for publication in the new-issue prospectus.

We do so first by examining the physical characteristics of firms seeking quotation from the 1970s to the 1980s, and then proceed to examine the extent to which economies of scale in the issuing process continue to discriminate against smaller firms in the 1990s. This is not just a matter of the scale impact of expenses incurred but also that of Stock Exchange regulation which directly or otherwise restricts entry to quotation to firms which do not conform with their requirements. The scale effect, however, partly relates to that by increasing the costs of compliance for smaller firms in administrative expenses incurred but also reflects market pricing costs associated with smaller new entrants.

ACCESS TO THE UK NEW-ISSUE MARKET FOR PREVIOUSLY UNQUOTED FIRMS

Regulation by the Stock Exchange in the legitimate interests of investors had imposed conditions for admission to quotation incorporated in the Listing Agreement which represented a considerable barrier (distinct from cost alone) to potential new entrants in the 1970s (Wilson 1980: paras 759–761). Specific features of this included minimum size thresholds both for size of firm and size of issue, together with minimum proportions of equity to be marketed and minimum time periods for trading and financial history. It is hardly surprising, therefore, when these formal entry barriers were reinforced by scale effects, that very few small firms

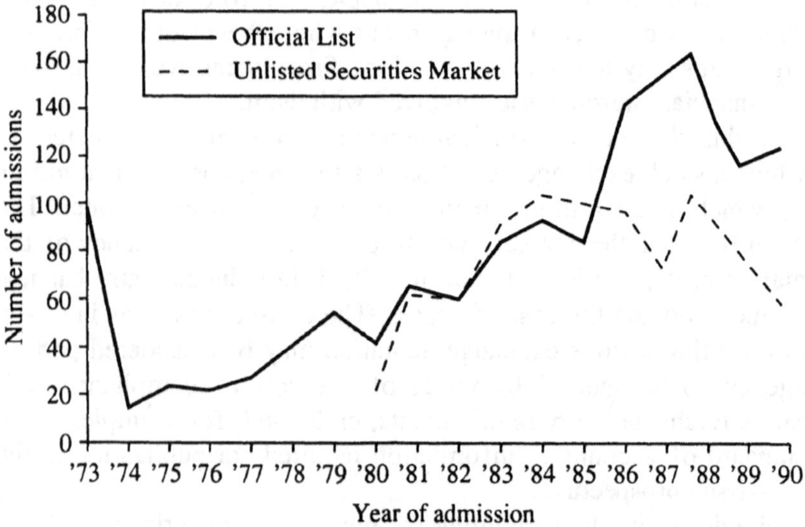

Figure 7.1 Admissions to the London Stock Exchange, 1973–90

Table 7.1 Grouped total assets of companies, by entry status
Figures are: number of firms in category, number as percentage of row, number as percentage of column, number as percentage of total

Assets	*USM entrant*	*From OTC or 163*[a]	*OL entrants*	*USM transfer*	*Row total*
Under £2.5m	152	6	10	2	170
	89.4	3.5	5.9	1.2	38.5
	52.1	18.8	12.2	5.7	
	34.5	1.4	2.3	0.5	
£2.5m–£7.5m	110	14	28	15	167
	65.9	8.4	16.8	9	37.9
	37.7	43.8	34.1	42.9	
	24.9	3.2	6.3	3.4	
£7.5–£15m	20	9	14	11	54
	37	16.7	25.9	20.4	12.2
	6.8	28.1	17.1	31.4	
	4.5	2	3.2	2.5	
Over £15m	10	3	30	7	50
	20	6	60	14	11.3
	3.4	9.4	36.6	20	
	2.3	0.7	6.8	1.6	
Column total	292	32	82	35	441
	66.2	7.3	18.6	7.9	100

Notes: 4 out of 16 (25%) of the valid cells have expected cell frequency less than 5.0 chi-squared = 132.73 with 9 degrees of freedom. Significance = 0.0000. Missing = 4.

	Mean assets for the average entrant (1980 £)[b]				
Mean (£000)	4,196.32	8,256.80	16,320.19	13,132.23	7,310.55
No. of firms	294	32	75	36	437
SD	7,064.11	6,393.47	27,326.92	15,813.56	14,374.51

Notes: F = 18.40, significance = 0.0000; K–W chi-squared = 104.10, significance = 0.0000.[c]

[a] Companies transferring from OTC markets or from quotation under Rule 163
[b] Data for OL entrants exclude 7 privatisation issues
[c] The F test compares means parmetrically, the Kruskal–Wallis (K–W) test non-parametrically
Source: Buckland and Davis 1989

sought quotation. The mean size of firm for 169 companies achieving quotation by means of an offer for sale during the period 1965–71 was £0.84 million, some three to four times the size of the Bolton Committee 'small firm'. The consequences of this may be seen (Figure 7.1) in the decline of new entrants to quotation in the early 1970s (also subject, of course, to the depressing influence of the national economic performance at that time) and the subsequent recovery of the new-issue market following the 1980 inauguration of the USM.

When in Table 7.1 we examine the size characteristics (measured by market capitalisation of equity) of companies entering the USM in the 1980s, comparing them with new entrants to the official list (OL), we clearly see that market capitalisations were lower for USM entrants than for new entrants to the official list, a finding which is only reinforced by a shift to a size classification based on the balance-sheet book value of total assets. Here the relative frequency of firms with total assets below £2.5 million is much larger for USM than official list new entrants, but there is still a degree of overlap. So, for example, 38 new entrants to the official list have size categories generally corresponding to the preferred USM size band. When, however, the relevant size classification was interpreted to be that of size of issue, the extent of such overlap effectively disappears with only 7 per cent of share issues on the official list falling below £1 million compared with nearly 50 per cent of USM share issues for less than that amount. When we consider costs, the stark extent of differences based on size of issue matters not only to the firm's view as to the worth of obtaining a quotation but also points to the fundamental problem of smaller companies' recourse to the Stock Exchange: that of the inherent illiquidity of small issues of stock.

THE SCALE EFFECT OF ADMINISTRATIVE COSTS

In a 1992 survey of USM companies (Abel 1993), 40 per cent of these firms indicated their intention of remaining on the USM, and for most of these (86 per cent) the principal reason was because the cost of transfer to the official list was too high. In this section we examine how, despite the innovation of the USM, fixed costs of entry still constitute a significant entry barrier to smaller firms. As a starting point we can consider administrative costs for the London new-issue market in the 1960s and in the USM and official list in the 1980s. Buckland and Davis (1989) investigated the extent to which the innovation of the USM had lowered threshold costs of entry. They found (Tables 7.2 and 7.3), after allowing for differences in method of issue, in particular the much greater popularity of placings on the USM, that the percentage costs of obtaining a placing on the USM were significantly lower than a placing on the official list. But there was a continuing clear size effect in relation to the size of issue involved: while the USM appears to have helped entry of smaller firms to quotation it has not altered the fact of significant economies of scale in the issuing process.

It has been argued (Jenkinson and Espenlaub 1991) that, following relaxation of Stock Exchange admission requirements, direct costs incurred on offers for sale are on average only 1 to 2 per cent more expensive than similar-sized placings, except for very small issues. This does not take sufficient account of significant differences within averages recorded. Despite overlaps in the size ranges of new entrants most USM entrants throughout the 1980s were significantly smaller than new entrants to the official list and *ipso facto* incurred significant differences in direct cost attributable to their small size.

Table 7.2 Administrative expenses as percentage of gross size of issue
Figures are: unweighted mean expenses, number of firms in category, standard deviation of expenses

Entry	*Placing*	*Offer for sale*	*Tender*	*Other*	*All methods*
USM	12.3	8.57	6.54	10.44	11.62
	209	22	9	26	266
	14.04	5.33	2.06	8.8	12.91
Transfer to USM	0	0	0	9.09	9.09
	0	0	0	2	2
	0	0	0	0.99	0.99
OL	16.11	7.71	6.31	8.33	8.36
	10	37	26	3	76
	8	6.42	3.13	3.08	6.38
Transfer to OL	7.86	2.14	0	7.42	4.89
	1	2	0	1	4
	0	0.02	0	0	3.18
All entrants	12.45	7.84	6.37	10.06	10.81
	220	61	35	32	348
	13.8	6	2.87	7.99	11.76

Source: Buckland and Davis 1989

Table 7.3 Relative significance of administrative expenses for USM placings

(A) As a percentage of issue capitalization, by size of issue

	Under £200,000	*£200–400, 000*	*£400,000–£1m*	*£1m–5m*	*Over £5m*	*Total*
Mean	63.2	19.46	12.44	7.91	1.2	12.59
No. of firms	5	33	76	93	3	210
SD	67.91	9.77	4.45	4.19	1.02	13.8

Notes: $F = 34.97$, significance 0.0000.
K–W chi-squared = 93.55, significance = 0.0000.

(B) As a percentage of issue capitalization, by size of firm (market capitalization)

	Under £2.5m	*£2.5–7.5m*	*£7.5–15m*	*Over £15m*	*Total*
Mean	18.09	12	8.32	11.5	12.49
No. of firms	49	109	48	4	210
SD	24.93	8.17	6.28	6.31	14.08

Notes: $F = 4.22$, significance 0.0064.
K–W chi-squared = 32.62, significance = 0.0000.

(C) As a proportion of entrant capitalization by size of firm (market capitalization)

	Under £2.5m	*£2.5–7.5m*	*£7.5–15m*	*Over £15m*	*Total*
Mean	4.71	2.34	1.09	0.52	2.57
No. of firms	49	109	48	4	210
SD	2.94	1.47	0.49	0.5	2.2

Notes: $F = 36.73$, significance 0.0000.
K–W chi-squared = 106.05, significance = 0.0000.[a]

[a] The F test compares means parametrically, the Kruskal–Wallis (K–W) test non-parametrically.
Source: Buckland and Davis 1989

MARKET-PRICING COSTS: THE SIZE EFFECT

Beyond the existence of entry barriers attributable to simple administrative expenses alone, there is the separate but related phenomenon of market pricing costs which may also effectively discriminate against smaller firms. This arises from the levels of introductory discount generated by the difference between the issue price and the expected equilibrium market price. For the London new-issue market in the 1970s Davis and Yeomans (1976) found a significant size – discount relationship: the market effectively required a significantly higher level of introductory discount (means of around 25 per cent) on offers for sale involving issues by firms with assets less than £250,000. Firms with assets in excess of £1 million exhibited mean levels of discount at least half that level. For quotation on the official list in that period, of course, the Stock Exchange required that 25 per cent of the issue be offered to the public, involving, therefore, potential (opportunity) losses to existing shareholders either through direct sale of old shares or dilution if new money issues were involved.

The USM recognised this problem by allowing its new entrants to offer a much smaller proportion of equity (10 per cent) so that vendor shareholders need not incur significant potential losses by being forced to offer for sale a substantial proportion of equity in a market likely to discriminate against such issues. However, notwithstanding this important dispensation it is remarkable how many USM firms issued more than the statutory minimum. For the 263 USM entrants between 1980 and 1985, mean values for the proportion of equity issued lie at 28 per cent (34 per cent for official list entrants). Some 70 firms issued more than 30 per cent of their equity; and 21 of these issued more than 50 per cent. In that context Buckland and Davis (1989, 1990a) found that the USM required higher discounts on issues where relatively low proportions of equity were involved, as well as lower issue size. The smaller USM issues revealed very high levels of introductory discount while those issues by USM firms of equivalent issue size to official list entrants recorded discounts consistent with the 'senior' market levels. Further analysis (Buckland and Davis 1990a; Keasey and McGuinness 1992) found a relationship between the level of discount and the quality of accounting information provided in the prospectus, with issue prices of entrants with inadequate records of past performance or forecasts being significantly marked down.

THE ILLIQUIDITY OF SMALL-FIRM EQUITIES

The persistence of thin trading in small-company shares

The question of pricing of issues by smaller firms, whether on the USM, the Third Market, the OTC or the official list is, of course, critically related to the size of issue and the inherent illiquidity and volatility of small-firm securities. We have already noted the sharp differences between the sizes of issues offered by USM and official list new entrants. We can also observe substantial differences in the average value of bargains, and their frequency, for USM vis-à-vis official list new entrants together with significant differences in the concentration of ownership. Table 7.4 indicates the average values per USM bargain expressed as a percentage of OL bargains between 1987 and 1992.

Table 7.4 USM mean bargain values as percentage of OL mean bargain values, 1987–92

1987	*1988*	*1989*	*1990*	*1991*	*1992*
19.2	22.97	23.2	25	22.6	19.3

Source: Adapted from *Stock Exchange Quarterly*

When lower sizes of issue are expected to attract purchasers from a UK equity market characterised by a heavy concentration of institutional ownership it is hardly surprising that the scale economies involved in such institutional purchase militate against effective demand for smaller-firm securities. The typical UK small quoted equity is therefore characterised by infrequent trades within thin markets involving risk-accepting individual investors and a relatively small number of institutional specialists (Wells 1992) willing to hazard the greater illiquidity and volatility of such securities in return for significant introductory price discounts and prospective greater yield. The vulnerability of markets in smaller issues was apparent even before the stock-market collapse of 1987. Indeed the phenomenon is hardly new and had been noted by Gupta as long ago as 1969 in terms of the greater volatility of smaller-firm equities in a bear market when compared with larger firms (Gupta 1969). The liquidity of smaller USM entrants' shares would not have differed to any material extent from that of the OTC, while the introduction of the Third Market and its subsequent termination did nothing to alter the fundamental problem – that of ensuring adequate liquidity for smaller-firm shares. This problem has been further compounded by the consequences of deregulation, an implicit reduction in the depth of market-making capacity available to smaller firms and consequent increased transactions costs, such that the shares of many such firms are exchanged on an infrequent matched bargain basis, with little practical advantage of the public quotation.

Indeed, this context seems a more plausible explanation for the decline of the USM rather than the greater accessibility of the official list, given as the principal reason by Abel (1993). While the latter undoubtedly holds to an extent, it would be quite misleading to infer that, because equivalent numbers of new entrants below £50 million market capitalisation were choosing quotation on the official list rather than the USM, this had solved the equity gap for smaller firms. It is clear that the effective demand by entrants for a market quotation up to 1987 came from firms well below £50 million and, indeed, within the £10 million size category (Buckland and Davis 1989). It is for firms of this size distribution that the transfer or raising of new equity on a UK exchange is problematic, notwithstanding recent innovations by the Stock Exchange designed to improve facilities for trading small-firm equities. Offsetting such improvements is the reduction in number of market makers, while the post-1987 economy has only underlined the relatively greater risks and costs associated with small firms' equity, particularly those firms of below £10 million market capitalisation.

Attempts at mitigation: innovation in security trading and bulletin boards

The relative centralisation of the UK new-issue market contrasts with that of the US OTC market with its extensive regional dealer network, and the rejuvenated regional exchanges of the French Second Marché (Buckland 1989; Buckland and Davis 1989). Such variations seem unlikely to work within the UK, however, and the evidence over two decades and more suggests that smaller firms continue to encounter significant threshold costs or barriers to entry to quotation arising from inevitable scale economies in the issuing process. Reduction of the latter, even if publicly acceptable, would only incur additional costs and risks for investors and would inevitably, therefore, be passed on to the firms themselves.

CONCLUSION

The USM innovation demonstrated a need; it also demonstrated the continued existence of scale economies and the greater price

Table 7.5 Departures from USM

	1980	*1981*	*1982*	*1983*	*1984*	*1985*	*1986*	*1987*	*1988*	*1989*	*1990*	*1991*	*1992*	*Total 1980–92*
Transferred to OL	0	0	6	11	25	10	28	28	20	6	32	30	13	209
Acquired	0	0	2	4	6	17	21	39	22	29	23	28	9	200

vulnerability of small-firm equities. Given that Stock Exchange regulations provide effective parity of access for small and large firms, the effective problem continues to be that derived from scale economies and costs. The solution to that lies partly within the firms themselves, to defer quotation until greater size is obtained, but also through other forms of financial innovations considered elsewhere in this book.

An indication of the benefit which an effective market in small-firm equity affords may be gathered from Table 7.5, which illustrates over a 13-year period the numbers of companies with quotations on the USM (a) which transferred to the official list and (b) which were acquired by other firms. In effect the latter phenomenon forms the more conspicuous, if smaller, part of the market for corporate control with direct trade sales making up the bulk. For entrepreneurs and shareholders in both groups of firms concerned with transferring part or all of the equity of their firms, motivation is bound to be affected by the ability to realise values in the relatively open market conditions of the exchange. While the quoted equity markets' liquidity imperfections (more properly attributable to their size) may constrain fair values it still provides a superior benchmark for assessing the costs of capital of comparable unquoted firms. Given the limits to the market's capacity for processing small-firm equity, particularly below £10 million, it seems that in effect the gap for firms seeking capital below this size will simply be passed down the line, as venture-capital and other financial intermediaries are unwilling to finance investment significantly below this threshold or endure the longer payback periods required to bring firms to an economic size. This has corresponding implications for entrepreneurs themselves and their motivation given the likelihood of significantly higher costs of capital for firms within this size category.

8

CHARACTERISTICS OF SMALL FIRMS FLOATED ON THE USM 1980–83

An inter-temporal study

Graham Hall and Patrick Hutchinson

INTRODUCTION

Traditionally, studies of stock-market flotations have concentrated on the underpricing of initial public offerings (see Tinic 1988 for a review). The creation of the unlisted securities market (USM) has provided the opportunity for a broader range of studies including those dealing with smaller firms. Buckland and Davis (1987) have investigated the significance of administrative expenses as barriers to entry to the USM. The same authors (Buckland and Davis 1990a) considered the influence of firm size in the context of the information content of new-issue prospectuses and the pricing of USM new issues. Buckland et al. (1989) investigated debt management by companies entering the USM. Keasey and McGuinness (1991, 1992) considered the issue of prospectus earnings forecasts, the reputation of entrants' auditors and the pricing of new issues on the USM. Hutchinson et al. (1988) provided an analysis of the financial characteristics of small firms which achieved quotation on the USM.

In this chapter we examine how the financial characteristics of small firms entering the USM between 1980 and 1983 inclusive differed from those that remained unfloated; and we compare these differences with those between firms of similar size floated on the official list and those remaining unfloated between 1970 and 1973. Given that a major reason for establishing the USM was to provide equity for small firms, especially those with a track record of growth, it would seem useful to explore what sort of small firms have, in fact, attempted to benefit from the new opportunities represented by access to the USM and to compare these firms with those of similar size that gained official listing in a period before the establishment of the USM.

The next section of the chapter provides a brief review of the USM and its role in small-firm financing. The third section considers the relationship between financial characteristics and stage of development of the firm, including stock-market flotation. The remaining sections present the method used, the results and the conclusions of the study.

THE USM AND THE FINANCING OF SMALL FIRMS

The ability of small firms to raise long-term finance has long been a matter of concern both in the UK and overseas. The Macmillan (1931) Committee of Inquiry into Finance and Industry in the UK gave rise to the term 'finance gap' to describe a situation where a small firm had grown to a stage where it had made maximum use of short-term sources of finance but had not yet reached the stage of being able to acquire longer-term finance by means of stock-market flotation. Many attempts have subsequently been made to close the finance gap. The Industrial and Commercial Finance Corporation was set up in the UK, as a direct response to the Macmillan Report's findings, in order to provide long-term debt and equity finance to smaller firms. Following investigations into the financing of small firms in the UK by the Bolton (1971) and Wilson (1979) committees, further developments have included the Business Expansion Scheme which grants tax relief to individuals buying equity in new small firms and the Small Firms Loan Guarantee Scheme (Taylor 1985: p. 209).

The creation of the USM was motivated partly by the slump of London Stock Exchange flotations in the 1970s (Davis and Pointon 1994: p. 328) and partly by specific concern for the growth of small firms. The discussion document issued in December 1979 by the London Stock Exchange (Peat, Marwick, Mitchell and Co. 1980) stated that it was becoming clear that smaller, growing companies were no longer inclined to apply for listing on the Stock Exchange as had been the normal pattern in the past. The reasons for this decline in interest by small companies were thought to be increased costs and formalities. In response to this problem, the London Stock Exchange introduced a three-tier market covering listed and unlisted securities. The USM was created to fit in between the official, 'main board', listing and the procedure by which bargains are matched under the then Stock Exchange Rule 163 covering occasional bargains matched by brokers. To enter the USM a company must normally have been trading for at least three years, and provide financial information for five years (or for the period of trading if less). Securities traded are not officially listed on the Stock Exchange. Transactions are matched either in-house by the stockbroker, or negotiated with another stockbroker. These requirements are less onerous and more flexible than for official listing and, since most entries to the USM are by placings which do not require underwriting or public advertising, they are cheaper. Access to the USM is restricted to smaller firms by means of maximum monetary limits on the market value of initial placings. Between 1980 and 1983 around two hundred companies were floated on the USM. The average market value of the USM firms at flotation was just under £10 million. The average market value of firms obtaining a full Stock Exchange listing was almost four times higher at £38 million.

STAGE OF DEVELOPMENT AND FINANCIAL CHARACTERISTICS

Weston and Brigham (1978: p. 963) considered the financial implications of five stages of development, namely: formation, rapid growth, growth to maturity, maturity and decline, with stock-market flotation being viewed as a watershed in the financial development of the small firm. This analysis was not taken to imply that all firms go through all of these stages. Clearly, maturity and decline can take place at any point from formation onwards. Also, some enterprises are able to short-circuit some of the stages by, for example, being formed and floated on the Stock Exchange at the same time. The use of the term 'growth' as a stage of development is somewhat misleading in the case of firms, as opposed to living organisms, since growth can and does continue during the maturity stage (Stanworth and Curran 1976). Nevertheless, it is useful to examine the stages that the small firm goes through as it grows from formation to flotation and beyond in order to theorise about the effects on financial characteristics.

According to Weston and Brigham, the major sources of finance at formation are the owners' personal resources. The major financial problem likely to arise at this stage of development is that these resources are not sufficient and that the business is thereby undercapitalised. Growth beyond formation is likely to be financed by retained earnings, trade credit and bank borrowing. The major financial problem at this stage is that growth may outstrip financial resources, leading to over-trading and liquidity crises. Growth may also cause the firm to face a 'finance gap' where it is forced to rely too much on short-term finance because of a lack of long-term finance. Further growth may require a stock-market flotation in order to overcome the finance gap. This might not always be welcomed by the owners of the business because a stock-market flotation could lead to their losing control over the business as outsiders bought shares. Once a stock-market flotation has been made the firm has all sources of finance available. The major problems that are then faced are those involved in maximising shareholder wealth, namely, ensuring adequate return on investment and achieving optimal gearing and dividend policies. Failure to do so may lead to decline, resulting in take-over or eventual bankruptcy.

It is, therefore, plausible that the lack of availability of certain types of finance, particularly long-term debt and equity, at certain stages of development will have a direct effect on the financial characteristics of the firm. If a finance gap exists then it may help to explain why small (unquoted) firms have different financial characteristics from large (quoted) firms. A finance gap could particularly distort the financial characteristics of small firms which grow rapidly. The argument is that such firms would have to rely more on internally generated funds than large firms and, therefore, there would be a higher correlation between profitability and growth in assets. Lack of long-term finance would force reliance on short-term sources of finance, thereby reducing liquidity. Lack of equity finance, because of lack of access to the stock market, would result in higher overall levels of leverage. In other words, not only would short-term debt be substituted for long-term debt but also for unavailable equity.

Empirical studies of newly quoted small firms suggest that they do have financial characteristics which are different from other small firms and from large firms. Walker and Petty (1978) found that small firms preparing to enter the US public stock market had a significantly different financial profile from that of large corporations. The differences for small firms entering the stock market were lower dividend payout, lower liquidity and higher profitability. Buckland et al. (1989) used data drawn from the quotation of small firms on the USM to examine their debt position. It was concluded that newly quoted firms were financially imbalanced at their quotation but that this was only weakly related to their size, industry, growth, riskiness and yields. Clear evidence existed that entrants moved towards target debt ratios, but that these targets were only poorly related to characteristics of firms suggested in the finance literature to be of importance in capital-structuring decisions. Hutchinson et al. (1988) identified the financial characteristics of small firms which achieved stock-market quotation on the USM by using principal component analysis and multivariate analysis of variance. The findings suggested that these firms had higher growth rates, used more debt financing and invested less in liquid assets than small firms which did not achieve quotation.

METHOD

From the previous section, it appears that there may well be differences between small firms which achieve flotation and those which do not, in terms of their financial characteristics. This study required a method to test the extent to which the financial characteristics of small firms which achieved USM flotation in 1980–83 differed from small firms which did not achieve flotation and to compare these differences with those between small firms which acquired stock-market flotation on the official list in 1970–73 compared to those which did not. The period 1970–73 was chosen for the purpose of comparison as it was the most recent period during which small firms had been floated on the official list market. After 1973, and before the creation of the USM in 1980, there was a slump in stock-market flotations with virtually no small firms being floated.

The method involved:

- comparing selected financial characteristics of a sample of small firms that achieved flotation on the USM with a sample of small firms that remained private;
- establishing the relative importance of these characteristics in increasing the probability that such firms would be floated on the USM;
- comparing the differences between the financial characteristics of small firms floated on the USM, and remaining private

1980–83, with those between small firms floated on the stock market and remaining private between 1970 and 1973. This study provides comparisons of these characteristics in the year of flotation, T, and the fourth year preceding flotation, $T-4$.

The following subsections describe the samples, variables and statistical methods used in the study.

Sample

Data were collected for four samples, each with 30 firms. The first was drawn from the population of firms that achieved flotation on the USM during 1980–83, the second from those that were floated on the stock market in 1970–73, and the other two represented control groups of companies which, during these respective periods, remained private.

One hundred and eighty-five companies were floated on the USM between 1980 and 1983. Since this study employed financial data, a decision was made to eliminate companies with unusual financial characteristics, namely mining and oil exploration, financial services, property, construction and subsidiaries of overseas companies. This left 120 firms.

Invoking the Bolton Committee's (1971) definition of a small firm – that it should be earning at 1971 prices under £200,000 of revenue – reduced the sample of companies floated on the USM to 30 companies. Clearly, whilst an important reason for establishing the USM was to serve as a vehicle for increasing the supply of equity to small firms, the latter represents only a small minority of its entrants. The sample of firms floated between 1970 and 1973 was drawn from the same industrial sectors and, in real terms, the same size range.

The control groups for both periods were matched by size, industrial sector and age. The last is important because there are both *a priori* and empirical (Storey et al. 1987) reasons for supposing both that flotation will, on the whole, be limited to companies that are neither very new nor very long-established and that, in turn, financial profiles may be loosely related to age. Indeed, in both periods the floated companies were typically in their teens or early twenties. It might also be of interest to note that in both periods most of the floated firms were drawn from the South of England followed, in roughly equal numbers, by firms from the

North and Midlands. Flotations by firms from Scotland, Wales and Northern Ireland were very rare.

Variables

It would seem self-evident that small firms enjoying a high rate of growth are the most likely to seek an injection of equity capital to fund future growth. Growth was measured by the proportionate increase in the book value of total assets over the year prior to flotation. Changes in sales, the measurement of which is less susceptible to the idiosyncrasies of accounting measurement than that of the value of assets, would have been a preferable measure of size, but it was not always provided in company accounts.

It was hypothesised that the firms most likely to seek flotation would be those whose owners believed that lack of capital was currently acting as a constraint on their achieving their full earning potential. It would seem reasonable to assume, furthermore, that it would be the capital market's expectations of future earnings which would be an important influence on whether a company's attempt to achieve flotation proved successful. Both owners' and the capital market's expectations of earnings were proxied by the book value of profits before interest and tax as a percentage of the book value of total assets in each relevant year.

One aspect of the finance gap confronting small firms which was discussed by the Macmillan (1931), Bolton (1971) and Wilson (1979) committees was their lack of opportunity to raise equity. If they were unable to overcome the barriers around full listing, they faced little alternative, given the absence until the 1980s of any significant venture-capital industry (see Murray in Chapter 6), to raising fresh equity from friends and relatives. The Wilson Committee, in particular, underlined the shortage of such 'Aunt Agathas'. As a consequence one would expect small firms to incur higher-than-average levels of gearing. The evidence on this is mixed with respect to small firms in general but would appear stronger with respect to small firms that are growing rapidly (Bolton 1971; Ray and Hutchinson 1983). This reliance on debt, in turn, leads to the cost of debt rising (Gupta 1969), in particular from the fear of insolvency. Hence, growing small firms might be expected to join the USM not only to gain injections of equity capital but to increase their attractiveness to potential lenders. Gearing has been defined here as the book value of debt as a percentage of the book value of total assets.

A second aspect of the finance gap discussed by the Macmillan (1931), Bolton (1971) and Wilson (1979) committees was the limited availability to small firms of long-term loans. These would clearly have provided them with more flexibility in the management of their cash flow. There is also some evidence (Robson Rhodes 1984; Keasey and Watson, Chapter 4) that, even within the limited scope offered by short-term loans, bank managers display a lack of sympathy for the problems faced by the owners of small firms. The result is that they might be expected to face severe problems in achieving an optimal degree of liquidity, especially if they are attempting to increase the size of their firms. Flotation on the USM would represent a means of redressing the balance. Liquidity is measured as the book value of net working capital as a percentage of the book value of total assets.

Directors of a small firm must choose the proportion of its profits that they will distribute as their remuneration – the payment of dividends was a rarity within the samples – and the proportion they will leave as equity. One might expect that the directors of growing small firms, confronted by the problems of funding the growth, will be more likely than others to display a temporary sacrifice in the level of their immediate benefits from remuneration, in the hope of achieving a higher level in the benefits from the long-term growth in the value of their equity. Not surprisingly, the second most commonly cited first reason provided in prospectuses for joining the USM (17 per cent against 23 per cent for 'capital-market access') was 'cash for shareholders' (Buckland and Davis 1987). This variable is defined as directors' remuneration as a percentage of the book value of total assets.

All data were acquired from the company accounts maintained at Companies House and have been collected on the year of flotation, and for the fourth year prior to flotation.

Methodology

It was decided to use a multivariate statistical technique to assess statistically significant differences both between the small firms which achieved flotation and those which did not, and between the two periods, the 1970s and the 1980s.

Because the study involved modelling the process leading to the outcome between two possible events, flotation and non-flotation, least squares regression would not have been appropriate. The requirement that the error term should be normally distributed would have been violated. Nor would coefficients be constrained to lie between 0 and 1. It was therefore decided to use a qualitative response model.

Qualitative response models are becoming increasingly common within the economics literature (Amemiya (1981) provides an excellent survey). They usually either assume a standard normal distribution for the probability functions of the occurrence of their dependent variable or a logistic distribution. Models assuming the former distribution are called 'probit' and those assuming the latter 'logit'. The two distributions are so similar that choice between them is almost a matter of indifference. In this case, probit was chosen.

It should be noted that in probit the coefficients are not directly interpretable as marginal probabilities. These can only be estimated by differentiating the probability function with respect to a change in each of the variables.

All data have been standardised with respect to their population mean value for that period. This is warranted on the theoretical grounds that the capital market evaluates the information value of a financial datum with reference to what is normal at the time but produces the fortunate spin-off that the interactive dummies which assess the differences between the 1970s and 1980s are more amenable (that is, more amenable than is usually the case with qualitative response models), to the interpretation afforded by least squares regression. Hall and Hutchinson (1993) provide a full technical explanation of the methodology adopted.

RESULTS

Comparison of means

As a starting point, the means of the four samples will be compared (see Table 8.1). This may prove helpful to the extent that it does not require any statistical expertise. However, as will be shown in the next section, such univariate comparisons can produce a misleading picture about the actual relationship between variables and the probability of flotation.

The difference between the means would be as hypothesised, in both T and $T-4$, with respect to profitability, directors' remuneration

Table 8.1 Financial characteristics of quoted and unquoted small firms, 1970s and 1980s: means

All figures are percentages of total book assets, except growth rate, which is percentage increase over prior year

	1970s			
	Four years before quotation (T – 4)		*At quotation (T)*	
	Quoted	*Unquoted*	*Quoted*	*Unquoted*
Change in total assets	45	17	64	10
Net working capital	15	19	18	18
Total debt	60	52	56	55
EBIT[a]	19	8	18	9
Directors' renumeration	5	7	2	8
	1980s			
	Four years before quotation (T – 4)		*At quotation (T)*	
	Quoted	*Unquoted*	*Quoted*	*Unquoted*
Change in total assets	77	32	48	15
Net working capital	4	18	17	16
Total debt	76	71	57	67
EBIT[a]	14	11	18	5
Directors' renumeration	9	11	5	9

[a] EBIT = earnings before interest and tax

and, most strikingly, growth in assets. The difference in working capital is, as would be expected, in $T - 4$ but not T, whilst differences in total debt would confirm expectations in three of the four samples but confound them with respect to T in the 1980s.

Probit analysis

A more precise picture emerges from the application of probit analysis. Table 8.2 shows the coefficients on variables derived from pooled data for both periods, with interactive dummy variables referring to changes between the 1970s and 1980s.

Table 8.2 Probit result

	Four years before flotation	*At flotation*
Constant	−3.2937* (2.52)	−0.4840* (−1.80)
Constant Dummy	1.8261 (1.31)	0.3118 (0.96)
Change in total assets	1.4229 (1.50)	0.3873 (1.51)
Change in total assets Dummy	−0.8036 (−0.78)	0.0158 (0.049)
Net working capital / Total assets	−0.6123 (−1.44)	0.1545 (0.92)
NWC / Total assets Dummy	−0.6274 (−1.68)	−0.1128 (0.43)
Total debt / Total assets	0.0725 (0.23)	0.1987 (0.78)
Total debt / Total assets Dummy	−0.1513 (−0.37)	−0.0465 (−0.15)
Earnings before interest and tax / Total assets	1.0327* (2.22)	0.4662* (2.21)
EBIT / Total assets Dummy	−0.4829 (−0.97)	−0.2648 (1.05)
Directors' remuneration / Total assets	−3.5326* (−2.21)	−0.7972* (−2.23)
DR / Total assets Dummy	2.1224 (1.25)	0.7353* (1.95)
	$R^2 = 0.20$	$R^2 = 0.47$

Notes: Numbers in brackets refer to *t* statistics.
* Significant at 5% level

Growth still appears important, as reflected by the value of its coefficient, especially in $T-4$, with no statistically significant changes apparently taking place in the interactive dummy between the 1970s and 1980s. The *t* statistic on the pooled data is, however, also not statistically significant, which indicates that growth is not a particularly reliable discriminator and, indeed, inspection of the data reveals outliers of high-growth unfloated, and low-growth floated firms.

The application of probit confirms the importance of profitability in explaining flotation but does not suggest any significant change in its influence between the 1970s and 1980s.

Relative shortage of working capital at the time of flotation was clearly not a characteristic of floated firms during either period but there is some suggestion of a difference between the two samples in $T-4$ during the 1980s.

Directors of small firms which achieved flotation are shown to have paid themselves a lower proportion of the value of their firm during the 1970s in both T and $T-4$, but the statistically significant interactive dummy shows that such self-denial, at least at point of flotation, would not appear to be the case during the 1980s.

Most startling of all, levels of debt were not statistically significantly higher amongst floated firms in either T or $T-4$ during the 1970s or 1980s, a conclusion that would not have been reached from a simple comparison of the mean values of data referring to $T-4$.

COMMENTARY

Our results provide useful insights into some aspects of the operation of the USM with respect to small firms. They represent only a minority of all firms floated on it, which, given the background of the USM, is in itself rather surprising. However, those small firms which did seek flotation are not necessarily the fastest growing; and the establishment of the USM would not appear to have made any difference to the relationship between the growth of a small firm and its probability of achieving flotation. Similarly, whilst small firms that were floated on the USM in 1980 to 1983 were clearly usually more profitable than those that were not, profitability would not appear to have had any more impact on the probability of flotation by a small firm than would have been the case during the 1970s.

One fallacy which our results should firmly nail is that small firms seeking flotation during either the 1970s or 1980s were motivated by high debt or low working-capital ratios. At best, small firms floated during the 1980s may have experienced shortages in working capital four years earlier; otherwise, the decision to float would appear to have had little to do with liquidity or gearing.

Of some interest to sociologists is the change that had apparently occurred between the 1970s and 1980s in the willingness of directors of small floated firms to accept lower levels of remuneration than those of small firms that remained unfloated. Self-denial would not appear to be a feature of entrepreneurs during the early years of Thatcherism.

9

DEBT TARGETING AND BANKING RELATIONSHIPS IN THE FINANCIAL BEHAVIOUR OF NEWLY QUOTED FIRMS IN THE UK

Roger Buckland and Edward W. Davis

INTRODUCTION

This chapter sets out observations from a two-stage research project investigating the debt behaviour of UK firms newly admitted to quotation on the USM and the official list. The objective of the research is to examine whether UK smaller and medium-sized firms resorted to a stock-market quotation to transform their debt capacity. This could be a result of prior external or self-imposed capital rationing, arising from the UK banking system's monopolistic supply of small-firm debt. The question of capital-market adequacy, currently known as 'short-termism', is of long-standing concern, with previous versions considered in the Macmillan, Bolton and Wilson committee reports. This produces a situation in which firms' ability to fund development is constrained either by reluctance of lenders to provide finance or by a corresponding reluctance of firms to borrow. The latter phenomenon may be linked to the debt-targeting hypothesis put forward by Marsh (1982). His analysis of the issuing behaviour of UK firms indicated that when raising new capital, firms appeared to be targeting their debt : equity ratios, with those targets related to size, bankruptcy risk and the firms' asset composition. The relationship between size, gearing and growth within new entrants to the UK new-issue market has been investigated by Hutchinson et al. (1988) who found that growth small firms are characterised by 'their high gearing and low liquidity which are indicative of the financial stress of growth'.

Hall and Hutchinson (Chapter 8) explore the links further, this time casting doubt on the debt hypothesis.

Quoted status not only provides the smaller firm with access to sources of equity and debt capital previously denied to it, but it also improves its credit-worthiness and financial standing, and enables it to restructure its whole financial base to achieve 'target' financial-policy levels. Managers, in choosing a particular financial structure for the business, may be thought to be guided not by the first-best wealth-maximising principles of Modigliani and Miller's (1958) arguments, but along second-best principles within which the level of corporate gearing is regarded as one element of a package of signals from manager–insiders to investor–outsiders (see, for example, Leland and Pyle 1977; Miller and Rock 1985; John 1987). In such a transactions-cost, principal–agent and signalling view of the firm, the debt behaviour of new entrants to equity markets becomes of great importance. Theoretically, the choice of debt ratio acquires a role of signalling management's confidence and expectations to the less well-informed, outsider providers of finance.

BANKING RELATIONSHIPS WITH SMALL FIRMS

Agency theory (Jensen and Meckling 1976) suggests that suppliers of debt will seek to bond owner–managers by contractual relationships which seek to limit their power to transfer wealth to themselves. One form which such bonding can assume is that of the taking of security, which for many smaller UK borrowers is normal banking practice (Binks et al. 1988) and which in turn depends on the asset cover available to the borrower.

Cosh and Hughes (1994) follow Myers and Majluf (1984) in finding that the financial structures of smaller firms compared with larger enterprises is consistent with the latters' interpretation of a 'pecking-order hypothesis'. Thus capital raising by such businesses utilises internally generated equity and debt before recourse to new issues of equity. As a result small firms are found to be characterised by a relatively greater reliance on short-term loans and overdrafts and much less reliance on equity capital than larger firms. Our concern, however, shared with Hutchinson et al. (1988), is with that population of high-growth medium-sized firms eligible for a stock-market quotation. While the pecking-order hypothesis will apply to such businesses, transactions costs (market as well as administrative scale effects) involved in the new issue of equity (Davis and Yeomans 1976; Buckland and Davis 1989) inevitably imply a forfeit of value of such magnitude that it is hardly surprising that owners of such firms seek to finance growth as far as possible by retained earnings plus debt. In the period under investigation this strategy is likely to have been reinforced by tax considerations (see King 1977: p. 207; see also Binks and Ennew, Chapter 3; Keasey and Watson, Chapter 4). In this context, therefore, where bank overdrafts constitute the most accessible source of external capital, the question of banking relationships with smaller firms is critical.

RESEARCH METHODS

Our methodological approach seeks to relate quantitative and qualitative dimensions in the analysis of smaller-firm debt behaviour. The relevance of the former is that it enables us to derive objective measures of risk and statistically valid sample selections of groups. The latter affords a richer understanding of the processes, particularly behavioural, behind financial decisions which ultimately are measured in financial accounts. Ample justification for this approach in financial research may be derived from, for example, Tomkins and Groves (1983); Roberts and Scapens (1985); Rickwood et al. (1987).

The methodology employed involves both cross-section analysis of the accounts of newly quoted companies (IPOs) obtaining quotation in the 1980s (Stage 1) together with a subsequent longitudinal case-study-based investigation (Stage 2) of a subset/sample of such firms selected by reference to their debt behaviour, as revealed in Stage 1 of this research.

The stage 1 research studies the population of all entrants to the UK new equity issue markets (the unlisted securities market, or USM, and the official list, OL), from the inception of the USM in November 1980 until the end of March 1985. Information is available upon entrants' financial characteristics and history and upon their financial activity for subsequent years. Financial structure is proxied by calculation of the ratio of total company indebtedness to the book value of capital employed. This is chosen in preference to measures calculated using net indebtedness, long-term debt, or only short-term debt, since those three disaggregated measures are all structurally related to company size and because the term structure of debt will be likely to change systematically over a period of new quotation. Book values are adopted in line with the considerations that, first, at the time of initial quotation market values of financing assets are unobservable; and second, that book-value measures are closer to the information conveyed in company accounts and used by managers (Marsh 1982: p. 131). This gearing ratio is recalculated at an interval of 12 months after quotation commences, to identify movements in financial structure subsequent to quotation.

By the inclusion of both USM and OL entrants, this sample allowed analysis of the USM firms to be compared with a control sample of OL entrants. There is, on the other hand, no control for or consideration of firms which do not enter the markets (for one study which attempts elements of such a comparison, although with a substantially smaller sample, see Hutchinson et al. (1988)). The analysis proceeded by investigation of the characteristics of these issuing firms, their behaviour and the links between that behaviour and their financial structures. The statistical methodology adopted proceeds from means analysis of levels of gearing at quotation to analyses utilising multiple regression and principal component analyses of the changes in gearing linked to various features of firm characteristics and performance.

Stage 2 of this research uses the information provided in Stage 1 to identify 20 USM companies with different financial characteristics and behaviour which were selected for subsequent interviews designed to examine further motives affecting debt behaviour. In particular, equivocal evidence on capital rationing, whether self- or externally imposed, could be illuminated by reference to firms' own explanations. As a control group, 20 official list entrants were also selected. These larger firms provide a basis for assessment of standard behaviour, first, in terms of 'normal' relationships with capital markets and, second, in terms of cultural stance adopted towards financial systems and the quality of financial management.

By using a longitudinal case-study methodology we focus on the specific reasons why, for example, firms' gearing ratios change after quotation, using both conventional sources and uses of funds statements and case investigations, establishing the extent to which debt behaviour is related to external market constraints or is internally generated by managerial risk-aversion.

THE EVIDENCE ON DEBT TARGETING

Preliminary evidence on debt restructuring

Across the population in Stage 1 there is evidence to support the general financial restructuring hypothesis. When opening gearing, for both the USM and OL groups, was grouped into four sub-ranges (under 35 per cent, 35–50 per cent, 50–65 per cent, over 65 per cent) it emerged that companies initially in the highest gearing category reduced their average gearing level quite dramatically (in the USM by 16.25 per cent, in the OL by 13.8 per cent) over the three-year period. At the other extreme, companies initially in the lowest gearing category increased their gearing ratio on average (by 17.82 per cent for USM companies and 10.12 per cent for OL entrants). The pattern was also revealed, to appropriately decreasing degrees, for the remaining two opening gearing categories.

Regression to a mean level of gearing was quite pronounced for the USM group. While regression to the mean also occurred for OL entrants, it was less marked. The inference may be drawn that restructuring was a more important motive in seeking quoted status for companies in the smaller size group characterised by the USM than for those employing the more traditional OL route. Table 9.1 summarises the movements towards 'targets' among the groups of entrants.

The influence of firm size on debt behaviour

There should be significant associations between entrants' size and their gearing if the hypotheses of financing gaps, and especially of

Table 9.1 Gearing levels and behaviour in Stage 2 sample firms
Levels defined as for Stage 1, USM in brackets.

Level	*Low*	*Medium*	*High*	*All*
Behaviour				
Rises	4(4)	0(4)	0(0)	4(8)
Unchanged	4(4)	3(5)	3(1)	10(10)
Falls	0(0)	3(0)	3(2)	6(2)
All	8(8)	6(9)	6(3)	20(20)

'gap closure' at entry, are to have any validity. As part of the Stage 1 investigation attempts were made to uncover statistical regularity and association between gearing measures and entrant size and are reported here as follows. There is evidence of links between gearing and size, particularly between the funding from creditors and accruals. Smaller USM entrants relied relatively less on long-term debt (6.51 per cent for entrants under £2.5 million total assets, 11.32 per cent for those over £15 million; but this was not statistically significant), with creditors and accruals 27.50 per cent against 21.71 per cent (same size groups; here $p<0.05$). Size differentials in gearing changes following entry were significant: −12.45 per cent compared to +1.17 per cent, with $p<0.01$.

However, the picture was less straightforward when alternative measures of gearing were introduced. If one considers that quotation permits the use of market values, or capitalisation, as a measure of equity backing for corporate debt, then gearing measures based upon market values become significant. The smallest USM entrants (under £2.5 million total assets) had an average debt : equity ratio, at historic written-down book values, of 139 per cent. Their average debt : equity ratio at market values one month after issue was a mere 28 per cent, very significantly smaller than the overall USM average of 52 per cent and the OL average of 58 per cent. Smaller entrants were unambiguously lower geared than larger entrants when approached by market values.

This evidence of direct links between size, financing positions, and financing behaviour is equivocal. Entrants in general were not as highly geared as the contemporary sectoral averages; and on average much less financially extended than the medium-sized firms in the *Business Monitor* samples. In both markets the smallest size category of entrant displayed higher debt levels than did other firms in the samples; and these smallest firms made the biggest reductions in their debt : asset ratios (Buckland and Davis 1989: Chapter 6). But the question remains: where were entrants going or attempting to go in their gearing behaviour?

Prima facie, the evidence of means classifications pointed to entrants having distorted financial structures at the time of their entry to the market. In Marsh's analysis of issuing behaviour, target financial structures were associated with company size, risk and asset composition (Marsh 1982: p. 121). Previously, the debt ratios of firms have been related to their size, industry, riskiness and asset composition (Briscoe and Hawke 1976). In Hutchinson et al. (1988)

also, firm size and firm growth rates were found to affect financial structure, with newly quoted firms displaying both higher growth rates and higher debt ratios than did a matched sample of unquoted businesses. We proceeded to test whether debt positions and debt behaviour are significantly associated with the variables variously hypothesised in the literature.

Several measures are correlated with each other as well as being related to firm's debt. Variables could also have a non-linear relationship to each other. Even if this were not the case for the underlying firm characteristics it could still apply to transformed variables chosen as proxies. By comparing parametric (Pearson's product–moment correlation) and non-parametric (Spearman's and Kendall's rank, or associative) statistics, tests are conducted on the potential superiority of various log-linear, exponential or hyperbolic associations between variables at the bivariate level.

As a result, transforms of the basic variables which more precisely reflect the variability in entrants' characteristics are generated and form the basis of our subsequent analysis. However, because many of the bivariate links were weak, even in the non-parametric approach, while many associations between non-financial variables are as strong as or stronger than those between them and the gearing measures, with attendant risks of multicollinearity in any multivariate analysis, a multivariate analysis was required. This allows the use of a statistical methodology such as multiple discriminant analysis, which presumes independence of variables, focused upon a set of proxies for data characteristics freed from any multicollinearity. Thus, firm growth is proxied by the price : earnings (P : E) ratio, by past profits growth and/or by forecast growth, recognising that these are inevitably imperfect surrogates for the anticipated growth in the value of the firm's equity. Risk is measured retrospectively by systematic (beta) risk and by the specific risk of equity returns, together with profits and share-price variability.

Using principal components analysis the underlying and independent characteristics within the sample are examined. The data are fitted to a model which extracts principal components with a subsequent varimax orthogonal rotation of the factor matrix to enhance individual factor loadings of the principal components, while maintaining the independence of the components. Table 9.2 shows the results of factorising the complete sample, with the first four principal components, the amount of variability explained for

Table 9.2 The UK population of IPOs, 1980 to 1985: principal components analysis

		Factor statistics			
Variable	*Communality*[a]	*Factor*	*Eigen-value*	*% variation explained*	*Cumulative % explained*
Total assets	0.87	1	2.73	18.2	18.2
Equity capitalisation	0.83				
Issue size	0.62	2	1.99	13.2	31.4
% new money	0.4				
% equity issued	0.74	3	1.65	11	42.4
β risk[b]	0.44				
Specific risk[b]	0.58	4	1.25	8.3	50.7
Profit variability	0.13				
Profit growth	0.27				
Capitalisation/assets	0.7				
Subscription ratio	0.07				
Discount on entry	0.15				
Forecast dividend yield	0.65				
Forecast dividend cover	0.46				
P:E ratio	0.72				

Factor loadings for rotated factor matrix, ordered by coefficient size

	Factor 1: yields	*Factor 2: size*	*Factor 3: issue*	*Factor 4: risk*
% equity issued	**0.84**[c]	−0.03	−0.01	0.17
Forecast dividend yield	**0.75**	−0.02	−0.27	−0.06
P:E ratio	**0.74**	0.15	0.35	−0.15
Forecast dividend cover	**0.58**	0.17	0.23	−0.19
Equity capitalisation	−0.01	**0.89**	0.17	−0.03
Total assets	−0.08	**0.84**	−0.28	−0.28
Issue size	0.26	**0.74**	−0.07	0.08
Capitalisation/assets	−0.1	−0.01	**0.82**	0.15
Profit growth	0.04	−0.09	**0.47**	0.18
% new money	−0.1	0	**−0.45**	0.42
Subscription ratio	0.09	−0.02	**0.19**	−0.14
Specific risk[b]	−0.28	−0.08	0.11	**0.7**
β risk[b]	0.08	0.27	0.22	**0.56**
Discount on entry	0.08	−0.06	−0.07	**0.37**
Profit variability	−0.05	−0.06	0.04	**0.34**

[a] Communality measures the percentage variation in data explained by the variable.
[b] As published after entry by the London Business School Risk Measurement Service.
[c] Bold type identifies variables that load heavily onto the principal components.
Source: Adapted from Buckland and Davis 1989, Chapter 6 where variables and method are further defined.

each variable (communality) and for the data set as a whole (percentage variation explained). These four independent principal components explain 51 per cent of the variability in the raw variables, with forecast yields, firm size, risk measures and the proxies for issuing process revealed as the main sources of variability within the data.

Table 9.2 further indicates the factor loadings or strength of relationship between the principal component scores and the raw variables, after rotation of the factor matrix. The correlation of the principal components with financial structure variables is reported in Table 9.3 from which it appears that gearing reductions following quotation were strongly linked with the level of opening gearing reported in the prospectus.

Using multiple regression analysis it is possible to test whether the size of gearing adjustments is related to general prospectus information, to performance or risk characteristics, and in particular, whether there are any significant influences other than opening gearing in determining subsequent gearing adjustments. Regression analysis can also test whether there are systematic multivariate associations between newly quoted firms' opening or target debt levels and other firm characteristics, such as industry, yields, riskiness, and firm size in addition to opening gearing. From Table 9.4,

Table 9.3 The UK population of IPOs, 1980 to 1985: correlation of principal component scores with gearing measures of entrants

	Gearing measures				
	A	*B*	*C*	*D*	*E*
Gearing measures:					
A Prospectus	—	0.46**	0.09	−0.59**	0.04
B 12 months after entry	—	—	0.26**	0.45**	0.32**
C 36 months after entry	—	—	—	0.15**	0.12*
D Change over 12 months	—	—	—	—	0.24**
E By market values[a]	—	—	—	—	—
Principal components:					
Yields	0.29**	0.21**	−0.01	−0.11*	−0.15**
Size	0.05	0.01	−0.03	−0.02	0.04
Issuing process	0.16**	0.04	0.06	−0.12	−0.26**
Risk	0.07	−0.16**	0.05	−0.23**	−0.05

[a] Total debt in balance sheet as ratio of equity capitalisation at entry.
* Significant at the 5% level
** Significant at the 1% level

Table 9.4 The UK population of IPOs, 1980 to 1985: gearing adjustment regressed on entrants' debt ratio, size, industry and issue characteristics

Stepwise regression, critical value of 1% change in R^2

Independent variable	*Entry step*	*Change in* R^2 *(%)*	t *statistic*	*Level of significance*	*Beta*
USM:					
Opening gearing	1	35	13.82	0.000**	0.53
Total assets	2	5	6.29	0.000**	0.26
Energy-sector dummy[a]	3	5	−5.57	0.000**	−0.24
% new money	4	2	−4.67	0.000**	−0.19
Subscription ratio	5	2	−3.77	0.000**	−0.15
Issue size	6	2	−3.75	0.000**	−0.16
Official list:					
Opening gearing	1	19	−4.16	0.000**	−0.35
Profits variability	2	4	−2.33	0.021*	−0.17
% equity issued	3	3	−3.42	0.001**	−0.34
Forecast yield	4	4	2.2	0.030*	0.21
Energy-sector dummy[a]	5	3	−2.2	0.030*	−0.18

[a] Only entrants in the energy and minerals SICC categories display any statistical regularities: see Buckland and Davis 1989, Chapter 6.
* Significant at the 5% level
** Significant at the 1% level

however, it is clear that the last variable accounted for 35 per cent of the variation in gearing changes for USM entrants in stepwise designs. Newly quoted USM firms indicated a significant size effect, with the sign on total assets being positive and significant, and indicating that the smallest firms make lower reductions in their gearing. With gearing definition changed, to provide for a market-based debt : equity ratio instead of one based on a balance-sheet debt : total assets ratio; while the R^2 remains similar to that for a balance-sheet constituted measure, an interesting finding arises from this alternative measurement of gearing. Most of the variation explained is attributable to the market premium of equity value over net assets, which has a strong negative regression coefficient. USM quoted firms with low asset backing for their market value have relatively low debt : equity ratios. Equity capitalisation itself, with a negative sign to the coefficient is significant also; smaller firms have higher debt : equity ratios than larger ones with the same share price : net assets per share ratios.

Overall these findings support the hypothesis that firms' asset composition is a critical factor, with resultant differences in eligible security they possess for borrowing. They also strongly support the hypothesis that smaller USM entrants have higher gearing ratios than larger but otherwise similar firms. Contrasting results of the same regression design upon official list entrants provide further support, with market-value-based models explaining more of the variation in financial structure ($R^2 = 36.5$ per cent one year after entry); with observed variation again dependent upon the market price : net assets per share ratio; and with even stronger crude size effects. For these firms also, the debt : equity ratios of larger OL entrants are significantly lower than those of smaller firms.

QUALITATIVE EXPLANATIONS FOR GEARING BEHAVIOUR

Stage 2 of this research project is intended to seek qualitative interpretations for the equivocal behaviour indicated in the preceding quantitative analyses. Given the known limitations of annual accounting data it was believed that interviews directed towards newly quoted firms with debt characteristics identified from Stage 1 would provide important insights.

The Stage 2 sample is drawn from the same population of UK companies which gained quotation between 1980 and 1985, a time period that was one of relative national economic stability. The criteria for selection are that the sample, comprising entrants to the unlisted securities market (USM) and also entrants to the official list (OL) of the International Stock Exchange, contains a range of opening debt positions – high, average, and low levels of leverage – and a range of subsequent, post-entry debt behaviours. Stage 2 firms, therefore, are not statistically representative of the population as a whole, and inferences will not be drawn about population characteristics from the qualitative data. Where research questions are raised and inferential evidence is required, recourse to statistically representative samples is called for. Here, our attention is directed to the nature of the research problem rather than to its quantification.

Including the perspectives of entrants which had not (by 1991) survived as independent quoted businesses introduced a major complication. In considering the interaction of quotation with financing and external performance pressures, one of the key outcomes of problematic financing is corporate failure, take-over, acquisition or merger. For some newly quoted firms, quotation may be effected with the objective of maximising shareholders' future proceeds in the market in corporate control which quotation opens up; for many others, ambitions of continued independence may be frustrated by exposure to the market in control, or their performance may be such that failure or take-over solutions are adopted. It was determined that such businesses should be represented in the research: crucial dimensions of entrants' experiences would be lost were one to research only those whose histories were, by and large, financially or managerially unproblematic or crisis-free.

Two samples of 20 firms were drawn. From the initial Stage 1 companies were prioritised for access by reference to criteria identified in Stage 1. Access was sought at the level of senior management, with the priority being: (a) the financial director of the time of first quotation; (b) managing director/chief executive of that time; (c) successor at that level. Interviews were to be conducted by two members of the research team, at the respondent's workplace or other site of their choice; access was negotiated by a written approach, with telephone follow-up, using registration data held on the FAME company database.

Table 9.5 Case status and respondent function for Stage 2 sample entrants

	USM	*OL*	*All*
Continuing in market	5	6	11
Moved to OL	5	—	5
Taken over	9	14	23
In receivership/liquidation	1	0	1
Total	20	20	40
Founder shareholder/Chairman/CEO	6	7	13
Finance director[a] now and at quotation	5	4	9
Finance director[b] now	9	7	16
Other director[c]		2	2
Total	20	20	40

[a] Includes 1 financial controller (OL)
[b] Includes 3 financial controllers (OL)
[c] One corporate affairs director in OL company; one non-executive director of (OL) business services company, since taken over by business now in receivership.

In the pair of samples from USM and OL segments of the London Stock Exchange strict matching was not attempted, since, almost by definition, the market segmentation splits entrants across size and experience characteristics. While the populations of USM and OL entrants overlap, it is not desirable to restrict oneself to the bigger USM entrants and the smaller OL entrants, when the research questions at issue are those of financing relations and behaviour, not merely of the effectiveness of market segments.

Table 9.5 summarises the case status and the level of seniority of access gained for the Stage 2 sample. Several issues arise here that are worthy of comment. More than half this sample had died through take-over prior to being researched. The rate of attrition does not appear – from these admittedly small samples – to be itself related to debt performance: some entrants which reduced gearing were taken over, as were some which kept gearing uniformly low, or which increased their gearing levels.

EVIDENCE ON BANK FINANCING

Newly quoted firms

A key preoccupation in sampling these firms was to examine their managements' perception of the relationship of quotation to *financing stresses*. As was observed in the quantitative data at Stage 1 of the research, the evidence of such a link is equivocal and weak, notwithstanding the assertion in the literature that newly quoted firms are suffering from and may be reacting to financing stress when becoming quoted. Respondents were questioned closely about the firm's relationships with financing sources, the adequacy of those sources prior to quotation, and the effects of becoming quoted on the access to and costs of funding. By design, the samples are not uniquely of low-, or of high-geared businesses. Indeed, as a result of the sampling process described above, the sample consists of a mix of cases exhibiting the full range of opening gearing and post-quotation gearing behaviour. Table 9.1 above has summarised the position and movements that were involved.

In the OL, these cases are biased towards debt- and gearing-reducing firms, whereas the USM cases include more which increased their levels of borrowing upon quotation. Prima facie this should be in line with the stress hypothesis considered in Stage 1: the relatively smaller, less well-known firms (USM entrants), which faced direct capital rationing by their banks sought after quotation to increase their borrowing; the larger, well-established OL entrants sought to reduce it. The issue is plainly not clear, however: one can equally sustain the argument that the OL businesses were over-extended prior to entry, compared with USM firms whose use of debt had been restricted (the levels of formalised, long-term debt found in Stage 1 above, and reported for these cases in Table 9.6, bear this out).

Gearing 'culture' – attitudes towards gearing and banks

Reporting of financing stress linked with quotation (or move to quotation) was rare. In the majority of cases, external funding was of minor and peripheral concern: entrants were in general highly cash-rich, cash-generative businesses, financing high rates of growth from internally generated funds. Low levels of formal debt are mirrored in managements' attitudes to banks and other lenders. Here qualitative data illuminates and informs our understanding of the gearing culture in newly quoted businesses. Only four USM entrants report 'stress'. One design business chose quotation to establish its reputation and status, after difficulties in funding an MBO from its retailing parent: but the crucial funding stress had already been resolved by private-venture funding prior to quotation, and quotation was a stage in growth rather than a prerequisite to funding. Two microchip businesses used quotation to alleviate the financial stress of very rapid growth; but in one case this represented resistance to dilution of owners' control, using the market evaluation of the equity as a base for further debt funding. The second chip business was the first to display the symptoms of classic growth stress, having relied upon a mixture of venture capital and debt from leasing, HP, and term loans on the high street

Table 9.6 Stage 2 cases' capital and income gearing measured at entry

		Zero	<10%	10–20%	20–30%	>N 30%
USM:	Capital	6	6	1	3	4
	Income	3	12	3	1	1
OL:	Capital	3	5	2	6	4
	Income	0	14	4	0	2

Source: Datastream and Issue Prospectuses

before restrictions imposed on debt access prompted quotation to restructure and enhance access. A third entrant, in consumer products manufacturing and marketing, was spun off by its parent, to whom it had substantial inter-company debt prior to quotation: its USM entry was the vehicle for restructuring it (or, equally, indirect restructuring of its already-quoted parent). The other stressed case from the USM was a venture in mining exploration, where relationships with debt providers were only marginally of relevance, and where the USM is seen in its role as a regulated market in the shares of high-risk ventures.

For the official list entrants there are but two cases of 'distress'. In these two cases entry was associated with repayment of specific lenders, banks whose lending was imposing restrictions either upon owners or on business strategy. In the former, a firm of estate agents, owners were burdened with personal guarantees for the partnership's extensive borrowings, and the creation of the quoted company was a vehicle for freeing shareholders from such onerous personal liability.

Elsewhere, when gearing was reported as a factor, respondents did not perceive it as stressful. One such was a financial-services firm that had been financed largely from borrowing from a merchant bank; however, the business itself was highly cash-positive and generative, and it was the lender's desire for an exit rather than difficulties in servicing high gearing that drove the decision. In the second, very rapid rates of growth of the business (in electronics) necessitated working-capital demands which had, pre-quotation, sometimes occasioned problems; quotation was partly a response to that, in providing equity, but more especially in enhancing access to larger quantities of bank facilities. This last was also the factor in the final two OL entrants to speak of financing strain. One, an electronics trading business, used extensive trade finance as a commercial weapon in its strategy, and sought quotation to continue to run such a high-geared operation at a larger size; the other, a property company, saw quotation as a route to higher borrowing capacity from international and syndicated sources.

These cases can be categorised into three distinct groups:

1 those which had no need of borrowing,
2 those which abhor and avoid borrowing,
3 those which treat the firm's gearing as though it was not present.

Around half of respondents saw themselves prior to quotation as being opposed to corporate debt, as a result of their experience or perception of the agency problems that debt introduced into their management responsibilities. One business-services firm joining the OL had previously found bank finance, only for the regional manager to be countermanded by his superiors, resulting in a makeshift, quasi-'equity' arrangement with the bank's venture-capital arm; another (USM) entrant had sought bank financing, but became disenchanted with banks' inability to perceive any solution to their agency problem vis-à-vis his operation. For one USM respondent, this was acute, and stemmed from previous personal or corporate experience with lenders who had exerted influence over corporate affairs and destiny:

> We were really saying 'We were beholden to a bank manager once, never again.' We don't like bankers, we treat them as a shop with three brass balls hanging on the outside, and we are not going to use their money again.

This leaves a bare majority of respondents where some bank or lender relationship was accepted prior to quotation, where the corporate culture accepted such an outside interest. Here a pattern can be perceived, in that many such firms possessed extensive security in the form of tangible, saleable assets: property, franchises, marketable securities; but there is also a factor of a sponsoring relationship – venture-capital or state-agency involvement or both – which produced an acceptance of debt in respondents' firms. For example, two USM entrants which came to the market as ventures took on remarkably little debt, and such debt as existed was more than outweighed by their strong cash position during initial periods of losses. An entrant from an established venture in microchip technology, in contrast, had acquired a culture of relatively high gearing while supported by the banking and state-agency venture institutions: a culture carried over into its quoted existence. Similar entrants in their field without that equity–debt 'partnership' background eschewed debt, using cash reinvested from the high margin activity as their funding source.

Gearing is not linked solely to asset composition, to the professionalisation of management, or to operating gearing and margins. There is a diversity of cultural attitudes towards taking on debt, and this is predominantly antithetical to debt in the case of newly quoted firms. This inhibits the expansion of financing pre-quotation and could, it may be argued, prevent growing firms from reaching a stage where quotation is possible. In the cases here it was noticeable that the early involvement of venture-capital institutions and state agencies made respondents less resistant to taking on lender relationships. Otherwise, the cases display the bias in quotation towards businesses that are capable of financing high growth from self-generated cash: where businesses exploit this 'window' of uncontested high margins and rapid growth stages to gain quotation.

The development of bank relations post-quotation

Generally, respondents see quotation positively as enhancing their banking relationships. Many observe that their quote, whether USM or OL, widened and deepened access to funds, and lowered costs both in percentage and in agency terms. This was reported most actively by the OL 'trader' companies, which relied upon borrowing to fund substantial levels of stocks and debtors. Here it was reported that quotation allowed entrants to shed restrictive security backing for their lending, to broaden the range of bank suppliers, and to reduce costs. Where firms had expressly gained quotation to get access to borrowing, they were satisfied that this had occurred, at least initially. Entrants often reported that, after quotation, they found lenders eager to offer more and cheaper facilities: indeed, several respondents found banks cold-calling them with facilities in the mid-1980s: 'From an access point of view I would say we were able probably to increase our facilities by 50 per cent because of it [quotation]. That was automatic.'

Table 9.7 shows that 'debt problems' were reported by only a minority of respondents: 9 out of 40. However, it is noticeable that there are some fault-lines here: the culturally conservative USM entrants tended to be the survivors there, while this was less so in the OL cases; and in the OL problematic debt relationships with the bank were often related to take-over activity.

Most USM entrants continued to avoid an agency relationship with the bank after quotation: banks were seen as a major consideration in ten USM cases, and where banks were an important source of funding, four of the ten saw banks as a problem, as a contribution to some deleterious change. Three USM cases were observably affected by breakdowns of their lines of bank credit: one had relied upon borrowing from a long-standing bank relationship for expansion, and was driven into receivership by the withdrawal of support as the recession deepened in 1991; one had used debt routinely from its pre-quotation days as a source of long-term

Table 9.7 Stage 2 cases' reporting of problems in agency relationships between entrant and banks

	USM			*OL*	
	Continuing on USM	*Moves to OL*	*T/o or fail*	*Continuing on OL*	*T/o*
Number of cases	5	5	10	6	14
Conservative culture	5	1	4	1	8
Accept short-term debt	2		5	2	6
Accepts debt, resulting in:					
Problems		2	2	1	4
No problems	2	2	2	4	2

Note: Categories in this table are not necessarily exclusive

investment and was forced to restructure financially, then was taken over following loss of bank support; one had expanded by acquiring retail freeholds backed by (unsecured) bank borrowing and the demands for securitisation of this persuaded the firm into retrenchment and divestment of assets. To these three might be added the case of one firm which, having been taken over, saw the bank pushing its parent into restructuring, leading to the original USM entrant's managers using bank support to finance an MBO of the subsidiary. They now perceive their bank as a 'loose cannon' in the firm's strategy which might upset their calculations at any time. Their objective is to eliminate this rogue element in strategy, which may only be achievable by a further take-over of their firm. In the other six firms, management either foresaw difficulties and took action to avoid them by degearing, or they retained strong asset backing which had not been overextended in the mid-to-late 1980s.

Dividing entrants into categories of those which 'survive' as USM quoted, those which have 'progressed' to OL status, and those which have 'died' through take-over or failure, Stage 2 does not support hypotheses that entrants with problematic bank relations are taken over, or that the low-geared firms survive. In the USM, it appeared that the continuing USM quotes were all conservative in their attitude to gearing.

For OL cases, eighteen of the twenty had or had developed significant dependence on bank funding, significantly more than in the USM. For some, again, this was largely unproblematic. For the two 'trader' firms, bank facilities for working-capital finance were enhanced by quotation and they continued to be available throughout the period. For two others, quotation resulted in bank borrowings being repaid; and while the relationship with the bank continued there was no perception of this being strained (both of these OL firms had been taken over before the onset of recession, and thus may not have been under equivalent pressures).

Another three cases displayed bank relationships dominated by preservation of net positive positions: levels of capital gearing offset by balances deposited with the banks, described by one respondent as 'net nil gearing'. This latter respondent saw no difficulties in the firm's bank relationship; the former had both, again, been taken over (and saw themselves as being 'milked' for cash by their new and highly geared parent firms).

Of the remaining eleven cases, two firms continued in existence and respondents saw no problems in their bank relationships. One used bank finance (in joint ventures) with property backing; the other had developed extensive leasing and hire-purchase relationships during the 1980s, but this had been run down as franchise renewal approached, and the firm had avoided term lending for reasons of the levy regime applied to its profits (a similar consideration affected the financing stances of two USM cases). Three others had been taken over, and respondents reported no role of the bank in that, although one should note that one of these was later placed in receivership due to unfundable lease obligations. One case had extended itself through gearing in the mid-1980s, funding its rapid expansion by that means, but took the decision at board level to wind gearing down in anticipation of credit restriction at the close of the decade. This leaves five OL cases where respondents saw banks as a factor in their problems. One firm was hampered by the issue process: when quoted, it experienced drastic undersubscription, producing a disaffected shareholder group; it was burdened by a decision pre-quotation to structure it with relatively high gearing for its sector; and it was necessary to build new banking relationships at that time. When margins fell on its business, the firm was in no position to borrow further or to make any rights issue: it was taken over after four years of existence. Another case had expanded by acquisition and organically, by reinvesting cash from operations: its founder used bank financing to buy out problematic equity partners, but the firm itself was lightly geared. Its difficulties arose from relocation into debt-funded property, bought at the height of the 1980s boom and funded out of reduced margins and earnings when property values had crashed. Although the business had, to date, survived, the debt had stripped away the founder's controlling interest in the firm.

The final three cases of gearing problems highlight the role of banks in precipitating change. In one case, gearing had been habitually used to fund expansion, with banks lending against contracts signed with reputable clients. As the business diversified, gearing increased and bank constraints were a factor in the company's sale (although the buyers were themselves debt-burdened also). Another business used bank finance in retail-property expansion, but could not defend its margins against a predatory competitor. Although both firms were equally highly geared, the predator was diversified and could withstand the temporary loss of margin in this portion of its business: the more specialised OL entrant was driven into an agreed take-over to escape being forced into liquidation by its bank. The final case here concerns a firm which had, as the respondent saw it, escaped from bank pressure and restrictions through the use of a rights issue in the mid-1980s, but then dissipated that cash in a misplaced and misdirected strategy of expansion in the USA. Without either cash or bank backing, the firm became a take-over target and lost its independence.

CONCLUSIONS – BANK FINANCING FOR THE NEWLY QUOTED FIRM

This chapter has drawn on findings of a two-stage investigation into financing behaviour of UK newly quoted firms. It confirms and enriches understanding of the links between bank finance and corporate financing in several key areas.

Previous research has suggested that fast-growth firms are denied bank finance for expansion plans (Storey et al. 1989) and that secondary equity market entrants, particularly USM entrants, are stressed by over-borrowing or by denial of access to funds (Hutchinson et al. 1988). On the contrary, in the 1980s and overwhelmingly, UK newly quoted firms display that, at quotation, they are typically free from financing stress, and that they are in general conservative in their attitudes to borrowed funds. The firms that attain quoted status are typically cash-rich: they are financing rapid growth from high margins and do not, in the main, require additional funding alongside quotation.

Respondents' cultural attitudes toward bank financing were conservative, to the extent that several treated borrowing as 'net' gearing, after taking account of cash balances: some respondents viewed their own relatively high-geared firms as low-, or even zero-geared. This reflects the UK cultural attitude towards debt in general, and after quotation most USM entrants, and many OL firms, retained their antipathy to bank debt, remaining sceptical of the attractions of borrowing and preferring to stay free of what were seen as unnecessary complications from the agency relation with a banker.

This is consistent with the experience of bank relationships where entrants developed or depended upon them as a part of long-term funding. Significant numbers of these entrants were taken over, and in one case failed, after becoming dependent on the bank relationship. The number of respondents who viewed their banker positively was small, and confined to cases where bank funding was restricted to the support of short-term, trading assets.

The data supports the Wilson Report proposition that funding gaps are less discriminatory than attitudinal: that the provision of funding in the UK to growing firms stems from institutions not adequately addressing the agency problems which need to be resolved. It supports, also, the research reported elsewhere in this volume, that the banking 'finance gap' is attributable as much to a failure of demand as one of supply.

10

EFFICIENT PRICING OF IPOs

Roger Buckland

Initial public offerings (IPOs) have been extensively researched, and no aspect has received more academic attention than the processes of pricing them. In the US, one might note the work by Scholes (1972), Ibbotson (1975), Rock (1986), Tinic (1988) and many others.[1] In the UK, IPO pricing in the London (later the International) Stock Exchange was examined by Henderson (1950), by Merrett et al. (1964), then analysed by Davis et al. (1974). Dimson (1979) introduced rigorous examination of option elements, and Levis (1990) has profitably applied Rock's asymmetric information analysis to UK data. Buckland et al. (1981), Buckland and Davis (1984, 1989, 1990a) have been consistently critical of the discounting revealed in UK pricing practice, particularly in terms of advisers' pricing and the pricing of privatisation issues.

The practical impact of these studies has, to date, been minimal. The mechanisms of issuing in London markets have been largely unaffected by the academic debate. New issues where companies have an existing exchange quotation are made by rights issues, targeted at the existing shareholders pro rata to their existing holdings, while UK issuing houses and brokers have continued to market IPOs by traditional methods of sale: the placing (shares sold to brokers' clients), the offer for sale (shares offered to bidders at a fixed price), and the offer by tender (as an offer for sale, but with the price struck, or fixed, by the demand of offerors, who bid for shares at prices above an advisery floor). The Stock Exchange has built up a body of regulation for these processes, involving the publication of prospectuses containing audited accounting information, notices of contract, directors' reports, and forecasts of performance (see the rules enshrined in the Listing Agreement and the General Undertaking, both published by the International Stock Exchange in London).

Any significant alterations have resulted, primarily, from the attractions of low-cost placings of equity over public-offer methods, which prompted the relaxation of size limits on placings in 1987 (from a maximum of £3 million to £15 million); and secondly, to the innovations derived from the very large-scale demands placed upon London's IPO market by giant privatisation issues during the late 1980s. The latter pressures have produced two strands of changed procedures:

1 explicit marketing, discounting and targeted design of offers to enhance their appeal to the retail mass-investor market; and
2 advances in pre-sale book building and conditional tendering among institutional purchasers in order to lock in their high-volume demand.

In using the stock market to facilitate transfer of ownership from the public to the private sector, the UK government posed great problems for issue advisers. Processes which were designed to cope with IPOs of the scale of tens or even hundreds of million pounds, mixed with larger issues of 'seasoned' equity in rights issues, were quite inadequate where unseasoned issues of many billions, representing 50 or even 100 per cent of the firm's equity, were involved. Most early privatisations involved massive wealth transfers to new shareholders (see Buckland 1987), encouraging stagging and distracting from any positive gains in productive and allocative efficiency or in the generation of wider share ownership. Latterly, large issues have employed contingency arrangements for institutional bidders, novel tendering procedures to reduce eventual discounting and internationalisation of IPO marketing.

THE EVIDENCE OF PRICING INEFFICIENCY

The extent of price adjustment in UK IPOs

The market price of IPOs tends to stand at a substantial premium to the offer or selling price (or shares are offered at a 'market discount'). Studies since the 1950s have established that the London markets consistently underprice IPOs. Buckland and Davis (1989 – hereafter 'B&D') studied the behaviour of entrants and the markets over five years, for both the main London market (the official list, hereafter OL) and for the then novel second-tier market in equities (the unlisted securities market, or USM). Between 1980 and 1985 the market price of shares sold stood on average at +23.76 per cent (B&D: p. 95) over the issue price, representing substantial losses of wealth to the vendor shareholders.

To understand whether there can be changes to the issuing process that could benefit vendors it is necessary to first understand how those price shifts come about, second to determine why they arise, and finally to consider whether there are alternative mechanisms through which quotation could continue without such penalties to vendor shareholders. Empirical research gives little credence to the industry's casual justification for discounts on IPOs: the typical broker's comment that one needs to give at least 5 per cent in order to attract the buyer. In an efficient capital market, excess returns are clearly not necessary to shift volumes of equity, and the classic 'price–pressure' hypothesis, where a discount exists because a high volume or proportion of equity is changing hands on the one day, has been conclusively disproved in successive studies of issues of both existing quoted and newly quoted shares (cf. Scholes 1972; B&D: p. 139). Discounting stems rather from the process of uncertainty resolution at the time of first quotation, and this underlies most contemporary analysis of IPO pricing (Rock 1986; or Levis 1990).

The shares being sold are almost certainly those of an established business with trading records as unquoted plcs. Directors and shareholders have decided to gain quoted status: this may be because the firm has encountered a capital constraint on its debt or equity financing, because it wishes to use its equity as negotiable paper in acquisitions, because it seeks the status and publicity associated with quotation, or because some shareholders wish to realise the value of some or all of their stake in the business. Thus it may be that at the time of entry the business wishes to raise capital by sale of new shares, or that some shareholders wish to sell existing shares; it may also be necessary to sell shares upon quotation, if the Stock Exchange requirements on a 'wide' holding of equity are not otherwise met: without a spread of holders, potential buyers and potential sellers, there is unlikely to be a ready market in the shares after quotation.

The pricing problem with an IPO is essentially a marketing one: the public knows little of the business beforehand upon which to base a price; there is an element of 'forced sale' in order to reach targets for breadth of shareholding or of raising new capital through the issue. The prospective investor is offered a set of information, contained formally in the prospectus, but joined (of course) by press comment and by broker briefings and reports. They are also offered a set of signals to help in their evaluation of the share: what confidence is expressed in the retention of shares by vendors, or by managers? What gearing and dividend policies have been or are being followed? What earnings multiples are offered by similar, but already-quoted businesses and at what price are professional investors willing to underwrite the shares being offered? From all of this information prospective purchasers' decisions will be translated into bids for shares, in advance of the market makers' eventual judgement upon a market clearing price. It is that eventual price which establishes the worth of the equity and the returns being offered. The price paid determines the vendors' wealth and crucially will reflect back upon such investors' willingness to invest in unquoted business.

We can illustrate this by reference to the pricing record of the 427 new equity issues made on the London market between November 1980 and March 1985, the first years of operation of the USM. The period was one of sustained bull market, with share prices rising after several years of stagnation in the late 1970s. There is, indeed, no time trend visible in the pricing of the entrants over these years,[2] but some features of the issues are clearly associated with the levels of discount experienced. The most important of these is that of the method of issue itself. In Table 10.1 the market discounts on IPOs are recorded, measuring them as excess returns in relation to the equity market as a whole. The significant differences displayed here suggest that the method of issue may be crucial in determining the size of vendor shareholders' losses at the time of market entry – in answering the 'why' question about discounting. Where pricing and initial holders are closely controlled by the issuing broker, as in the placing method, discounts are on average substantially higher than otherwise; where the price and the purchaser are influenced by an open tendering process, discounts are substantially lower than otherwise.

This evidence mirrors that from earlier periods in the UK: from studies in the 1950s and 1960s and from those at the beginning of the 1970s (Merrett et al. 1964; Davis et al. 1974; Buckland et al. 1981; Vaughan et al. 1977); issues by the placing method consistently involve vendors in higher costs by the loss of wealth implied

Table 10.1 Average recorded discounts, classed by method of issue and by market status

Figures are: mean percentage, number of firms, standard deviation

	Average, November 1980 to March 1985		
Method of issue	*USM entrant*	*Official list entrant*	*Row total*
Placing	27.92	8.46	27.1
	205	9	214
	52.01	14.92	51.13
Offer for sale	5.59	21.74	15.68
	21	35	56
	19.46	28.22	26.31
Offer by tender	12.13	10.36	10.9
	10	23	33
	28.12	16.74	20.39
Other methods	32.08	8.43	29.55
	25	3	28
	61.74	13.82	58.8
Column total	25.92	15.72	23.76
	261	70	331
	50.78	23.46	46.52

Notes: Chi-squared = 142.73 with 3 degrees of freedom.
Significance = 0.00.
Missing = 3 entrants.
Source: Buckland and Davis 1989

in discounting the IPO. Such losses, moreover, cannot be explained in terms of any other features of the issues or of the firms, such as their size, profitability, growth, riskiness, or industry (B&D: Chapter 7). Although it is in the interests of brokers' clients (as purchasers of IPOs) to maintain this state, why otherwise would clients (as vendors) continue to accept the advice to use the placing method? In other words, can the disparity in discounts be explained?

It has already been mentioned that there is a widely held institutional view that discounts are necessary to shift high volumes or proportions of shares in IPOs: this pervades brokers' and issuing houses' attitudes, but has perhaps surfaced most markedly in the IPOs of privatised businesses over the last decade, where discounts have been justified in terms of the volume of shares being made available. It has also been mentioned that there has been adequate academic disproof of the proposition, and that discounts cannot be justified by this argument. It remains true that IPOs arise in a context where quotation is being gained simultaneously with a share sale: there is some uncertainty resolution about the market value of the share at the time of issue. Several have argued that this uncertainty resolution could explain discounting, most notably Dimson (1979) in his study linking discounts with option elements within IPOs. On the other hand, the recent research shows discounts to be unrelated to risk measures, whether those indicated in prospectuses' balance sheet or earnings records, or those in market measures subsequent to issue (B&D: p. 107; Keasey and McGuinness 1991: p. 141).

When analysing the discounts on these IPOs, it is also clear that there are some structural differences between the prices at which issues are being sold by tender and those where the sale price is fixed in advance by the issuing house or broker. Not only are the average discounts different, but discounts are associated with different features of the entrant. In particular, regression analysis shows that discounts on tender issues were not influenced by the prospectus variables that are associated with discounts on placings and offers for sale: a strong indication that advisers are creating discounts in their reaction to prospectus information, without any evidence that the wider market requires discounts for such features (B&D: Chapter 7; Keasey and McGuinness 1992).

Traditional methods of issue

Differences in methods of issue are important in that the methods relate to key differentials in entrants' needs and motivation. Here the various methods of issue involved are analysed, to determine what their objectives, effects, merits, and drawbacks might be. Three broad axes distinguish IPOs: first, whether there is any necessity to broaden shareholding; second, whether advisers dominate the issue process; and third, how the initial shareholder list is controlled at and after issue. Figure 10.1 provides a summary of these distinctions. Here the features are exposed and their impact upon the issuing process is considered.

Public availability of shares?

For some potential entrants to exchanges the firm's equity is already sufficiently widely held amongst investors prepared to trade, and there

Characteristics in **bold**; methods in *italics*

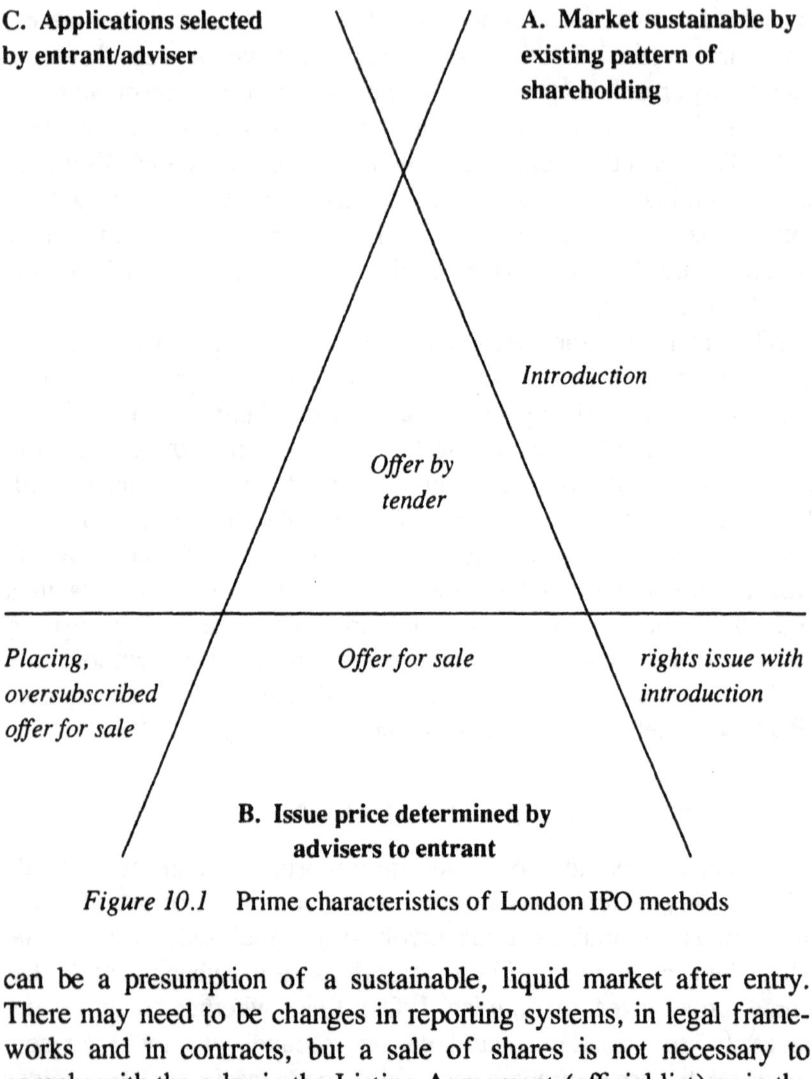

Figure 10.1 Prime characteristics of London IPO methods

can be a presumption of a sustainable, liquid market after entry. There may need to be changes in reporting systems, in legal frameworks and in contracts, but a sale of shares is not necessary to comply with the rules in the Listing Agreement (official list) or in the General Undertaking (USM). Entrants can minimise their costs of entry by being 'introduced' to the market, with a minimum of two market makers agreeing to trade in the equity from the outset. With average entry costs of £58,000 (in both USM and the official list, at 1980 prices, 1980–85) the introduction offers access to organised secondary markets at remarkably low prices (B&D: Chapter 5).[3]

However, there appears to be no restraint upon the ability of market makers to initiate pricing of equities introduced. The variability of prices within the first trading week, or across the first trading month, is no more than for entrants where shares were priced at entry, and in a competitive system of market makers there is perhaps room for argument over the importance of the 10 per cent (USM) and 25 per cent (OL) thresholds: if licensed market makers are prepared to quote unconditional two-way prices on an equity, is there any reason to inhibit the company from adopting the introduction method? For the official list, in particular, the requirement that 25 per cent of equity be 'widely held' is limiting.

One powerful reason, of course, has nothing to do with the technical capacities of the markets, but is connected rather with the company's motivation in seeking a quotation. Rarely do entrants report that their objective in joining an exchange is to maximise shareholder wealth, or even to minimise the cost of equity capital; they cite instead status, funds requirements, or the needs of particular shareholders (B&D: Chapter 2). In the USM, in particular, entry has frequently been associated with an expansion of the equity base (64 per cent of USM entrants raised some new money, 42 per cent of official list entrants) and an Introduction would not serve such a purpose. Equally, if entry is associated with a shareholder's desire to sell shares, an Introduction is inappropriate.

Advisory or market pricing?

In London, the three dominant modes of IPO are the placing, the offer for sale, and the offer by tender. Their common feature is that they seek to sell shares – often newly created shares – while effecting a resolution of uncertainty surrounding the value of those same shares. The means of achieving those objectives are radically different in nature and in effects, however. At this point the second axis differentiating methods comes into play: the extent of influence of the entrant's advisers in setting a price for the IPO. In the UK, IPO shares are sold either at a pre-determined placing or offer price, or the price is 'struck' after an inspection of applicants' orders for shares at various tender prices.

As the predominance of placings and fixed-price offers demonstrates, issuing houses and brokers persist in providing advice on fixed-price issuing, but the evidence is that their advice is of little merit. Advisers' prices are found to accentuate features which are not of interest to the wider market: over 1980–85 the observable influences on pricing of placings and offers for sale in London were 'past growth signals, yields, and variability – joining an emphasis on size, security of information, and specific risk ... we cannot find confirmation through the tenders sample that these are reasonable factors (in the sense that USM investors treat them as important)' (B&D: p. 103; see also Buckland and Yeomans 1977). In similar vein, Beatty and Ritter (1986) and Keasey and McGuinness (1992) find weak evidence for the value of auditor quality as a price signal, but none for the sponsor/broker.

When pricing is predominantly error-prone (and especially when advisers are hoping, even trying consciously to induce oversubscription in order to exert control over the shareholder list) then there will be a strong tendency to underprice. This is seen most clearly in London on the USM, with its high and very widely variable discounts. Not only is this disadvantageous for vendors in terms of their immediate wealth, but where advisers are over-optimistic the process may affect the survival of the business: there has been a marked tendency for those USM entrants which were overpriced (that is, resulting in undersubscription and negative discounts) to fail, be taken over, or lose their quotation: 'adverse experience with a public sale in the USM has very often been followed by an early withdrawal from the market' (B&D: p. 104).

In the offer by tender there is a shadow form of tâtonnement process. Advisers will determine a floor price, itself usually underwritten; but applicants can bid for shares at prices at or above this floor. The brokers can then construct a demand schedule from the bids, selecting a striking price at a point where bids at that price clear the shares made available.[4]

A tendering process will typically result in a sale price close to the eventual market price. Over 1980–85 the discounts on tendered issues averaged 10.90 per cent; over 1965–71 the average was only 4.62 per cent (B&D: p. 93). This is clearly advantageous for vendors at the time of entry (their wealth is enhanced by the lower discounts); and it is also clearly advantageous from the point of view of investors in unquoted equities which may become IPOs in the future: a higher and more certain exit price reduces the cost of capital for the unquoted firm with aspiration to eventual quotation.[5] The tendering process is also transparently equitable as between applicants. Any who are attracted by the equity's returns can bid; and those applicants with the highest evaluations can secure shares by raising their bid accordingly. The price received by the vendor is determined by an effective simulation of a market process rather than by some adviser's opinion of the market outcome.

Control over purchasers?

To set against these powerful advantages of some form of tendering process (and the London Stock Exchange's version of the tender is by no means the only possible one), there are offsetting disadvantages. From the point of view of the market, seeking depth and liquidity in the shares of IPOs, the tendering process may leave too high a proportion of the shares sold in 'firm' hands, with relatively few mobile shareholdings in the initial phases of quotation. If the prospectus gives all conceivable useful information, and applicants bid firm for the shares which they are allocated, there is little reason to anticipate willing sellers or buyers prior to release of substantive new information about the entrant.

Of more substantive interest to the entrant might be the third axis: the control over shareholder lists. This is intimately involved in the tender process. In being equitable between applicants, one is neutral as to their identity, even to their scale of interest in the equity. In the extreme, this can be a serious embarrassment, as the UK government found in its role as vendor of all the shares in Enterprise Oil: in setting the underwritten floor price to the tender relatively high, and with a deterioration in oil-sector share prices before application day, the terms of the issue removed any incentive for applicants to buy the independent business. As a consequence, one potential predator seized the opportunity to apply for a controlling interest in Enterprise at the underwritten price, confident that, in the absence of full subscription at that price, the government as vendor would be obliged to sell. In the event, this opportunistic take-over bid was thwarted by the vendor disallowing the raider's application. The shares, however, had then to be taken up by the underwriters (who were not pleased to be forced to assume that responsibility when a willing buyer existed). The list of Enterprise Oil's shareholders was both relatively short – with little of the desired individual holding – and unstable – with reluctant holders bent on minimising losses and rapid disposal, rather than on exploiting a privileged position in actions such as the reinvestment of earnings, or by participation in future rights issues.

That extreme example highlights the key disadvantage of the tender: even when the pricing and sale is a 'success', with all offered shares taken up by subscribers at a price close to the subsequent market valuation, the firm – or at least, its management – may seek more active control over the nature and scale of their shareholders. It is a nice question in the field of agency problems as to whether vendors (and particularly their agents, the management) have any proper concern with such positive choice of buyer, but it is apparent that IPOs are presently managed with such choice in mind. This is the case not only in the privatisation issues of the 1980s, but for issues in general.[6] In striking a balance, much will depend upon the issue's scale: how large does the IPO need to be to meet any objectives of stock exchange regulation, or of the company's capital requirements? How substantial is the resulting sale of shares in relation to the existing pattern of control? Are there legitimate reasons for pursuing actions which will result in inequities between applicants and impede a freely competitive issuing environment?

The costs of UK methods

Given that IPO management does pursue such objectives (and we return to the propriety of such action in the conclusions to this chapter), let us then consider how the London market sets out to achieve them, and with what results. Consider first the London Stock Exchange placing, where the firm's advisers are engaged to determine a price, at which brokers are paid to act as intermediaries in seeking buyers for the shares issued. A proportion of the shares will be made available to the Stock Exchange via other brokers, but the bulk of the shares will be 'placed' with clients of the issuing broker. Such clients will take their purchase decision according to the advice on this specific issue, to their past experiences as clients for placing, or after their own evaluation of prospectus and other information.

For the entrant/issuer and for the broker, the advantages of the placing are: first, the low costs involved in finding buyers, and second, the opportunity given to control the initial shareholder list following entry. From 1980–1985 the average cost of a USM placing was £90,910, and in the official list £175,620 (both 1980 prices: B&D: p. 56). Costs are minimised because public advertising is informational, rather than marketing-oriented; and investors receive a signal of the value of the offered equity directly from the broker rather than from other investors. Initial shareholders may be selected for purposes of promoting an active after-market – for example, placing some shares with known intending sellers, some with investors known to wish to purchase more – but it is equally possible to manipulate the shareholder list for the issuer's interests by fragmenting minority holdings, securing against future bidders, or in placing shares with investors who value the implicit option elements such as pre-emption rights in future equity issues.

The demerits of the placing are also pronounced. First and foremost, a placing excludes the 'public' from participation in an IPO: they must in general enter the market after issue (usually at greater dealing cost, and without any discounting incentive) in order to become shareholders. This restriction has led the London Stock Exchange to limit the size of IPOs made by placings. The restriction to £3 million until 1987 (when it was raised to £15 million by the Stock Exchange) effectively confined the placing to entrants under £12 million in capitalisation on the OL (selling the minimum 25 per cent), or £30 million on the USM (based upon the guideline minimum of 10 per cent). The relaxation of this restriction is one sign of the Exchange's willingness and desire to see more entrants using this method. Also it may begin to remove one of the placing's main defects, which is the relatively high cost presented to vendors. Although the administrative costs may be insubstantial in absolute terms, they still represent a substantial barrier for IPOs of small scale. The costs as a percentage of issue size are higher for the placing than for any other method, in both the USM and the OL (B&D: p. 58), and remain so as a percentage of equity capitalisation: over 1980–85 the average placing incurred a dead-weight administrative cost of 2.56 per cent of entrant capitalisation (2.49 per cent USM, 4.14 per cent when used in the OL), compared to 1.80 per cent for other methods of entry (B&D: p. 59).

Any increase in the scale allowed for placings will allow these percentage costs to fall sharply, since there are many fixed-cost elements in administrative expenses. However, when discounting costs are considered, the penalties of the placing become more marked. Over the period 1980–85, shares sold by the placing route were underpriced on average by 27.96 per cent on the USM, 27.10 per cent when including the OL, in comparison to 17.65 per cent (18.60 per cent) for other sale methods (B&D: p. 93). Such high average costs present the vendors – either as individuals, or in terms of the class of stake holder in the unquoted business – with a formidable disadvantage, transferring a substantial fraction of their wealth to the new shareholders at the time of market entry. It has been shown that the USM placing transferred some 3.29 per cent of a firm's capitalisation from existing to new shareholders over the 1980–85 period, compared to 1.5 per cent for USM tenders and 0.91 per cent for USM offers for sale (B&D: p. 142).

The common alternative to placing shares is to determine a fixed price of sale, to arrange to sell all the shares involved at that price by having it underwritten, and then to invite the public to apply for the shares on offer. This offer for sale has long been the dominant method for large-scale IPOs in the official list, and has also been used by several larger issues on the USM. For the entrant, one advantage lies in the provision of a signal, in the underwritten price, that the shares are at least that valuable. This reinforces any prospectus information and brokers' recommendations to applicants, and is absent from the placing. The offer for sale also eliminates any uncertainty about the size of receipts from the IPO, were that to be relevant for capital tax or inheritance planning, for example. The major disadvantage lies in the higher absolute cost of the offer for sale over the placing, and the continued discounting penalties of setting a sale price in advance of experience of the market price for the share. Over 1980–85, the average administrative cost of an offer for sale in London was over £500,000: £235,110 on the USM, £716,400 on the OL (B&D: p. 56; the OL figures contain outliers of high costs in privatisation issues, however). Costs are higher partly because the public offer element necessitates more rigorous advertising of the terms of sale, but also because the entrant purchases the underwriting insurance (and signal value), at a cost of some 0.5 per cent of issue capitalisation.

However, despite both fixed and variable elements of costs being higher, the tendency for IPOs by offer for sale to be larger and by larger entrants meant that from 1980 to 1985 the percentage costs of using the method were less than those for the placing, at 8.57 per cent of issue (2.27 per cent of capitalisation) in the USM, 7.71 per cent of issue (2.23 per cent of capitalisation) in the OL (B&D: pp. 58–9). As noted above, this 'advantage' has prompted the Exchange to raise the maximum size of placing, allowing its percentage costs to compete with those of the offer for sale.

Turning to the discounting procedure, the offer for sale has displayed lower discounts than the placing: an average of 15.68 per cent compared to 27.10 per cent in London markets between 1980 and 1985 (B&D: p. 93; this is also consistent with the evidence from 1965–71, when the figures were 13.80 per cent and 17.48 per cent respectively). As already noted in the context of placings, this gives the offer for sale an advantage in terms of the wealth which vendors transfer to new shareholders upon entry.

Given the open nature of the application process, it may at first seem surprising that this method has been classed as one offering control over shareholding. The route by which this is indirectly attained is by the inducement of oversubscription, after which different classes of applicant can be favoured in a graduated allocation process. Commonly, applications are graded by their size, sometimes by nature of the applicant (individual, employee, institution, for example), and available shares are rationed according to the shareholder profile desired by the company (or, more probably, by the company's management). Thus the issue is seen to have important sub-goals for the issuer: not only to enter a quoted market, not only to raise capital, but also to shape the shareholder profile, to reward and provide incentives for employees, to introduce share option arrangements for management. In the privatisation issues of the 1980s the process has become ever more sophisticated. Applicants have been allocated different forms according to their status, there have been complex and costly incentives to some classes of applicant (free or bonus shares, preferential allocation rights, discounts for customer shareholders: see Buckland (1987) for a discussion). The process has become institutionalised as a part of the entry process, with complex controls – even prosecution – for evasion of the allocation procedures, and extremely high rates of oversubscription (again, see Buckland 1987).

Derived from this is the fundamental issue as to whether companies should control their shareholder lists in any fashion other than by the workings of the market: the allocation of shares upon entry is perhaps the last chance offered to them to achieve this control. There is little or no hard evidence available on the effects of exerting such control: whether fragmentation of holdings benefits the operation of the market or not; whether it is effective in resisting hostile take-over; whether the influence of minority interests is changed by bias in allocation; whether any gains in such areas, or in publicity at the time of issue, offset the losses of vendors' wealth transferred to the fortunate applicants. Such evidence as does exist (primarily for the evolution of share registers in privatised businesses) suggests that the profile engendered by allocation biases decays rather quickly (see Buckland 1987); while the record on take-over behaviour is not promising. Privatised firms Britoil and Jaguar Cars have lost their independence; British Aerospace has acquired the privatised Royal Ordnance Factories and the Rover Group (later sold in a trade sale to BMW AG). British Airways, on the other hand, has exerted its power in the private sector by taking over several of its UK competitors (British Caledonian, Dan-Air); it has absorbed Brymon Airways and Birmingham European Airways into its operations, and further expanded through equity holdings in TAT of France, US Air in North America and Deutsche Air in Germany. In the absence of positive evidence, it is difficult to conclude other than that the attempt to control shareholding during entry is costly, transitory, and probably ineffectual.

ISSUING METHODS FOR THE 1990s

While London's entry methods may bear comparison with others (for example, the entry discounts on French IPOs are notoriously high (Dubois and Dumontier (1988)), they do present costs to vendors which would appear to be avoidable by appropriate innovation in issuing practice. The offer for tender stands always as a reminder that massive oversubscription of public issues is not necessary, and that vendors could expect to receive a sum close to the market value of their shares if they wish to exit during the firm's entry. The ease with which market makers adjust to pricing shares which are introduced to the market also suggests that liberalisation of access to this procedure would be in entrants' interests, particularly where they might judge that the temporary publicity upon entry was unnecessary.

A detached observer, however, might find something more fundamentally awry with London's practices. Issues priced by advisers are high-cost and advisers are seen to discount inappropriate features. One must conclude that the production of a fixed issue price is not the best solution to the problem of the resolution of price uncertainty at entry. Dimson (1979) and Rock (1986) have long established that it is an option element that necessitates any discount, but only the tender process has been designed to allow applicants any role in pricing that option. One more logical approach would be simply to determine the discount offered in advance, by inviting applications for shares at the eventual market price, less a percentage. The percentage – effectively the 'discount' – is then determined either by the adviser exerting their proper role in reaching a judgement upon the degree of difficulty involved in valuing the share, or the applicant is invited to determine it by tendering. Administratively this would present few problems. Applicants could bid for the shares required and deposit a cheque for a sum larger than the anticipated cost. Applicants' cheques could be cleared, with an offsetting transfer of the balance (amount deposited, less the sum determined by the market price net of discount allowed) to their accounts. Alternatively, and building upon the increasingly prevalent practice of part-payment for IPOs (a practice which currently effectively levers upwards any discount offered or allowed), the initial fixed payment deposited with the applicant could be followed by a variable closing payment determined by the actual market price, less discount allowed.[7] Vendors would be assured that, on selling their holdings at the IPO price, they would receive a full market value, net of discount determined by the judgement as to price uncertainty at the time. Applicants would be assured of a premium for facing the price uncertainty, but also assured that they were purchasing a share free of the returns distortions introduced by introductory discounting, just as with a tender issue.

Equally, the market could introduce a variant of the tender issue, whereby applicants made bids at varying discount percentages rather than at varying issue prices. Such a procedure with Enterprise Oil and Britoil would have freed those issues from their dependence upon the level of prices within an unstable oils sector and obviated the problems of undersubscription which they faced.[8] There is no reason, in either of these cases, why an entrant should not pay for the signal of an underwritten issue price, or why the procedure should not be adapted to the case of the placing. Indeed, if there are advantages to entrants in terms of the clientele effects available in the placing, one might expect to find that the discount allowed through this method would be lower than through alternative methods aimed at the investor at large.

The advantage of innovation of this nature in IPOs is that it relates the entry and pricing process to the problems involved, rather than confusing those problems with other complexities which are demonstrably beyond the capacity of advisers. Were the entrant to pursue secondary objectives such as share-register management (as with the privatisation programme, for example), the impact of that upon discounting would be transparent; in placings, equally, the merits of using a closed broker clientele compared with open public offer would be transparent in the advice as to the discount being offered.

The disadvantage, if it is one, would be that the entry process is stripped of some of its mystique, and certainly of some of its immediate excitement. Issues would no longer be the subject of short-term speculation, and applicants would be seeking long-term returns rather than the quick turn on an underpriced offering. The market makers' task would be unaffected or even ameliorated: since offer prices are at present not connected systematically with the market price, their pricing problem is unchanged; while the increased stability of subscription levels and the absence of stagging would reduce the present problems faced in management of the early, destabilised markets, there would be radically fewer instances of rapid disposal by stags, less incentive for 'flowback' in issues where application has been geographically segmented, fewer problems from overhangs of shares held by underwriters.

One further alleged disadvantage may be that issues made at conditional rather than firm prices would not be understood by investors. It is, however, the investors' uncertainty that drives the discounting process in IPOs, and investors are as capable of dealing with this information as they are with any other prospectus details; investment professionals and advisers, in particular, would be aided by concentration upon the merits of the entrant equity as an investment, rather than as a short-term speculation. In Table 10.2 the merits and demerits of the various methods – those existing and those proposed here – are summarised.

With this, unweighted, list of features the relative disadvantage of the conventional methods is graphically clear. The conventional placing delivers a balance of pluses and minuses on this scaling: any alternative scores more positively. A change away from adviser involvement in pricing makes substantial differences, but a switch to this chapter's version of 'conditional pricing', with advisers or bidders determining a discount from eventual market price, rather than establishing a price *per se*, is visibly advantageous: +5 for the tender or offer versions. Within the range of features, we would argue that the choice between methods will be strongly influenced

Table 10.2 Merits and demerits of issue methods for IPOs

		Fixed price			*Conditional pricing*		
	Introduction	*Placing*	*Offer for sale*	*Offer by tender*	*Offer by tender*[a]	*Placing*	*Offer for sale*
Equity between applicants	—	N	N	Y	Y	N	Y
Maximises receipts from any sale	—	N	N	Y	Y	N	Y
Price set by market forces	—	N	N	Y[b]	Y	Y	Y
Price underwritten by investors	—	N	Y	Y	Y[c]	N	Y[c]
Entrant can control who buys	—	Y	Y	N	N	Y	N
Entrant can offer incentives[d]	N	Y	Y	Y	Y	Y	Y
Some willing buyers frustrated	—	Y	Y	N	N	Y	N
New shareholders are long-term	Y	?	?	Y	Y	?	Y
Administrative costs are low	Y	Y	N	N	N	Y	N
Discounting costs are low	Y	N	?	Y	Y	?	Y
Involves a sale of shares	N	Y	Y	Y	Y	Y	Y
Balance of Y–N	1	0	1	5	5	3	5

[a] Tendered by varying bids for discount rather than price
[b] Or, by a tâtonnement process prior to competition by market makers
[c] Could still be if signal regarded as valuable
[d] Reward systems for employees, or to induce bias in application
? Depends upon adviser's success and pursuit of other goals

by their particular perspective upon the quotation problem. Advisers will rank highly features such as frustrated buyers, since they provide a pool of future demand for the stock in the market, where broking commissions are made; similarly, advisers will be less concerned to see new shareholders taking a long-term view of ownership, since it is the transfer of shares between owners that generates broking income.

From the vendor's point of view, maximisation of receipts is strongly favoured by change, but vendors who retain interest in the control of the firm's equity may find the loss of potential influence over buyers and, even, the influx of long-term shareholders a detrimental factor. For the wider community, equity in share allocation, the direct involvement of market forces in pricing from the outset, the absence of vendor/management control over future ownership, and, in the context of short-termism, the enhanced involvement of long-term equity investors, are all positive aspects of prospective change.

For management, in contrast, many of the plus points in this table are, directly, immaterial. Their interest in share prices may be direct, as vendors during the sale; however, they are as likely to be affected by option elements based upon future share prices, and be interested to minimise the apparent value of shares at quotation. Certainly one can say that the lower the equity's value is at quotation, the easier it will be to deliver large percentage increases in earnings per share thereafter. Management will also be concerned to influence the nature of future shareholders, with a view to impeding take-over, reducing the enforcement of principals' interests over their own. They will be unconcerned by the existence of frustrated potential buyers.

CONCLUSIONS: REFORM OF ISSUE METHODS FOR IPOs

It is not for academics to tell a stock exchange the details of what a workable system of IPO management should be, but it is our role to highlight the defects of present issue methods and to identify the issues and features that the issue method, as one service of a stock exchange, should address. Here it has been demonstrated that London's current range of methods does not serve vendors' – or even most potential applicants' – best interests. The methods persist in providing entrants with expensive advice which has been demonstrated to be of poor quality. The USM reinvigorated London's IPO market in the 1980s but it did so solely by liberalising the access hurdles (size, profitability, profits record), and by reducing the administrative costs of entry. However, the range of methods of issue remains as dated as it was in the 1960s. Changes that have been made – the increased size of the placing, the detailed management of applications – have not addressed the fundamental problem, which is that the methods used are inappropriate to offering unquoted firms an entry procedure during which those firms' shareholders can expect to realise the full value of their shares, or avoid transferring substantial parts of their wealth to new shareholders. During the 1980s, IPO management has destabilised entry procedures, with the encouragement of stagging, especially in privatisation issues. Through the placing process entrants have acquired quotation at a high cost in terms of wealth transfers, and there is no evidence to justify those costs.

The present range of methods, moreover, is increasingly oriented not so much as to enhance access to low-cost capital, but rather to fulfil two questionable corporate goals. The first is to convey as 'success' a situation where applicants have been sold a valuable asset relatively cheaply, accompanied by a clamour of unsatisfied applicants, preferably with media coverage of the queues of people delivering last-minute subscription forms, and followed by a substantial price premium in the aftermath to entry. The second objective has become one of vendors – or management – exploiting a last opportunity to exert control over shareholding, by allowing management or its agents to select new participating investors at the time of entry.

Neither objective is consistent with vendor shareholders' best financial interests, nor are they consistent with the principle of free and equitable access to secondary markets in equity. They raise difficult issues of how vendors control the impulses of management to build defences against shareholder influence during and after entry. The previous section of this chapter outlined the features of a reformed system of market entry. IPOs should be made by introduction where possible and appropriate. Where a simultaneous sale of shares is necessary, there will need to be a resolution of the uncertainty as to the price of those shares. Presenting applicants with a specific adviser-determined price is not a process which has been shown to succeed; neither can it be expected to succeed, when it is the discount not the price that affects applicants' reluctance to value the returns on offer. By designing issue methods to concentrate the attention upon this uncertainty, either through a tender process based upon discount percentage, or through a process of application at prices conditional upon market outcomes, IPOs could be conducted in a way that improved the position of vendors (and hence made investment in unquoted equity indirectly more valuable) and which produced more orderly after-markets, without the destabilising sales by stags or the purchases by frustrated applicants.

NOTES

1 For example, Ritter (1991), Grinblatt and Hwang (1989), Welch (1989), Keasey and McGuinness (1991), Levis (1992). See also Dubois and Dumontier (1988) on France, Finn and Higham (1988) on Australia, Nahmijas and Pera (1988) on Italy.

2 In contrast with the 'hot issue' year of 1987, when discounts in the London IPO market were abnormally high by historic standards (Keasey and McGuinness 1991).

3 However, only 34 of those entrants made their entry directly from unquoted status: the others already had established trading either in the over-the-counter sector or on the USM itself prior to official list entry (the average cost for these direct entrants was higher over 1980–85 – £78,000 in 1980 prices).

4 The striking price is typically pitched marginally below the clearing price, however. The underwriting process provides, first, an assurance to the vendor that the sale will be accomplished (even if only to temporary holders); and, second, a signal to applicants that the value of the equity is acceptable to the investment community.

5 The higher the exit price anticipated, the higher the present value at the time of the original investment; and the higher that present value, the lower the then required return. Equally, the lower the variability of the exit value, the lower the risk premium attached to the original required return.

6 Note the emphasis on employee ownership in the Alexandra Workwear IPO of 1985 and the emphasis on fragmented ownership of the Bairstow Eves Group in 1982.

7 Thus, an IPO would be offered at, say '1 million shares, for sale at market price less 5%; applicants to send £1 per share on application; issue underwritten at 90p per share'. If market makers determine prices averaging £1 per share over the first week of dealings, successful applicants receive a refund of 5p per share, unsuccessful applicants have their cheques cancelled, returned, or refunded.

8 Or the offer could invite tenders from investors, 'Based upon an underwritten price of 90p per share, tenders to state the applicant's required number of shares and the percentage discount in integer

amounts from −10% upward; applicants to pay £1 per share for each share applied for'. Thereupon the issue would be allocated at the level of discount which cleared the shares available, with the strike price determined according to that percentage and the subsequent market price of the shares.

11

SOCKS, BUBBLES AND CRASHES

A financial analysis of the Sock Shop

Anthony Steele

Sophie Mirman and Richard Ross were unsuccessful in selling 49 per cent of their start-up business for £40,000. They eventually raised a loan of £45,000 under the government's Loan Guarantee Scheme, and with £2,000 of their own they opened their first shop, a kiosk in Knightsbridge tube station. Four years later, on 29 April 1987, Capel-Cure Myers offered for sale 20 per cent of the ordinary shares in their business, The Sock Shop International plc, at 125 pence each. This would turn their original £2,000 into £2.5 million in cash, whilst still leaving them with 80 per cent of their company. The business was worth £27.5 million at the issue price.

The lists closed on 7 May and the issue was 53 times over-subscribed. The shares opened for trading on the unlisted securities market at 205 pence. In a hectic first day of trading one million shares changed hands, the price at one point touching 290 pence, ending at the close at 257 pence. The shareholders' wealth had doubled in one day. In 1988, still only 31 years of age and now the mother of two children, Sophie Mirman was voted Businesswomen of the Year. The Sock Shop must be one of the exceptional business stories of the 1980s. At its launch 'it was an identikit USM new issue' (*Investors Chronicle* 1987). The marketing formula was one used by a cluster of businesses founded in that decade: Body Shop, Knickerbox, Flash Trash, Shave Shop, Tooth Booth, Blouse House, Tie Rack, Shirt Rack (Urry 1990).

By February 1990, the shares were worthless. Administrators were appointed under the Insolvency Act as the company crashed owing £16 million in short-term debt. The bubble had burst.

Is it legitimate to identify Sock Shop as a bubble stock, one whose share price was inflated on an irrational mania of enthusiasm, beyond levels justified by any realistic analysis of its expectations? The overwhelming majority of empirical findings support the view that the major stock markets are mainly rational (Fama 1970; Merton 1987). The rational markets hypothesis implies that the market price of a security can be understood as the expectation of the present value of future cash flows available for distribution when the quality of information embedded in that expectation is high relative to the information available to the individual participants in the market. This is the dominant paradigm for explaining a range of stock-market phenomena such as the random fluctuation of prices, the inability of professional investors to generate superior performance (even before expenses charged to investors) in the funds they manage, the pricing of derivative instruments, and the market reaction to cosmetic accounting changes. Evidence that does not fit the rational market model is considered to be a puzzle or an anomaly. Anomalous evidence includes the 'PE effect', where low price-to-earnings stocks seem systematically to earn higher average returns than high price-to-earnings stocks (even after correcting for risk differences), 'the small stock effect', the 'January Effect', 'The Weekend Effect'. The argument in this chapter is that the Sock Shop was an instance of the 'bubble effect'.

The focus of the chapter is not on the company failure and the events leading up to February 1990; unhappy as those were, we instead examine the euphoric events of 7 May 1987. The drama of bringing Sock Shop to the USM is re-examined, together with the public-policy implications of the speculative enthusiasm which it generated. The characteristics of the USM which make it conducive to the formation of speculative bubbles are identified, as is the threat this poses to its economic role in the chain of corporate finance for embryonic and growing ventures.

This is a controversial undertaking since the theoretical literature has yet to agree on a definition of bubbles or indeed on whether they are possible. For economic historians, such as Kindleberger (1978, 1991), positive feedback, in which price increases both cause and are caused by speculators' expectations of price increases, exists as an historical phenomenon. Rational expectations theory (Flood and Garber 1980), on the other hand, holds that prices are formed within the limits of available information, and prices cannot diverge from fundamental values unless the information proves to be widely wrong. In this chapter we explore the expectations implicit in the pricing of the Sock Shop and consider whether they were rational.

This chapter is set out in six sections. The next section describes the dimensions of the Sock Shop's achievement as set out in its prospectus. The third section considers the limits to growth for the business. The fourth section lays out the model for valuing a growing business with a time-varying growth parameter. The fifth section presents the estimates for the model and the inference that the Sock Shop was astronomically overpriced on issue. The last section deals with the implications of this case for understanding the nature and role of the USM.

THE PROSPECTUS

By the time of the company's introduction to the USM, the husband and wife who founded Sock Shop had achieved remarkable success. In the four years since its first outlet was opened, the growth had been explosive. The average number of shops had risen each year as 2, 8, 22, 43. The turnover growth had been equally impressive, from £613,000 in the first seventeen months' trading to a forecast of £12.5 million for the year ending September 1987. This was entirely organic growth from a business they had created from a zero base. Profits after tax had leapt from £27,000 to £1,073,000 over the same interval. With a 100 per cent reinvestment rate, net assets also grew exponentially.

The financial performance is summarised in Table 11.1. For completeness the subsequent results are supplied, although the analysis which follows is based only on the achievements up to the prospectus. Academic analysis does not lend itself easily to marvelling at accomplishments, but it is evident even to a jaundiced eye that the financial results were almost unparalleled.

The formula that the founders hit upon was to take a hitherto unimaginatively retailed product, and to market it with both design and flair. Hosiery had a dull image. Clothing retailers might give a small area to a junior buyer or designer to cut their teeth on, but did not give the goods either a prominent location or promotion. Marks and Spencer was the leading retailer in a fragmented market, as Table 11.2 indicates. The fragmentation of distribution was matched by the lack of branding and differentiation in the product.

Table 11.1 Financial results of Sock Shop

	16/7/83 to 30/9/84 17 months £000	*Y/e 30/9/85 £000*	*Y/e 30/9/86 £000*	*6 months 31/3/87 £000*	*Prospectus 12 months 30/9/87 £000*	*Actual 12 months 30/9/87 £000*	*Actual 17 months 28/2/89 £000*
Turnover	613	2,080	6,171	7,358	12,500	13,984	44,373
Profit after interest and tax	27	140	478	807	1,073	1,155	2,416
Earnings per share (EPS)	0.14p	0.70p	2.39p	4.04p	5.17p	5.56p	7.75p
Net assets	26	166	644	1,451	—	3,443	5,510
Retail price index	90.1	95.4	98.3	100.6	102.4	102.4	111.8
Real terms EPS at 31/3/87	0.1563p	0.7367p	2.4459p	4.04p	5.17p		

Source: Prospectus 1984–87; FAME database 1988, 1989

Table 11.2 Estimated sales of socks by type of outlet

Outlet	*% by value*
Marks & Spencer	20
Other variety stores (Littlewoods, BHS)	7
Clothing multiples	22
Independent clothing outlets	8
Market stalls	16
Department stores	5
Mail order	2
Other outlets	20
Total	100

Source: Harvest database

Table 11.3 indicates that, by the time of Sock Shop International flotation, advertising levels on press and on TV were relatively low and decreasing.

Market estimates (Mintel: May 1985) estimate that the women's hosiery market averaged around 540 million pairs per year. Demand was basically static with only some 3 per cent variation in volume terms around that average over the previous seven years. Consumer surveys (Table 11.4) indicated how 92 per cent of respondents acquired socks in the previous years. Into this mature and stolid market, the Sock Shop formula was to take a dowdy necessity and

Table 11.3 Main media advertising on socks

Year	*£000's*
1980	123
1981	203
1982	184
1983	217
1984	60
1985	60
1986	116
1987	70
1988	31
1989	49

Source: MEAL database

Table 11.4 How hosiery was acquired in the last year

Bought self	47%
Received as gift	60%
Bought by another	53%
Acquired in any of these three ways	92%

Source: Mintel survey 1983

to be fashionable, to be a designer brand, to be prominent, to be expensive and to make hosiery a gift item. The outlets were also accessible, located in areas of high pedestrian traffic, such as tube and mainline stations, airport terminals and prime high-street sites.

The prospectus lists the location, selling area and lease details of 49 outlets. As Table 11.5 shows, the modal size was under 200 square feet of selling area. For example, the outlet at Terminal 1, Heathrow Airport, was 175 square feet, for which the rental was the greater of £90,000 or 20 per cent of sales. The concession had just a year remaining. The outlet at Waterloo Station was 30 square feet, for which the rental was the greater of £18,000 or 9 per cent of sales. The lease in this instance was a periodic tenancy with six months' notice.

As the business grew, the average length of lease extended, but the properties were essentially short-lease booths inside mass-transit terminals. Table 11.6 shows the increasing average length of lease; most of these were subject to more frequent rent reviews. The premiums paid to obtain leases, whilst not disclosed separately in

Table 11.5 Distribution of actual and proposed retail sites by net selling area

Area (square feet)	*Number of sites*
Under 100	4
100 – under 200	18
200 – under 300	13
300 – under 400	7
400 – under 500	0
500 – under 600	3
600 – under 700	3
Over 700	1

Source: Sock Shop prospectus

Table 11.6 Analysis of growth of outlets

Year	*No. of outlets opened*	*Average length of lease (months)*	*Marginal net assets per store*[a]	*Marginal sales/net assets*[b]
1983	1			
1984	4	7.3	6.5	23
1985	11	6.5	12.7	10
1986	20	12.85	23.9	8.5
1987	13	11.79	67.3	7.8

[a] Net asset increase/no of outlets
[b] To approximate the effect of each year's expansion, net asset turnover is calculated as the increase in sales divided by the increase in net assets
Source: Analysis of prospectus

the prospectus, were also believed to have risen. The increase in the net assets per store is consistent with such a belief. The sales generated per net asset investment, whilst falling, were many times the performance from mature retail businesses. Table 11.7 gives comparative figures.

Table 11.7 Comparative operating ratios for Sock Shop and leading retail multiples, 1984–87

	Marks & Spencer	*J. Sainsbury*	*Tesco*	*Sock Shop*
Sales : net assets ratio:				
1984	1.62	2.77	3.39	25.5
1985	1.74	2.55	3.44	12.5
1986	1.89	2.44	2.99	9.6
1987	1.97	2.38	2.86	8.6
Sales margin:				
1984	10.4%	4.7%	2.8%	4.4%
1985	10.3%	5.2%	2.9%	6.7%
1986	9.9%	5.5%	3.0%	7.8%
1987	10.1%	6.3%	4.1%	11.0%
Return on equity:				
1984	13.7%	18.8%	12.7%	103%
1985	13.8%	19.4%	13.4%	84%
1986	15.5%	19.5%	14.2%	74%
1987	17.5%	20.2%	17.2%	55%

Source: Prospectus and Micro Extat database

The *Investors Chronicle*, in its review of the issue prospectus, reported from its briefing that sales per square foot in one store were as much as £3,000 with an average of £1,500 which compares to £450 per square foot at Marks and Spencer and £155 at Debenhams: 'Last year [1986], some 1.5m people squeezed into the 360 square feet of Sock Shop beneath Piccadilly Circus buying about 250,000 pairs of socks, stockings and tights' (Waller 1987).

The marketing success of Mirman and Ross was acknowledged by the city. The view of Keith Wills, retail analyst of the brokers Scrimgeour Vickers, was reported: 'it's a unique formula which no one's imitated, and it seems to have limitless growth possibilities' (Isaac 1987).

COMPETITIVE ADVANTAGES

The first step in financial analysis is to understand the sources and defendability of competitive advantage enjoyed by a business. A recognised property of all markets is that profits are eroded by competition, and that sustainable profits are founded on imperfect competition. Ability to erect barriers to entry prolongs the opportunity to earn excess returns and ensure that any competitive advantage is not transitory.

Identifying the sources of product-market imperfection provides a qualitative perspective on the limits to organic growth of a business. Porter (1979, 1980) provides a well-used taxonomy for understanding the degree of competition in an industry. In the Porter scheme there are five major sources of competitive advantage:

1 Economies of scale:
   (a) advantages of optimal size,
   (b) high capital requirements;
2 Product differentiation:
   (a) via enormous advertising expenditure,
   (b) via quality and service;
3 Cost advantages:
   (a) learning or experience curve,
   (b) ownership of technology – patents etc.,
   (c) monopoly control of raw materials;
4 Access to distribution channels:
   (a) organisational advantages,
   (b) geographical location;

5 Government policy:
   (a) protection,
   (b) incentives.

There are five factors which tend over time to erode competitive advantage:

1 bargaining power of buyers,
2 bargaining power of suppliers,
3 threat of new entrants,
4 threat of substitute products,
5 rivalry among existing firms.

The Sock Shop formula had some unique elements. However, it was never a manufacturer (unlike, say, the Body Shop); this might have given it some added defendable advantages such as the ability to franchise. Retailing is a fiercely competitive industry, and innovative style and design provide transitory advantages since 'there is no copyright on bright ideas when they are laid out on the high street' (Urry 1990). Fashion is also a fickle factor on which to found a fortune. Much as one is impressed by marketing innovation, it is not a sustainable source of growth and profit, unless it is protected. The major source of protection against competition in retailing is geographical location. The choice of location was the key element in the Sock Shop formula which gave confidence about the future. If Sock Shop occupied the nodal points of pedestrian traffic, imitators were precluded from entering their market.

The advantages that Sock Shop enjoyed with its property portfolio indicate that its growth possibilities were limited. There are only a finite number of locations in London, and even fewer outside, with the right characteristics.

The analysis in Tables 11.6 and 11.7, although indicating the high sales volumes and growth of sales, also hints that each successive generation of expansion is less attractive than the preceding. For a business to generate an average 55 per cent return on equity is impressive; however, if it was earning an average 74 per cent return a year earlier, then for the average to drop the marginal return on the expansion must be much less than 55 per cent. The information in the prospectus shows that the sites into which the Sock Shop was expanding, whilst still very good, were no longer prime locations. Even without this corroboration, considerations of competitive advantage help form expectations that the rate of growth was decaying.

The properties which Sock Shop needed were not available on freehold, being mainly within transport termini. The short duration of the tenancy agreements has two other implications for understanding how its competitive position might come to be eroded. The first was a constraint on its financial structure. Agency arguments suggest that the maturity of debt should seldom exceed the life of assets (see Timan and Wessels 1988), thus Sock Shop was unlikely to have access to long-term borrowing to finance its programme of expansion. The second implication was that, whilst location protects the Sock Shop from direct competition, it also exposes the enterprise indirectly to competition in the short-term property market.

The race to occupy prime sites might increase rents, and lead to premiums being paid to obtain leases. In the leasehold property market the rent is fixed for a period of time, but the owners of the freehold can require a premium payment when the contract is signed. The size of this premium increases with the commercial attractiveness of the property and the length of time before annual rent is next reviewed. In the Sock Shop accounts the premium is accounted for as a fixed asset and depreciated over the remaining life of the lease contract. This has the effect of smoothing the incidence of expense in the profit-and-loss account differently from the incidence of cash expenditure in the cash-flow statement. The success of a niche retailer like Sock Shop perversely has the effect of demonstrating the commercial attractiveness of the locations they want, which raises their cost. In Table 11.8, a cash-flow analysis of Sock Shop is presented, based on the technique described by Lee (1983); this lends support to these deductions.

The cash-flow picture is consistent with these speculations on the nature of the competition for short-duration tenancy agreements. The premiums being paid to acquire leases are accounted for as part of the purchase of fixed assets. The cash from operations is not sufficient in every year to cover these capital purchases. The uncovered cost of the expansion programme is being financed by overdraft and short-term borrowing.

A more prudent financing policy might have raised more equity in order to finance the high growth rate, given that long-term borrowing was not available to the company. However, the exposure of the company to competition for location, the rising costs of location, the limited number of sites with the correct attributes, the effects of seasonal sales patterns and changes in

Table 11.8 Cash-flow analysis of Sock Shop

	5 months ending 30/9/84	*Y/e 30/9/85*	*Y/e 30/9/86*	*6 months ending 31/3/87*	*Y/e 30/9/87*	*17 months ending 28/2/89*
Funds from operations	56	279	964	1,423	2,197	4,799
Changes in working capital	12	51	110	334	1,115	1,246
Cash from operations	44	228	854	1,089	1,082	3,553
Other sources						
New equity	2				1,825	
Sales of fixed assets						872
Total cash sources	46	228	854	1,089	2,907	4,425
Cash uses						
Purchase of fixed assets	87	240	1,135	1,360	3,731	12,427
Purchase of goodwill						794
Payment of taxation			8	53	318	681
Payment of dividends						616
Cash (outflow)	(41)	(12)	(289)	(324)	(1,142)	(10,093)
Overdraft and short-term borrowing:						
Opening balance	—	(41)	(53)	(342)	(666)	(1,808)
Closing balance	(41)	(53)	(342)	(666)	(1,808)	(11,901)

Sources: Prospectus 1984–87; FAME 1988, 1989

women's fashion, of exposure to short-term interest rates, and the reaction of rivals lead to a tempering of judgement about the limitless growth possibilities of the Sock Shop.

RATIONAL VALUATION

A series of papers, Garman and Ohlson (1980), Ohlson (1983, 1988, 1989a, 1989b, 1989c), have derived a theoretical model which characterises the relationship between value-relevant or fundamental information variables and rational market prices. This allows us to investigate the expectations implicit in the valuation of the Sock Shop. Linear Markovian information dynamics are used to model dividend expectations in terms of earnings expectations. Steele (1990) gives empirical evidence for the model. Using data from 1920 to 1983, 80 per cent of the long-run behaviour of shares can be explained from the time-series properties of earnings.

In general terms, consider a firm in an uncertain multiple-period economy. The information variables that describe the firm within a financial markets context are represented by an $(n \times 1)$ real-valued vector, Z_t at the current date. The stochastic evolution of Z_t, Z_{t+1}, ... is assumed to be governed by a Markovian linear 'lagged regression' system:

$$Z_{t+1} = (\Omega_t + \Gamma_{t+1})Z_t$$

where Ω_t is an $(n \times n)$ matrix of parameters, which may be time-varying, and Γ_{t+1} is an $(n \times n)$ matrix of zero-mean random disturbances of the system parameters.

A property of this characterisation is that predictions of future expected values of the information variables are a linear function of the current information set Z_t, since

$$E(Z_{t+\tau}/Z_t) = \Omega^{\tau} Z_t$$

for a constant parameter model or

$$E(Z_{t+\tau}/Z_t) = \{\Omega_{\tau}, \Omega_{\tau-1}, \Omega_{\tau-2}, \ldots, \Omega_{t+1}, \Omega_t\}Z_t$$

for time-varying parameters.

This system is referred to as linear information dynamics. Representing information as a dynamic simultaneous equation model permits considerable generality of formulation, embracing higher-order autoregressive processes if necessary. Garman and Ohlson (1980) prove that the market price of a share can be represented as a linear function of current information, that is:

$$P(Z_t) = B'Z_t$$

where $P(Z_t)$ is the share price now and B is an $(n \times 1)$ vector of valuation coefficients or multipliers.

The essence of the proof is that the market price of a share is the sum of discounted dividend expectations, i.e.

$$P(Z_t) = \Sigma w_\tau E(d_{t+\tau}/Z_t)$$

where w_τ is a discount weight.

Also, the information dynamics gives $E(d_{t+\tau}/Z_\tau) = e_d \Omega^\tau Z_t$ where $e_d = (0, 0, 1, 0, \dots)$ is a vector that extracts the dividend from the information set Z_t. It follows that the market price of a share is a linear function of current information:

$$P(Z_t) = e_d[w_1 \Omega + w_2 \Omega^2 + \dots]Z_t.$$

In applying this framework to the Sock Shop, in order to derive a rational valuation of the company, the information set Z_t is constrained to be a three-vector (x_t, y_t, d_t), where

x_t = earnings,
y_t = net asset value,
d_t = dividends.

The prospectus reveals very little about dividend policy, so let us assume that dividends may be predicted as a fixed-payout percentage of forecast earnings:

$$d_{t+1} = bx_{t+1}.$$

Earnings expectations consistent with our discussion of competitive advantage are predicted by an exponential growth model, but with a time-decaying growth rate,

$$x_{t+1} = (1 + g_t)x_t,$$

where $g_t = g_a - (g_a - g_n)t/2H$ for $t < 2H$

$$g_t = g_n \text{ for } t \geqslant 2H.$$

This growth-rate pattern has earnings growing exponentially, but at a decreasing rate. Initially at $t = 0$, the growth rate in earnings, $g_t = g_a$ is abnormally high at some rate g_a. As time evolves, the growth rate falls linearly until some time $2H$, when it reaches g_n, the normal or long-run growth rate, at which level the now mature business sustains its performance. The earnings growth-rate pattern is shown in Figure 11.1.

In order to apply this expectations model, it will be necessary to estimate g_a the initial abnormal growth rate for the Sock Shop. The terminal long-run growth rate g_n is taken as the real rate of growth of GDP, since in the limit the organic growth of mature retailing businesses will not out-perform the general economy. (Expectation about the time, $2H$, for Sock Shop growth rates to mature down to this limit will form the basis for the contention that the valuation on the USM was irrational.) This is one of the simplest models with a time-varying parameter on earnings growth. However, a property of this formulation is that dividend policy is exogenous. Future growth paths are unaffected by changes to dividend payout.

In Appendix I linear information dynamics are described in which changing the payout ratio does not alter future earnings. The conclusions of the chapter are unaltered by this elaboration since we show for this class of models that the persistence of abnormal growth rates will always exceed that implied by the equivalent simpler model. With an endogenous dividend policy, supernormal growth expectations implicit in the Sock Shop share price need to be even more unrealistic than the estimates to be presented in the next section. Expectations about net asset book values will be formed from the accounting identity:

$$y_{t+1} = x_{t+1} + y_t - d_{t+1}.$$

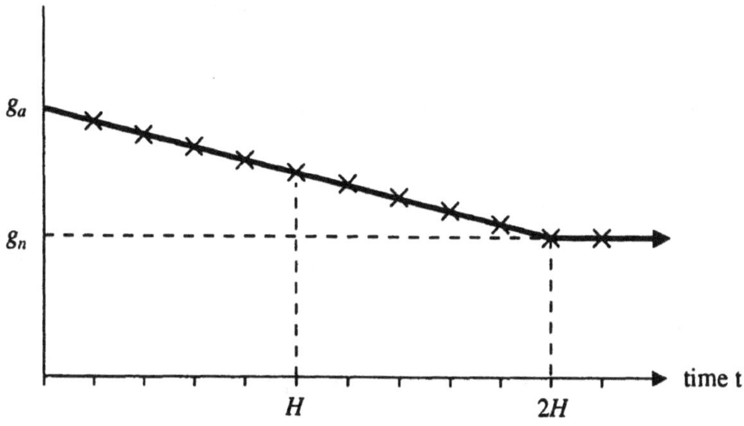

Growth-rate pattern for the *H* model

Figure 11.1 Growth-rate decay

The linear information dynamics can be written as:

$$\begin{bmatrix} x_{t+1} \\ y_{t+1} \\ d_{t+1} \end{bmatrix} = \begin{bmatrix} (1+g_t) & 0 & 0 \\ (1+g_t) & 1 & -b(1+g_t) \\ b(1+g_t) & 0 & 0 \end{bmatrix} \begin{bmatrix} x_t \\ y_t \\ d_t \end{bmatrix}.$$

From this it is evident that dividend expectations are forecast from current earnings as follows:

$$E(d_{t+\tau}/Z_t) = b\prod_{i=t}^{t+\tau}(1+g_i)x_t$$

Fuller and Hsia (1984) show that the sum of the present value of these changing dividend growth-rate expectations reduces to a simple form:

$$P(Z_t) = \left[\frac{b(1+g_n)}{k-g_n} + \frac{bH(g_a-g_n)}{k-g_n}\right]x_t,$$

where k is the discount rate.

The model is linear in the current information set Z_t, but with zero parameters on y_t and d_t. There are two elements to the parameter on x_t. The first takes the form of a Gordon growth model and can be interpreted as the component of value explained by the normal growth rate. The second element is the premium due to abnormal growth rates. The simplicity of the result derives from the average growth rate in the interval $(0, 2H)$ being $(g_a - g_n)/2$, because of the assumption about a linear decay in growth rates.

Rearrangement of this valuation equation in terms of H gives:

$$H = \frac{P(Z_t)}{x_t}\frac{(k-g_n)}{b(g_a-g_n)} - \frac{(1+g_n)}{(g_a-g_n)}.$$

It is this form, which we discuss below, that allows us to investigate the growth rates implicit in the valuation of the Sock Shop.

PARAMETER ESTIMATES

A simple but robust valuation model has been derived consistent with reasonable assumptions about the stochastic evolution of earnings, asset values and dividends. It requires a small set of empirical estimates in order to value a company. Rescaling by the number of shares on issue converts the model to a per-share basis, relating market price per share to earnings per share. The share-price behaviour on the USM subsequent to listing is shown in Figure 11.2. Its first-day performance was surpassed within 12 months. However, we take $P(Z_t) = 257$p, the closing price on the first day of trading, 7 May 1987. We shall establish that this was a 'bubble' value by making explicit the growth rates implicit in the price.

The EPS, x_t, is 5.17 pence, which was the prospectus forecast for the full year ending 30 September 1988. The discount rate k is given by the capital-asset pricing model,

$$k = \text{risk-free rate} + \text{beta} \times \text{market-risk premium}.$$

The risk-free rate in real terms is taken as 3 per cent, which was the return being offered by medium-term index-linked gilts. The beta risk measurement service gave industry betas as follows:

Deparmental Stores	0.84
Furnishing Stores	1.07
Stores Mail Order	1.04
Stores Multiple	1.00

Source: London Business School Risk Measurement Service (April 1987)

Sock Shop is a retailer, and so a long-run beta might be 1.00. There could be grounds to raise the beta, to adjust for its USM status, since the beta estimates are based on the main market. A value of unity would be conservative in the long run, which is not unrealistic given Blume's (1975) evidence that betas regress over time to the mean of unity.

The market-risk premium is difficult to estimate, since historically it is highly volatile as the analysis in Table 11.9 shows. Conventional practice in financial analysis is to take the forecast premium as the historical average (see, for example, Water Services Association 1992). For the UK this is 9.8 per cent. The discount rate for the valuation model is: $k = 3\% + 1 \times 9.8\% = 12.8\%$, say 12% to err on the side of overvaluation.

As was indicated, the long-run normal growth rate g is taken as the sustainable growth in GDP. The UK economy has had a variable performance:

Average growth per annum in real GDP

1968–73	3.2%
1973–79	1.4%
1979–86	1.4%

Source: OECD 1985, 1987

Taking g_n as 3 per cent would be a conservative growth rate, in the context of the valuation equation, but it could be justified if there were overseas markets in which the Sock Shop retailing formula might work.[1]

An estimate of the abnormal growth-rate parameter g_a consistent with the evidence is more difficult. There are only four years of EPS data (including one forecast). The EPS figures adjusted to real terms are given in Table 11.1. The postulated earnings predictor equation with a time-varying growth rate g_t is:

$$x_{t+1} = (1 + g_t)x_t.$$

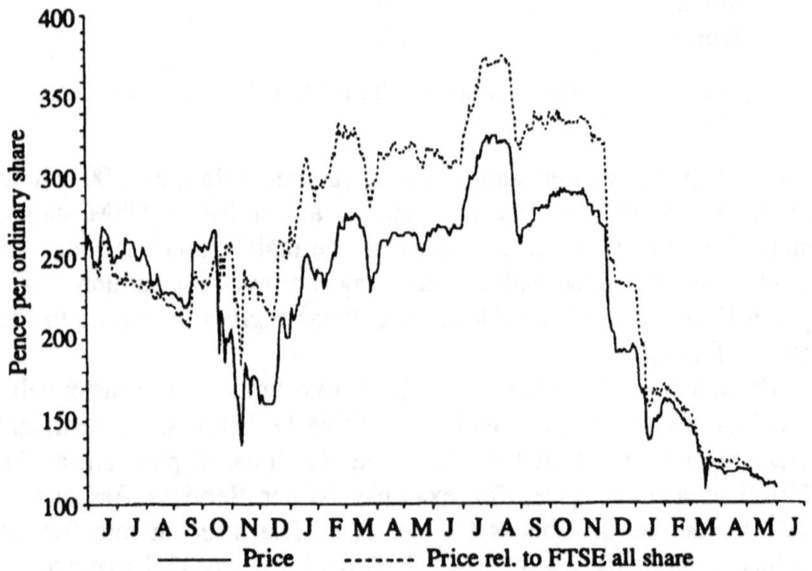

Figure 11.2 Share price and price relative for Sock Shop International plc, June 1987 to June 1989
Source: Datastream

The data for the model does reveal that the growth rate is time-varying:

Year	t	x_{t+1}	
1985	1	$0.7367 = (1 + g_1)0.1563$	hence $g_1 = 3.7134$
1986	2	$2.4459 = (1 + g_2)0.7367$	hence $g_2 = 2.3201$
1987	3	$5.17 = (1 + g_3)2.4459$	hence $g_3 = 1.1137$
1988	4	$? = (1 + g_4)5.17$	hence $g_4 = ?$

Table 11.9 Risk premium analysis

Year	*Equities (gross %)*	*Gilts (gross %)*	*Risk premium (%)*	*Risk premium (decimalised)*
1958	45.5	15.2	30.3	1.303
1959	54.8	0.9	53.9	1.539
1960	−0.1	−8.7	8.6	1.086
1961	−2.0	−11.4	9.4	1.094
1962	−1.9	21.9	−23.8	0.762
1963	17.3	1.8	15.5	1.155
1964	−10.2	−6.7	−3.5	0.965
1965	7.5	−0.2	7.7	1.077
1966	−8.8	0.5	−9.3	0.907
1967	34.7	0.1	34.6	1.346
1968	33.8	−7.8	41.6	1.416
1969	−15.7	−4.3	−11.4	0.886
1970	−9.0	−4.0	−6.0	0.950
1971	33.3	16.9	16.4	1.164
1972	13.1	−10.7	23.8	1.238
1973	−38.6	−17.6	−21.0	0.790
1974	−57.5	−28.8	−28.7	0.713
1975	99.8	9.5	90.3	1.903
1976	−14.0	−1.1	−12.9	0.871
1977	40.2	29.1	11.1	1.111
1978	3.4	−9.4	12.8	1.128
1979	−6.5	−11.2	4.7	1.047
1980	16.5	5.0	11.5	1.115
1981	0.2	−9.2	9.4	1.094
1982	22.2	43.6	−21.4	0.786
1983	22.0	10.0	12.0	1.120
1984	24.1	2.1	22.0	1.220
1985	15.0	5.0	10.0	1.110
1986	21.9	2.0	19.9	1.199
1987	4.5	12.1	−7.6	0.924
1988	5.6	2.3	3.3	1.033
			Geometric mean	7.43
			Arithmetic mean	9.81

Notes: All returns are adjusted for inflation. Figures assume gross dividends and interest are reinvested.
Source: BZW Equity – Gilt Study 1969.

The growth rate in EPS is decaying very quickly. The problem this presents for estimating g_a to start the model is to estimate g_4, the growth rate in 1988. The solution adopted is displayed in Figure 11.3. The prediction of g_4 is based on an exponential decay, $g_t = g_0 \exp(-gt)$ for constants g_0 and g. An ordinary least squares estimate[2] gives $g_0 = 7.0847$ and $g = 0.6021$. The prediction of g_4, and hence g_a, is $g_a = 7.0847 \exp(-0.6021 \times 4) = 0.6373$. The abnormal growth-rate parameter used in the model is 63.73 per cent. This will lead to an overestimate of value. The reason is evident from Figure 11.3. The parameters are being developed for the model in the previous section which postulates a linear decay in growth rates. The estimate of g_a is based on exponentially decaying time-varying growth rates, which will always be lower. The direction of the bias strengthens the case, since the growth expectations are still shown to be unrealistic, despite leading to an overestimate of value.

The payout ratio b is taken as 50 per cent, which is the rate Marks and Spencer pay.

Summarising the discussion so far, the valuation equation derived in this section is

$$P(Z_t) = x_t\left[\frac{b(1+g_n)}{k-g_n} + \frac{bH(g_a - g_n)}{k-g_n}\right]$$

and

$$P(Z_t) = 257\text{p},$$
$$x_t = 5.17\text{p},$$
$$k = 12\%,$$
$$g_n = 3\%,$$
$$g_a = 63.73\%,$$
$$b = 0.5.$$

Thus,

$$257 = 5.17\left[\frac{(0.5 \times 1.03)}{(0.12 - 0.03)} + 0.5H\,\frac{(0.6373 - 0.03)}{(0.12 - 0.03)}\right].$$

The value of H to be consistent with a share price of 257 pence is 13. This means that implicit in this share price is an expectation that the abnormal growth rates of Sock Shop would persist for 26 years. When Capel-Cure Myers advised Mirman and Ross on an issue

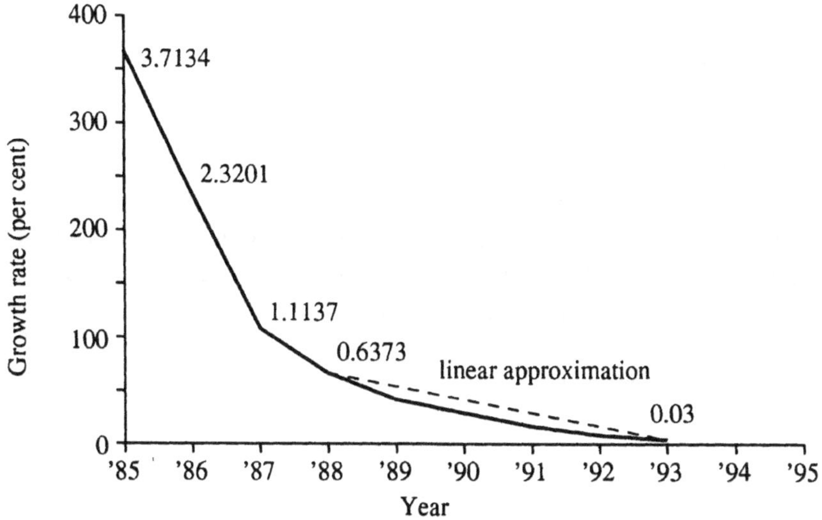

Figure 11.3 Exponential decay in growth rate, with linear approximation (leading to an overestimate of *g* within the period of estimation)

price, the value selected was 125p. The duration of supernormal growth rates implicit in this price was 11 years.

Having deduced estimates of the duration of supernormal growth implicit in the share price, the linear information dynamics equations allow us to simulate the growth pattern of the business.

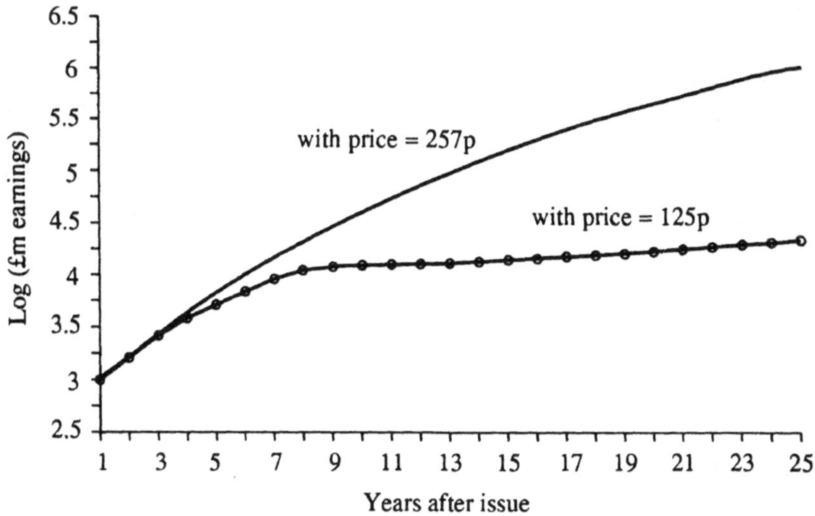

Figure 11.4 Earnings forecast as implicit in share price (using prices of (i) 125p and (ii) 257p)

The model was simulated without stochastic terms to find the mean growth path. The log of the earnings stream is plotted in Figure 11.4 for the two $2H$ values consistent with 257 pence and 125 pence. For the former price, Sock Shop's expected earnings and dividends at the end of the transitional growth phase of 26 years are £1,360 million and £678 million respectively in real terms.

If one believed that 257 pence was a reasonable price, and that Sock Shop's growth rate would decay in a linear fashion, then in 1987 prices consistent with those beliefs, in 26 years Sock Shop would dominate UK retailing. For comparison, the 1987 profits of the major retailers were:

	£m
Marks and Spencer	276
GUS	233
Sainsburys	158
Asda	129
Tesco	119
Debenhams	41
Lewis	39
	995

Another way of expressing the mania of these expectations is that earnings of £1,360 million would correspond to annual women's hosiery sales of 2,800 million pairs. This is five times larger than the total UK market.[3]

At the more sober issue price of 125p, the projections consistent with this would be £29.5 million earnings and £14.7 million dividends. It would be a notable achievement for a specialist retailer to join the ranks of the major chains in 26 years, but it is within the bounds of plausible expectations. For Sock Shop to dominate the UK economy is outside of those bounds.[4]

A massive premium on the first day of trading cannot easily be accommodated within the framework of a set of plausible expectations about growth. The alternative explanation is that the predictions of David Waller, writing in the *Investors Chronicle* on 17 April 1987, came true: 'So expect a stampede of stags when Sock Shop makes its debut, irrespective of pricing details and the company's growth prospects ...'.

IMPLICATIONS

The contention of the preceding analysis was that there was an over-reaction on the USM at the launch of the Sock Shop. Literature on excess volatility and over-reaction is steadily accumulating.

Lonie et al. (1989) provide UK evidence that the market usually overestimates future growth potential of past excellent companies, and draws precisely the opposite conclusion about non-excellent companies, tending to make pessimistic predictions. From the list of the top 200 UK companies in *Management Today* for June 1982 they formed a 'winner' portfolio of the top 30 companies. The bottom 30 companies were combined to form a 'loser' portfolio. There was a remarkable reversal in fortunes: investing in the loser portfolio for 1982 to 1987 would have given a return 1.5 times greater than for the winner portfolio.

Clayman (1987), investigating the companies originally selected by Peters and Waterman to demonstrate the excellence of outstanding performers in *In Search of Excellence: Lessons from America's Best Run Corporations*, found that they subsequently generated unimpressive returns, compared to a portfolio of non-excellent companies.

Fruhan (1979) and Malkiel (1963) present cross-sectional evidence that a number of high-return-on-equity firms faced quite impressive, and essentially unachievable, investor growth expectations.

Using aggregate market data Shiller (1981a, 1981b, 1984), LeRoy and Porter (1981), and Grossman and Shiller (1981) present evidence that the historical record of large variations in stock prices is inconsistent with the rational valuation of expected dividends.

Lehmann (1990), Zarowin (1990) and Pettengill and Jordon (1990) are three recent papers which use the CRSP (Centre for Research in Security Prices) returns data to investigate the question of whether investors over-react to new information. Over-reaction to good news would lead to abnormally high returns ('winners') as share prices are bid up, followed by abnormally low returns as share prices return to their normal levels. The opposite would happen to any over-reaction to bad news.

Based on their evidence, investment strategies which are constructed contrary to rational ranking or selection, investing in recent 'losers' and shorting recent 'winners', appear to show profits even after correction for bid–ask spreads, transactions costs, risk, seasonality and size. To quote Robert Heller, in his recent article in *Finance*, a news sheet for members of the investment analyst community in the UK: 'The conclusion is unavoidable, familiar, but still somewhat alarming: that the City over-values good performance, and then over-reacts to its own disappointment.'

Whilst the Sock Shop International case study is only a single anecdote, the plural of anecdote is data. A case example has the rhetorical power of a case in point (McCloskey 1986) and leads naturally to questions about the micro-market structure of the USM. Are there features of this junior market which make it prone to irrational pricing? What are the consequences of irrational prices? Are there alternative institutional arrangements which might better serve economic interests?

The first observation to make about the institutional arrangements of the flotation concerns the expenses of the issue. The expenses appear large in proportion to the cash being raised, representing 16 per cent of the net proceeds, or 2½ per cent of the market value of the company (see also Buckland and Davis 1989). The distribution of the proceeds was as follows:

To Mirman and Ross	1,925,000 @ 125p		2,406,250
To Company	2,000,000 @ 125p	2,500,000	
less expenses		(680,000)	
			1,820,000
Net proceeds of issue			4,226,250

These expenses cover the investigations and accountant's report associated with an initial public offering. They also include the pre-launch publicity and the underwriters' commission. The process of underwriting appears, at first sight, an arcane practice. At a more prosaic level it is entirely analogous to a manufacturer requiring wholesalers to go long in physical inventory in return for a discount on the retail price. The wholesalers guarantee the manufacturer the proceeds of the issue, net of their underwriting discount. The £680,000 is the price that Sock Shop paid to have access to the retail distribution channels for its shares. For orders of magnitude, this sum should be contrasted with the entire industry's main media-advertising spend given in Table 11.3.

The marketing of the company's shares was into a very thin market, where a few transactions could have a disproportionate effect on prices. The thinness of the market means that there is not the share turnover and potential brokerage income to interest independent brokers and analysts. The small size of the companies, and the low level of liquidity in the market, also mean limited interest from institutional analysts. Mispricing is more likely with under-researched investments, supported by pre-launch marketing.

The USM prospectuses need only to provide a limited number of years' trading record. The shorter the historical record, the more volatile and subject to 'animal spirits' is the basis on which expectations are founded. The Sock Shop prospectus gave no indication of a statistic as fundamental to any rational valuation exercise as the future dividend policy. The limited information, the lack of incentive for independent professional analysis, the thinness of the market, the pre-launch marketing are all contributory factors that made Sock Shop such a 'success' on the day, and the USM a 'failure'.

Such successes are not without cost. A serious consequence of a bubble stock is that it destroys confidence in a market. For the venture-capital industry, the junior market provides one route for eventually realising the capital gain on their investments.

In the last 30 years, venture funds acting as specialised financial intermediaries have emerged with an investment strategy unlike that described by classic Markowitz portfolio theory, concerned as it is with a relatively passive approach to managing indirect secondary investments in readily realisable securities. The goal is to achieve capital gains, as opposed to a running yield. Approximately 90 per cent of the net present value of a typical venture-finance deal is achieved as a capital gain on exit. Whilst the enterprise in which the fund makes a direct investment may have an indefinite life, the strategy is to grow the enterprise to a target size in a finite time. An active junior market is a useful ingredient to the operation of a venture-fund strategy. The junior market may not, as in the Sock Shop case, provide a significant direct source of capital to the growing business, but as a more convenient exit route it has an inventive value in promoting the financing of new enterprises.

Speculative bubbles followed by reality break this chain. The capital losses through the banking multipliers can damage the system of financial credit more widely. Consumption patterns and savings ratios alter as the market gives inflated wealth signals. When the mania subsides, risk capital is lost, and so are opportunities for subsequent serious and worthy ventures.

Over-reaction to a small number of transactions is a feature of thin markets, and the provision of an orderly junior market may involve more than the mere relaxation of official list requirements. The issue for the junior market is one shared by markets in antiques, fine art and real estate among others, and is to address the question: 'How should a thin market be organised?' Unless this issue is resolved, the public-policy aims of the junior market to enhance the supply of venture capital to fast-growing enterprises will be impeded by excess volatility, by bubbles and by crashes.

NOTES

1 In 1987, Sock Shop International opened its first US shop in central Manhattan, which grew to 17 outlets in Manhattan, New Jersey and Philadelphia by 1989. By the end of February 1989 the US outlets had lost £677,000. As Sophie Mirman reflected in *Management Week*, 27 November 1991, 'A major problem that we had was with drug related violence ... we had young kids coming into our shops and threatening sales staff, which meant that we had to have armed security guards in tiny little shops ...'. The New York underground did not prove a suitable overseas location in which to replicate the Sock Shop retailing formula.

2 With only three data points, ordinary least squares is as good a heuristic device for estimating the parameters as any. No goodness-of-fit statistics are reported because of the low degrees of freedom.

3 The UK market is 540 million pairs annually. The average margin on sales is 11 per cent, and the average price per pair £4.32, giving a net profit of 47p per pair.

4 This conclusion is robust, as sensitivity analysis of the parameter estimates indicates. Rearrangement of the valuation equation derived in this section gives the following.

Since the conclusion hinges on the view that the growth expectations implicit in the closing share price were implausible, we are concerned with minimum values of H:

$$H = \frac{P(Z_t)}{x_t} \frac{(k - g_n)}{b(g_a - g_n)} - \frac{(1 + g_n)}{(g_a - g_n)}.$$

Maximum and minimum values of parameter estimates are: beta (min 0.9, max 1.1); risk-free rate (min 2.5%, max 3.5%); market risk premium (min 8%, max 10%); hence k (min 9.7%, max 15.5%). For abnormal growth a 50% variation gives g_a (min 32%, max 95%). For normal growth g_n (min 0%, max 3%). Since the payout ratio and the abnormal growth rates interact (see Appendix I for further discussion), we consider a 50% variation in $b(g_a - g_n)$, (min 15%, max 45%).

The minimum value of H corresponds to minimum values of k, maximum values of $b(g_a - g_n)$, maximum values of g_a, and maximum values of g_n.

With a fixed-price earnings multiple $P(Z_t)/x_t = 257/5.17 = 49.71$, the minimum value of H is calculated as 6.3 years.

This estimate (unlike sensitivity analysis using Monte Carlo methods) has a very small chance of occurring, due to the compounding of small probabilities. That is, if each of the seven parameters are independent and have only a 1 per cent chance then the probability that H is as low as 6.3 years is 10^{-14}.

A persistence of abnormal growth rates for ($2H$) 12.6 years, where the initial abnormal growth rate is 95 per cent decaying to a long-run growth rate of 3 per cent corresponds to profits of £311.85 million in real terms in 26 years. This lower bound figure is less than a quarter of the 'best estimate' of £1,360 million, but its implausibility is indicated by the fact that it still represents earnings over 10 per cent greater than those of the most profitable UK retailer.

APPENDIX I
LINEAR INFORMATION DYNAMICS (LID) WITH TIME-VARYING PARAMETERS AND ENDOGENOUS DIVIDEND POLICY

The basic model employed in the chapter is

$$\begin{bmatrix} x_{t+1} \\ y_{t+1} \\ d_{t+1} \end{bmatrix} = \begin{bmatrix} (1+g_t) & 0 & 0 \\ (1+g_t) & 1 & -b(1+g_t) \\ b(1+g_t) & 0 & 0 \end{bmatrix} \begin{bmatrix} x_t \\ y_t \\ d_t \end{bmatrix} + \begin{bmatrix} e_1 \\ e_2 \\ e_3 \end{bmatrix}$$

which has the property $\delta E(x_{t+1}|Z_t)/\delta d_t = 0$, because in this specification change in dividends does not influence future earnings. A refinement of the model that penalised or rewarded future earnings if dividends were changed would imply $\delta E(x_{t+1}|Z_t)/\delta d_t = -r$. This in turn would alter the parameters of the LID to

$$\Omega_t = \begin{bmatrix} (1+g_t) & 0 & -r \\ (1-b)(1+g_t) & 1 & -r(1-b) \\ b(1+g_t) & 0 & -br \end{bmatrix}.$$

The new parameter r represents the replacement cost of capital distributed as dividends, either as earnings forgone or as the weighted average cost of capital. (Ohlson (1988, 1989b, 1989c) models a risk-free world, in which case the replacement cost of capital r is the risk-free rate of interest.)

Dividend expectations τ periods ahead would as before be given by

$$E(d_{t+\tau}|Z_t) = e_d\Omega_\tau\Omega_{\tau-1}\Omega_{\tau-2}\ldots\Omega_{t+1}\Omega_t Z_t.$$

With some algebra this can be shown to give

$$E(d_{t+\tau}\,|\,Z_t) = b\prod_{t=i}^{t+\tau}(1 + g_i - rb)x_t.$$

Using the Fuller and Hsia (1984) result, the sum of the present values of these dividend expectations reduces to a valuation equation

$$P(Z_t) = \frac{b(1 + g_n - rb)}{k - g_n + rb} + \frac{bH(g_a - g_n)}{k - g_n + rb}\,x_t,$$

or equivalently

$$P(Z_t) = mx_t - d_t,$$

where the earnings multiplier is

$$m = b\left[\frac{1 + k + H(g_a - g_n)}{k - g_n + rb}\right].$$

(This corresponds to an Ohlson (1988) 'permanent-earnings' valuation model I.)

Introducing a dividend effect into the model has not altered the basic structure. The model used in the chapter for valuing Sock Shop can be seen to be a special case obtained by setting the value of the parameter r to zero.

Rearrangement of the valuation equation in terms of the implicit half-life of the supernormal growth gives:

$$H = \frac{P(Z_t)}{x_t}\,\frac{(k - g_n)}{b(g_a - g_n)} - \frac{(1 + g_n)}{(g_a - g_n)}$$

$$+ \frac{P(Z_t)}{x_t}\,\frac{r}{(g_a - g_n)} + \frac{rb}{(g_a - g_n)}.$$

When the parameter r is zero, we obtain the estimate of H given in the Parameter Estimates section of this chapter. For non-zero values of r, the value of H is higher.

Further, $\delta H/\delta r = (P(Z_t) + d_t)/x_t(g_a - g_n))$ is positive, and thus the minimum value of H occurs when r is zero. It follows that the persistence of supernormal growth rates needs to be even more unrealistic in models in which dividend policy has an effect on future earnings.

12

SECOND-TIER MARKETS IN EUROPE

New markets for growing firms' equities

Mario Anolli, Roger Buckland and Michel Dubois

INTRODUCTION

The experience of the United Kingdom in the 1970s, when the numbers of initial public offerings (IPOs) on the London Stock Exchange collapsed (see Davis, Chapter 7), was not unique: the phenomenon was repeated across Europe. Indeed, the concerns about financing 'gaps' and about the barriers to independent growth of the small or medium-sized enterprise were common across European economies. In this chapter we seek to explore some examples of the various experiments in innovative arrangements for the listing of equities within Europe. In particular, we look at two continental European equities markets: France and Italy. These are chosen because they represent differing traditions of financial systems and differing historical frameworks of equity trading.

The United Kingdom is characterised by a unified and centralised secondary-equities market, with a major international business and a separation of the market and the state. The market is privately operated as a club of brokers and dealers, with self-regulation under a loose statutory system of oversight. Industrial finance is also largely free of state involvement, with an emphasis on equity as the core element of long-term financing and restricted involvement of the banking system in the control or governance of firms (Cox 1986; Lisle-Williams 1982).

In France, the equity market is both smaller and less internationalised. Historically, equities trading is conducted by state-controlled market authorities, with trading statutorily restricted to licensed broker/dealers. The market has only recently progressed from the ancient continental European model of order-driven, call-over trading. The French state has historically guarded control of credit closely, through closed 'circuits' of state-operated, sectorally focused lending institutions such as Crédit Nationale, the Sociétés de Développement Régionale (SDRs: set up to promote small and medium-sized firms regionally), or the Institut de Développement Industriel (IDI) of 1970 (Morgan and Harrington 1977; Green 1983, 1986). The French equity market entered the 1980s following a period of stagnation in new business, exacerbated by the nationalisation of major companies begun in 1981 by the incoming socialist administration.

In Italy, the fragility of the post-war retail and commercial banking system is still being addressed (Furlong 1986: pp. 158ff); relationships of finance with industry and the state have centred upon support for giant corporations by state-sponsored bodies: the IMI (Istituto Mobiliare Italiano) and IRI (Institute for Industrial Reconstruction) (see, for example, Monti et al. 1983). The stock exchanges of the fragmented states before the formation of the modern unified state continued in business, with that business dispersed among several centres: only Milan in the industrial North stands out as of (relatively) large scale; and trading continued in the tightly regulated state frameworks, with licensed broker/dealers accorded a monopoly of business in listed securities. There is, therefore, a spread here of stock exchanges with widely differing structures, widely differing regulation and different relationships to the growing firm's funding problems. In this chapter we draw together the work of Mario Anolli on the problematic emergence of a second tier in Italian exchanges and work by Michel Dubois on the reception of new firms by the French second-tier market in the 1980s.[1]

This is set in the context of wider change and harmonisation of securities markets in the European Union (EU). Not only have these been radically affected by the global forces of liberalisation, securitisation and internationalisation, but the creation of the Single Market in the EU has implied radical innovation and modernisation of securities trading by every national market. In part this is implicit in markets' response to the novel presence of competitors: where previously exchanges possessed protected monopolies of securities trading they must now open their market to fellow members of the EU. In part, also, markets have innovated in order to comply with the EU's harmonisation regulations, which have converged upon a system of price-driven, continuous-quotation securities markets, with liberalisation of traded securities.

EQUITIES MARKETS AND THE FINANCING GAP FOR SMALL AND MEDIUM-SIZED FIRMS

The UK's preoccupation with an equity funding gap, inhibiting the independent growth of emergent enterprises, is reproduced elsewhere within Europe. The diversity of state and institutional approach to industrial finance can be largely attributed to concern about the level of support for the emergent firms in economies (see, for example, Cox 1986: Introduction; Bayliss and Butt Philip 1980; Mayoux 1979; Wilson 1980). The European Commission, also, commissioned research to explore the relationship of the various securities markets to growth financing within the then Community (Schmidt 1984, for example). Subsequently, most stock exchanges and countries introduced additional, lower-tier segments to their equities exchanges as a means of enhancing the attractiveness of the markets to the small or medium-sized enterprise (SME) (Bannock and Doran 1991; Buckland 1989; Grenier 1988; Caprio 1989). The unlisted securities market of the UK, the Second Marché of France and Italy's Mercato Ristretto are the three involved in the research reported in this chapter; there are others in Holland, Germany, Denmark, Sweden, Spain and Portugal.

The common theme of second-tier equity markets is that they are intended to introduce firms to secondary tradability at an earlier stage of development, growth and maturity (Bannock, 1987; Buckland and Davis 1990b). This could operate by providing an alternative to the other options open to the emergent enterprise. Conventionally, these are either extended growth in an unlisted environment (where equity values remain uncertain, where the cost of equity capital is arguably higher and where there may be institutionalised financing gaps), or linkage with – even take-over by – established listed firms (where the entrepreneurial spirit of the growing firm may be compromised or extinguished and the impetus for growth lost).

Within the 1980s, it was fashionable to regard these innovations in market provision as successes (for example, Bannock 1987 and Daigne and Joly 1986). Their introduction precipitated (or coincided with) an upsurge in IPOs throughout Europe, bringing large numbers of new quotations of relatively small enterprises. From the perspective of the 1990s, however, the picture appears more complex and problematic. The stock exchange shock of 1987 had a differentially great impact upon the small, second-tier quotations;[2] and again there was a cyclical collapse in IPOs which particularly affected the second-tier entrants. As Davis (Chapter 7) comments, trading on second-tier markets remains chronically thin, while – at least in the UK – USM entrants have been lost in roughly equal measure to acquisition as to progression to the upper-tier listed market. Here, therefore, we critically examine some aspects of the new markets which reflect upon their relevance to the financing needs of the growing SME: criticisms which are relevant across the capital markets of the EU. In the next section we turn to the Italian experience of the Mercato Ristretto, where innovation attempted to address a confused history of restrictive regulation. Then we look at evidence from French markets of the chronic undervaluation of IPOs, using Rock's asymmetric information model as a reference point. This parallels similar study of the UK's USM by Levis (1990), where this adverse selection model was applied to IPO pricing.[3]

THE PERFORMANCE OF THE MERCATO RISTRETTO, THE ITALIAN SECOND-TIER SECONDARY MARKET

The regulatory background

The regulatory framework of the Italian securities secondary market has undergone a reform process, the motivation for which was the need for a rebalancing of the financial structure of Italian industrial firms. Policy makers believe this to be too unbalanced towards bank financing. The disequilibrium on the liabilities side of the balance sheet of Italian firms is a particularly important phenomenon for the small and medium-sized ones (Caprio 1989). Unofficial second-tier trading burgeoned in the post-1945 years (the Mercatino, or 'little market'), with over 100 companies traded on that unregulated over-the-counter market and with over 30 firms entering the official list subsequently. In the early 1970s its turnover surpassed that of the licensed exchange, and it was suppressed by a ruling of the Supreme Court in order to preserve official control over investor protection. An official second-tier secondary market – the Mercato Ristretto – was established through Law no. 49 of 23 February 1977, for the trade of securities 'not officially listed in the Stock Exchanges' and to promote a market for the raising of equity capital by smaller-sized firms (Cesarini 1979).

The model for the Mercato Ristretto minimised supervision while maintaining the stockbrokers' monopoly over trading. It arose from two considerations. First, it was widely believed that the official list did not represent the country's real economic structure, either in numbers of listed companies or in terms of the ratio of capitalisation to the size of the economy; hence the need for a market intended as a preparatory step towards listing on the official list. The Mercato Ristretto was thus seen as a seasoning market for small-sized firms aiming at a subsequent admission to the official list. Secondly, the Mercato Ristretto was intended to be the natural place where small-sized firms could raise equity capital and correct a classic finance gap. The Italian manufacturing sector was characterised by a myriad of small firms with a good entrepreneurial potential for growth, but that potential could not be exploited because of the lack of supply of equity capital by founders or by their 'extended family'.

These financing and seasoning functions entrusted to the Mercato Ristretto were outlined very clearly in the reports accompanying the law and the regulations which created the market.[4] The evolution of the regulatory framework and the market-performance indicators show that these objectives have been only partially fulfilled.

The meaning attached to 'second-tier' in the Mercato Ristretto

In common with all other developments in European second-tier market segments, the new Italian market presented entrants with a more relaxed regime of entry and reporting standards. Admission requirements are lighter than those needed for the stock exchange (net capital not less than one billion lire; positive net income for the previous two fiscal years; at least 20 per cent of securities to be listed distributed to the public). Moreover, trading in securities admitted to the market takes place on only one day a week, on the floor of the stock exchange, but at a different time from that of the official list meetings (the opening of the market was initially set at 15.30). Only official intermediaries were allowed to trade in the securities listed on the Mercato Ristretto; and settlement of the contracts had to be made on the third working day following the day of the trade.

At first the market did not yield the results expected, due to the minimal differences in the listing requirements and operating characteristics of the Mercato Ristretto when compared to the official list. In order to enhance segmentation between the two parts of the market, some regulations were reviewed in 1987. Listing requirements were lowered to one single year of net income; and a minimum public holding of ten per cent of shares to be listed was deemed adequate. The procedures and disclosure required were softened and requirements for the prospectus substantially simplified. Finally, the limit of the rolling method of settlement was expanded from three to ten working days and weekly trading was superseded by daily frequency in order to enhance the liquidity of the market. The choice of a ten-day delay in settlement of contracts was aimed at reconciling two opposing needs: hindering speculation, potentially destabilising in such a thin market; and easing settlement of shares traded because of the peculiar time-consuming way by which their ownership certificates are transferred.[5]

The 1987 reform moved in the right direction, but again failed to yield results. In 1990 the regulatory framework was revised again. The main adjustments were: mandatory audit of the balance sheet by a chartered firm; opening of listing to foreign firms; and delegation of control over some listing procedures to the Comitato per il Mercato Ristretto (a technical local supervisory body including representatives of intermediaries and of regulatory organisations). Shares whose transfer is not subject to any constraints were segregated in listing from those whose ownership status is subject to approval clauses and from shares which are not transferable by endorsement. There was further change in January 1991 during a general reform of the whole Italian securities industry.[6] The picture is completed by Law no. 207 of 17 February 1992, promoting easier trade in mutual banks' securities and facilitating registration and settlement by a central depository agency.

Performance indicators in the Mercato Ristretto

There are presently six markets (Milan, Turin, Rome, Genoa, Florence and Naples); the Milan Mercato Ristretto represents more than 99 per cent of the whole volume traded in all markets of this kind; moreover, on the other five markets there are only nine securities which are not simultaneously listed on the Milan list. This alone suggests the dominance of Milan in a horizontally segmented Italian equities market, and as the location of the vertical second segment of the market also. The performance analysis of the market will thus be restricted to the Milan Mercato Ristretto.

As Table 12.1 shows, the number of companies listed on the Mercato Ristretto has always been low. Indeed, listings and delistings have been infrequent: for Milan, if one disregards the 23 companies in the first year, the aggregate number is 40 listings and 26 delistings. Only 14 companies have come to the official list of the stock exchange via the Mercato Ristretto, compared to 142 companies which obtained listing over the period. Thus in only one out of ten cases has the Mercato Ristretto performed the seasoning task assigned to it. Moreover, in 1990 and 1991 six Mercato Ristretto new listings were companies entering after cancellation from the official list.

This criticism must be tempered, in that the market's seasoning potential relates only to a subset of the companies actually listed,

Table 12.1 Securities and companies traded on the Milan Mercato Ristretto (numbers at end of year)

	Securities			*Companies*	
Year	*Banking*	*Miscellaneous*	*Total*	*Milan*	*Other*[a]
1978	19	4	23	23	
1979	20	9	29	28	
1980	20	9	29	28	3
1981	27	10	37	36	1
1982	26	11	37	36	1
1983	25	11	36	35	1
1984	26	12	38	37	1
1985	26	10	36	35	1
1986	24	9	33	32	1
1987	28	9	37	35	0
1988	29	8	37	35	1
1989	28	9	37	35	4
1990	26	12	38	37	6
1991	26	17	43	41	9
1992	22	18	40	37	9

[a] Numbers excluding parallel listings, where also quoted in Milan.
Sources: Comitato del Mercato Ristretto di Milano; CONSOB

because of their peculiar composition. The list in fact is dominated by shares of mutual banks and of other banks, whose charters impose clauses hindering free transfer of their shares, and which cannot thus be admitted to the official list. The transfer of property rights in mutual banks' shares is restricted by the so-called *clausola di gradimento* (acceptance clause) and becomes valid only when the board of the directors of the bank has given its agreement to the admission of the purchaser of the stock into the company. Thus, although the market's contribution to the development of the stock exchange has been limited, this is not entirely an intrinsic fault of the Mercato Ristretto but a reflection of the dominance of its list by companies where 'seasoning' could not have been accomplished.

In terms of the size of the companies quoted on the Mercato Ristretto, the average values of registered capital and capitalisation of the companies listed on the Milan Mercato Ristretto at the end of 1992 were L 55.9 billion (£23 million) and L 342 billion (£143 million) respectively. The same values regarding companies listed on the Milan official list were L 276 billion and L 778 billion respectively. The typical company listed on the Ristretto is thus much bigger than the minimum size for entrants (net worth amounting to L 1 billion) and its capitalisation would rank it approximately one hundredth among companies listed on the official list. Fully two out of three companies listed on the official list at the end of 1992 had a capitalisation below the average capitalisation of Ristretto listed companies. This overlap of size – the differentiation of a market rather than its segmentation – mirrors that observed in the UK's USM (Buckland and Davis 1989). It stems from two factors: the stock exchange boom in 1985 and 1986; and the peculiar position of the mutual banks. During the mid-1980s boom some companies that (in size and by public holding of shares) were eligible for entry to the Mercato Ristretto instead entered the official list directly.

The rigidity of the structure of the Mercato Ristretto list is thus almost entirely explained by the difficulty of exit from the market and by the lack of appeal to potential new entrants, which have almost always preferred to be listed on the official list. The growth in capitalisation of the Mercato Ristretto is shown in Table 12.2. Two points are particularly worth mentioning: the limited rate of growth of the market, since, in real terms, the capitalisation at the ends of 1991 and of 1992 were even lower than that of 1979 (the first year of full market operation); and the market's extreme concentration in

Table 12.2 Capitalisation of the Milan Mercato Ristretto (billions of lire, at end of year)

Year	A Total	B Banks	B/A per cent	Real[a]	As percentage of official list	As percentage of GDP
1978	3,613	3,591	99.39	13,293	44.35	1.43
1979	5,672	5,533	97.55	17,424	54.86	1.83
1980	11,843	11,685	98.67	30,051	50.51	3.05
1981	16,873	16,644	98.64	36,322	58.69	3.64
1982	8,753	8,569	97.91	16,200	32.06	1.61
1983	8,046	7,849	97.55	13,208	22.54	1.27
1984	6,292	6,113	97.16	9,494	12.64	0.87
1985	7,885	7,492	95.02	10,955	8.03	0.97
1986	9,753	9,001	92.29	12,989	5.12	1.09
1987	10,211	9,714	95.13	12,940	7.26	1.04
1988	10,331	9,946	96.27	12,413	5.84	0.95
1989	13,599	13,111	96.41	13,241	6.32	1.14
1990	14,830	14,049	94.73	15,727	8.82	1.13
1991	14,434	12,793	88.63	14,434	8.14	1.01
1992	12,668	11,560	91.25	12,018	7.47	0.84

[a]. Valuation at end-1991 prices, by ISTAT consumer price index.
Sources: Comitato del Mercato Ristretto di Milano; Comitato Direttiva degli Agenti di Cambio della Borsa Valori di Milano; ISTAT

the banking sector. The value of the shares issued by banks has always represented more than 90 per cent of total capitalisation; inside the banking sector itself more than two-thirds of the capitalisation refers to mutual banks or to banks issuing shares whose transfer is limited by the company charter. The table also shows severe shrinkage of the relative size of the Mercato Ristretto compared to the size of the official list: when the Mercato Ristretto was created, the aggregate value of its listed companies was about one-half that of companies listed on the official list; from 1982 on, the percentage ratio of the markets has shrunk and touched little more than 5 per cent in 1986, the year of maximum growth of the stock exchange.

Share prices and trading on the second-tier market

The average price performance of the Milan Mercato Ristretto has been unsatisfactory. At the end of 1992 the CARIPLO index of Mercato Ristretto share prices was a little more than three times its level of 10 May 1978 (the first trading day of the Milan Mercato

Table 12.3 Turnover of the Milan Mercato Ristretto (annually, in billions of lire)

Year	A *Total*	B *Banks*	C *Non-bank*	B/A *per cent*	*Real*[a]	*As percentage of official list*	*Velocity*[b] A	 C
1978	13.4	13.2	0.2	98.51				
1979	54.5	51.5	3	94.5	167.42	1.9	1.17	2.16
1980	204	197	7	96.57	517.64	2.78	2.33	4.71
1981	245.3	231.8	13.5	94.5	528.05	1.99	1.71	6.98
1982	137.7	133.2	4.5	96.73	254.86	3.65	1.07	2.18
1983	88.6	83.6	5	94.36	145.44	1.51	1.05	2.62
1984	74.9	70.2	4.7	93.72	113.01	1.05	1.04	2.5
1985	154.9	132.8	22.1	85.73	215.21	0.59	2.19	7.73
1986	304.1	244.7	59.4	80.47	405	0.46	3.45	10.38
1987	356.6	291.2	65.4	81.66	451.89	0.85	3.57	10.46
1988	332.2	314.9	17.3	94.79	399.16	0.8	3.23	4.05
1989	808.4	765.5	42.9	94.69	787.13	1.51	6.76	10.15
1990	1,202.4	1,162.4	40	96.67	1,275.1	2.37	8.46	6.31
1991	625.9	552.5	73.43	88.27	625.92	2.02	4.28	7.23
1992	509.72	472.96	36.76	92.79	483.57	1.47	3.76	3.32

[a] Valuation at end-1991 prices, by ISTAT consumer price index.

[b] Velocity measured by annual turnover as percentage of market capitalisation (at end year).

Sources: Comitato del Mercato Ristretto di Milano; Comitato Direttiva degli Agenti di Cambio della Borsa Valori di Milano; ISTAT

Ristretto). In the same time span the MIB (Milan stock exchange) general index (and the relevant MIB banking-sector index) grew by between nine and ten times. The performances of the price indices have been surprisingly independent: in particular, Mercato Ristretto prices reflected only poorly the main market boom in 1985–86 and the following shocks in October 1987, October 1989 and August 1990. Trading volumes on the Milan Mercato Ristretto are shown in Table 12.3; volume has always been relatively low, although growing over the period. The turnover ratio is remarkably low, although showing strong growth in later years. During the whole period (excepting the initial year of 1978) it ranges from a minimum of 1.04 per cent in 1984 to a maximum of 8.46 per cent in 1991; both are much lower than in the Italian official list (from 25 per cent to 45 per cent) and lower than in other EU second-tier markets. Again, this is explained by the peculiarity of the securities traded: the predominance of bank shares. Growth of trading has also been hindered by banks' practices in the purchase or sale of their own shares: that is, by buying and selling at their branches, on their own account, shares their customers are willing to sell or buy, so taking business away from the Mercato Ristretto. That is a source of bias in price formation and may lead to conflicts of interest between the customer and the intermediary.

As for primary-market activity, Table 12.4 shows the raising of new capital to be comparable to that for the official list. The new capital-to-turnover ratios are seldom lower than 1 and are sometimes higher than 6, whereas the normal level of such a ratio is approximately 0.1 for Anglo-Saxon markets and around 0.2 for the Italian and French stock exchanges. This confirms the low level of trading on the Mercato Ristretto, but, on the other hand, it suggests that the funding policies of the vast majority of the companies listed on the Mercato Ristretto do not rely upon the support of the secondary market as such: issuers (that is, the banks, through their branches) have plenty of points of contact with potential subscribers other than the secondary market. Share issues by non-bank companies have been only 24 out of 147; and funds raised by non-bank companies have accounted for merely 5 per cent of the total (Bisoni and Ferretti 1991).

Future development of the Italian market

The Italian second-tier market, therefore, has not closed a finance gap for small and medium-sized firms. It provided a niche market for shares in banks, where restrictions on share transfer inhibited

Table 12.4 The raising of new capital at the Milan Mercato Ristretto (in billions of lire)

Year	A *New capital*	B *Turnover*	C *Dividends*	*A/B*	*A/C*
1978	83.77	13.4		6.25	
1979	64.96	54.5	77.93	1.19	0.83
1980	176.94	204	94.19	0.87	1.88
1981	742.86	245.3	135.45	3.03	5.48
1982	348.43	137.7	149.34	2.53	2.33
1983	163.66	88.6	188.23	1.85	0.87
1984	507.24	74.9	197.49	6.77	2.57
1985	72.5	154.9	254.12	0.47	0.29
1986	312.87	304.1	318.62	1.03	0.98
1987	310.59	356.6	405.67	0.87	0.77
1988	194.35	332.2	442.87	0.59	0.44
1989	596.08	808.4	478.12	0.74	1.25
1990	647.15	1,202.4	547.38	0.54	1.18
1991	631.75	625.92	784.99	1.01	0.8
1992	185.3	509.72	656.79	0.36	0.28

Source: Comitato del Mercato Ristretto di Milano

use of the official list. Its impact upon the problems out of which it arose – low numbers of new entrants and lack of attractiveness to the growing entrepreneurial firms in Italy – has been meagre. The aim of this section is to consider the foreseeable development of the second-tier secondary markets in Italy in the light of past experience, the recent evolution of the regulatory framework and the attitudes lately shown by the regulatory bodies.

There exist in Italy two second-tier markets: one official, the Mercato Ristretto, and the other unofficial and unregulated, the '*terzo mercato*'. There is also the possibility that the CONSOB may create local markets, where traders will be able to exchange securities not listed on the stock exchange (analogous to the London Stock Exchange's plans for a market in smaller companies' securities). In the Mercato Ristretto there have been moves towards a rebalancing of the list, with a decrease of the high weight of the banking sector and a redistribution of listed companies towards the manufacturing sector (Bini 1990). Thus recent legislation on mutual banks' share transfer and registration may provide for the free transfer required for listing on the official list and for management of share certificates by a central depository agency. As a result, many mutual banks – presently listed on the Mercato Ristretto – may apply for admission to the official list. In addition, banks, including those listed on the Mercato Ristretto, will no longer be able to internalise their customers' trade in shares listed on the official list and the Mercato Ristretto, except in very special circumstances. That should increase the turnover of the Mercato Ristretto, and its level of disclosure will rise because of the clear distinction of roles between issuer, consultant and trader.

These changes enhance demarcation of the segmented markets. Another line of action would transfer to the Mercato Ristretto securities suspended from the trading on the official list when some of the listing requirements are no longer satisfied: in 1991, for instance, three out of the six shares newly listed on the Mercato Ristretto were previously traded on the official list. The CONSOB could control more stringently the minimum flotation requirement, often broken by smaller listed companies. This would protect the market from thin trading: when the flotation requirement is not observed by small companies the thickness of the market is jeopardised more than in the case of securities with higher market value. In the latter case the relative scarcity of securities outstanding is balanced by their market value, which allows for thicker trading.

As far as the *terzo mercato* is concerned, its importance is beginning to decline: trading has decreased as well as the number of companies and securities traded.[7] In addition, the regulatory actions of the CONSOB will change this market. The CONSOB has repeatedly exercised moral suasion in order to encourage issuers of securities traded on the *terzo mercato* to apply for listing on the official list or on the Mercato Ristretto. The admission procedure to the official list has also been changed, speeding up admission to the list, which may be granted immediately, subject only to the publication of the prospectus. Many applicants have availed themselves of that provision, cutting down the time span between the IPO and the admission to the list, taking away from the *terzo mercato* one of its main sources of business. Finally, the future of the *terzo mercato* will be compromised by the creation of local markets for the trading of securities not listed either on the official list or on the Mercato Ristretto.

Local markets and finance for the growing firm

In regulating such markets, CONSOB will reflect its historic reservations towards the *terzo mercato*. The development of local markets will be subject to legal and economic factors. On the regulatory side, the solution will give exclusive access to trading to licensed securities traders (SIMs), banks and stockbrokers. The weight of banks as intermediaries will be overwhelming because SIMs, unlike banks, are geographically concentrated in Milan. Banks will take part in order to exploit their competitive advantages (a better geographical distribution than SIMs, enabling them to have better and more active information about companies) and to react to external constraints. Some banks may need to securitise part of their balance-sheet assets in order to meet the requirements of the EU large-loans directive and to comply with capital-to-asset ratios; securitised loans may eventually be introduced on the local market and the mechanism employed to reduce the exposure of the bank towards the firm. A more radical process, with banks assuming more responsibility for the management of firms' financial structure,[8] could see the bank offering to the firm a package of financial assistance aimed at the flotation of shares on the local market following a capital increase, first underwritten by the bank itself and then distributed to investors and bank customers via the local market.

The Bank of Italy itself seems to have seized the initiative in reshaping the relationship between banks and firms, by advocating a better balance between debt and equity for the small and medium-sized firms and a higher involvement of banks in the development of the equity markets (Banca d'Italia 1991, 1992, 1993). The admission of small firms to local markets could promote restructuring of their financial sources, a pattern followed to some extent by large Italian listed firms during the second half of the 1980s. Local markets could foster the creation of venture-capital intermediaries: local markets, along with the Ristretto, seem to be the natural outlet for the sale of the participations temporarily assumed by venture-capital intermediaries. The interest of the issuer in access to the local market would depend upon differentials in costs: for instance, in avoidance of external auditing and certification of company accounts.

Nevertheless, development of local markets is hindered on one hand by the possibility of electronic linking of markets (which may suggest as more viable and less costly the creation of a section of the list of the Mercato Ristretto dedicated to regional securities) and, on the other hand, by the tendency, observed in some more advanced financial systems, to avoid proliferation of segments of the secondary market and to have only one official market and one second-tier market, the latter possessing listing requirements notably lower than those of the main market. There may be more potential in the exploitation of screen-based entry of orders for small-firm securities, with periodic clearing of batches of orders within the system. Movement (in 1994) to the five-day rolling-settlement system across Italian exchanges should also promote liquidity, without the necessity of duplicated local information and trading mechanisms for segregated trading in small-company securities.

ARE COMPANIES GOING PUBLIC UNDERVALUED? THE FRENCH EXPERIENCE

The emergent, growing enterprise may regard quotation on secondary equities markets as an alternative to other forms of external financial support for its strategies, but the attraction of an IPO will depend upon many factors. One such factor is the extent to which the underlying value of issued securities is realised by vendors during an IPO: the question of the 'discount' experienced by issuers during the process of introducing shares to quotation.

This is not at all to neglect other crucial factors which will influence the firm's attitude to the use of secondary-equity quotation. It is apparent that factors such as control and family succession are influential across societies (see, for example, Chevalier 1989; Buckland and Davis 1989: Chapter 5); second-tier markets have been relatively attractive to family-controlled businesses because they permit quotation with lower thresholds of public (that is, non-family) shareholding and with lower administrative costs of market entry. The potential for future use of a quotation either in raising capital for accelerated organic growth, or in accelerated external growth by acquisition, may also be influential; and many IPOs are triggered by owners' or managers' search for status and publicity available through the exposure to analysts' and media scrutiny.

If assets are systematically underpriced during market entry, this creates a disincentive to new quotation as a route for continued firm growth: it also diminishes the rewards available to owners and venture-capital investors where they plan to exit from or realise investments during an IPO (see Buckland, Chapter 10, for an analysis in the UK context). Many IPO markets have been found to exhibit this discounting characteristic; this section of the chapter presents evidence regarding the underpricing of unseasoned issues in France. The question of rationing is taken into account and the market efficiency is tested. The sample consists of 277 firms listed on the Second Marché during the years 1983 to 1993.[9]

The survival of systematic underpricing in France

If there is systematic undervaluation it means a loss for the previous shareholders, which acts as a brake upon companies going public and an abnormal gain for the new shareholders, whose interest is to subscribe in order to make a quick profit. In freely competitive conditions such a market ought not to exist for any length of time: vendors will vacate the market. However, the opposite phenomenon is the norm: since the creation of the Second Marché, the rate of companies' introduction increased, year on year, until halted by external shocks to the exchange. Here we study this paradox through a model suggesting the possible persistence of undervaluation of companies during IPOs.

Almost all the French IPOs in the 1980s have taken place on the Second Marché (excluding privatisation-related issues; and even there the route for issue of securities in the various Crédit Agricoles régionaux was through provincial Second Marché quotation. As in the rest of Europe, there had been very few listings since the mid-1970s, particularly compared to the (greater) number of delistings. This situation, exacerbated by the 1981 nationalisations, brought the potential danger of marginalisation of the French stock market. The 'Special Unofficial Market' had not managed to act as a stepping stone towards the official list, and the stock-market authorities (the COB or 'stock exchange commission') decided to create a new, more liquid, market with less stringent access requirements than the official list.

Relaxation of access requirements principally related to three points:

- the shares made available to the public were to represent a minimum of 10 per cent of the company's capital (as opposed to 25 per cent on the official list);
- auditing of accounts was no longer to be necessary prior to introduction: but instead must be carried out within 3 years of entry;
- the prospectus for the public no longer had to be certified by the COB.

This substantially lowered the costs of going public. Lemée (1983) estimates that, on average, they have been reduced sixfold, from FFr 3 million for an official listing to FFr 500,000 for a flotation on the Second Marché. Access costs are thus considerably reduced for smaller-sized companies. The limited number of shares made available to the market (due to the small percentage of capital released to the public and the companies' smaller size) may lead to weak liquidity and thin markets. This underlay the provision of market-management arrangements – the 'syndicat de liquidité' – for each entrant company (see also Buckland 1989). These measures, helped by a bullish market, contributed to the dramatic increase in the number of IPOs in the mid-1980s. In this respect, the Second Marché apparently achieved its purpose.

French IPOs have long been characterised by discounting. In the first systematic study, MacDonald and Jacquillat (1974) studied 31 introductions between 1968 and 1971. On average, the extra return over that of the market reached 3 per cent on the day of flotation, 4.1 per cent at the end of the first week and 4.6 per cent for the first month. They conclude that the market reacts efficiently (since almost all the discount is absorbed on the first day of quotation); and the size of discount is, on average, small, with no potential for arbitrage profits in application. In a further study between 1966 and 1974, MacDonald et al. (1978) put forward a new model, involving investors' anticipation of the beta of securities. Again, they conclude that discounting generates abnormal returns below the transactions costs of available short-term investment strategies. This contrasts with contemporaneous research on the over-the-counter (OTC) market in the USA. The thrust of that research is that IPOs display an abnormally positive short-term market-adjusted return between 10 per cent and 30 per cent, depending on the study and the period under review.[10]

Most early studies ascribe undervaluation to the influence of the issuing bank. This proposition is counter-intuitive, because, in the aggregate, banks would not systematically privilege customers who are investors over those who are sellers: they are competitive intermediaries faced with two groups with contrary interests. A more plausible reason has to do with the nature of the US flotation procedure: the introduction price is unilaterally set by the offerers; since companies are keen to see a fully subscribed issue, it is conceivable that they may accept underpricing of the issued shares. Both the contemporary French studies concluded in favour of the superiority of the French listing procedure, a practice close to an auction. Undervaluation averaged about 4 per cent in France whereas it was 11.4 per cent in the US OTC (MacDonald and Jacquillat 1974; MacDonald et al. 1978).

When Dubois and Dumontier (1988) reported on IPO pricing in the early years of the Second Marché, therefore, it was striking to find high positive levels of discounting. This was also in line with other 1980s studies (for example, Beatty and Ritter 1986; Jog and Ryding 1987; Nahmijas and Pera 1988; Tinic 1988; Buckland and Davis 1989). Fresh effort to explain the phenomenon centred on information economics. Rock (1986) showed that the existence of investors better informed than the rest of the market (including the company's management) would provide a rationale for shares being underpriced when listed. He assumes that shares are sold by public offer for sale and that, if demand is in surplus, rationing is carried out by lot. The investor is either allocated the shares requested in full or not at all. Better-informed 'insider' investors are supposed to know the expected price with certainty; however, according to the hypothesis, their combined demand is insufficient to fully subscribe the issue. 'Outsiders', less-informed potential applicants, find themselves in an unfavourable situation: on the one hand they only know the value of shares in probability terms; and, on the other hand, the likelihood of getting overvalued shares is greater than that of getting undervalued ones (see Rock 1986 or Levis 1990 for a full exposition; and Keasey and Short 1992 for a critique).

This theory, although very appealing, requires that the introduced company is able to set the introduction price. This is true of US procedures, as for listings by public offer of sale (in the UK; and by the *Offre Publique de Vente* (OPV) in France), but it is not the case for the other procedures operating in France, which are characterised by an auction process. This raises the question of whether pricing of Second Marché IPOs is explicable through Rock's model. Here, we examine a sample of 277 flotations, taking place during the first ten years of the Second Marché from February 1983 till December 1993. Privatisation issues and the few companies listed on the spot market have been excluded, as are companies offering stock other than ordinary shares, and those which switched from the Special Unofficial Market to the Second Marché (for these there was a market price prior to the transaction).

There were some companies that could have considered direct admission to the *Cote Officiel*. It seems that relaxation of the procedures has encouraged some new companies into quotation (arguably more than in Italy, as seen above[11]). Excess returns at the time of the IPO are measured and modelled by means of the capital-asset pricing model (CAPM). Thus a share which has been undervalued is characterised by an abnormally high return given its risk level, and the CAPM can be used as a reference point to estimate the extent of undervaluation. In order to establish whether there is undervaluation or overvaluation one measures the difference between actual and predicted returns: if there is overvaluation the difference is significantly different from zero.[12] Over 1983–86 the excess return was calculated for the 99 companies successively over periods from 1 to 25 weeks following the IPO. If there is no systematic undervaluation the average excess return must be systematically nil and the linked hypotheses to be tested are, therefore:

H1: $\beta = 1$ and $E_{jt} = 0$ at $t = 1, \ldots, 25$

where β is the systematic risk coefficient and E_{jt} is the excess return for entrant j over period t.

Excess return is observed during the first week following flotation: it reaches 19.26 per cent on average, as opposed to 4.22 per cent in the MacDonald and Jacquillat study (1974) conducted on the spot market. The characteristics of the companies involved can explain such a difference, but not on their own; one must add to them the lesser number of shares made available to the public and less-competitive flotation procedures than the *Mise en Vente* (tender). The second week alone still shows an abnormally positive excess return.[13] There is further statistically significant reaction at the end of the fourth week, characterised by a fall of 1.31 per cent. This may be due to the prevalence of profit taking in a thin market. This fall remains small and does not bring into question the profits from early weeks. To conclude, if one keeps to applications serviced, the abnormal return found during the first four weeks is 21.2 per cent on average, of which 19.6 per cent are gained in the first week of flotation. There is, indeed, undervaluation of floated companies and, thus, a loss of wealth for vendor and existing shareholders.

The same results flow from tests on the full sample of 277 companies between February 1983 and December 1993. The mean abnormal return on the IPOs is 20.87 per cent, the median 10.77 per cent. These are statistically significantly different from zero on all conventional tests, but the distribution is clearly not normal: the standard deviation is 27.88 per cent, with skewness of 2.94 per cent and kurtosis of 15.41 per cent. This is generated by a small number of outlying IPOs with very high discounts.

How serious is this apparent underpricing?

For the firm, the higher discounting apparent in Second Marché IPOs may not in itself be more damaging than those experienced in the past. Since vendors need only sell a minimum of 10 per cent of shares in the IPO, the implied 'cost' in capitalisation terms can be limited to (on average) 2.12 per cent of equity capitalisation (the historic levels required 25 per cent public holding, or a limit of 1.5 per cent of capitalisation on the average discounts experienced). Arguably this is lower than the immediate benefit in equity value to be gained from quotation itself (see Buckland and Davis 1989: Chapter 9 for a discussion of the UK case).

For the individual applicant and investor, also, large average discounts do not imply equivalent realisable returns. There are two important elements of cost involved which relate to the Rock (1986) analysis: transaction charges and the opportunity cost associated with the 'freezing' of funds. The cost of freezing funds depends on the flotation. It is standard to freeze applicants' funds during the allocation process, but for some transactions the call for capital precedes the flotation; in other instances financial intermediaries demand cover equal to the total order. In this sample the call for capital took place in 146 out of 277 cases and the average length of freezing was three days.

The opportunity cost of frozen capital includes an amount equal to the cost of all the shares applied for, whereas gains on the transaction come only from the shares allotted. For example, if Company X is floated on 15 February at FFr 100 a share, and an investor announces the intention to buy 100 shares, for which there is a call for capital as from 11 February, then FFr 10,000 are frozen for 5 days. Assume that, subsequently, applications are granted at one for twenty; and then the shares held are subsequently sold on 16 February at FFr 125 per share. The investor's return from the operation, positing a market return of 2 per cent between the 15th and the 16th, are as follows:

	FFr	
Application for shares	FFr 100 × 100	10000
Purchase	5 × 100	500
Selling		625
Return before freezing funds		125
less: Return of FFr 500 in the market	500 × 2%	(10)
Costs of freezing FFr 10,000	10,000 × 1%	(100)
Transactions costs	500 × 3%	(15)
Excess return	125–125	0

Therefore a transaction which has a return for the serviced applications of 2 per cent becomes a break-even deal once the transactions costs (500 × 3% = FFr 15) are deducted. To test compliance with Rock's model, the excess returns for this sample were stripped of immobilisation and transactions costs. There are two possible opportunity costs of the frozen capital. If the investor wishes to invest the whole of available capital in the stock market, then by subscribing for shares in the flotation planned investment is postponed by a length of time equal to the capital freeze and the opportunity cost is, then, equal to the market return (with the assumption of all $\beta = 1$). Alternatively, if the investor anticipates reduction of the bid, only a fraction of the funds are at risk and the opportunity cost approaches the risk-free rate. The investor's position must also be studied in detail. We have identified two types of investor:

- the small shareholder who bears the cover charges (freezing of capital for one day) or the freeze cost; and
- the holder of a more substantial portfolio who only bears the freeze cost at the issuer's discretion.

After deduction of the transaction charges (assumed to be 3 per cent) excess returns were obtained. For 1983–86, over the first week there is only one case where the excess return is, statistically, equal to zero. Otherwise it is in the investor's interest to systematically subscribe for flotations. As Table 12.5 shows, we have shown that, even with a minimum, risk-free rate of return, the opportunity cost of frozen capital is significant, but flotations remain transactions of interest to investors in three out of four situations considered.

Table 12.5 Average returns from arbitrage in IPOs on the *Second Marché*, 1983–86

Percentage of investment, over period of arbitrage (not annualised); transactions costs assumed to be 3% of sale value; holding costs as in table.

	Opportunity cost = market return			*Opportunity cost = risk-free rate*		
Excess return (%)	*Mean*	*Standard deviation*	*t-statistic*	*Mean*	*Standard deviation*	*t-statistic*
Net of all frozen funds	3.1	48.98	0.63	11.53	17.2	6.67**
Net of specific funds frozen	12.39	31.96	3.68**	12.77	17.55	7.24**

** Statistically significantly different from zero, $p < 1\%$.

Source: Dubois 1989: p. 14

The choice of issuing method

The cost of freezing funds cannot explain discounting on its own. One should also examine whether the method of issuing has any impact. Prima facie every method should exhibit similar discounts, if competing financial intermediaries act in the issuers' interests. This null hypothesis can be tested through tests of analysis of variance on the abnormal returns in the sample, and Table 12.6 reports the results for such a test in the French context.

There are several difficulties in such a test, however. First, the French system permits IPOs to be tried under one system, then suspended and resumed under the same or a different method: thus there are groups of IPOs effected under one method alongside other

Table 12.6 Average returns from arbitrage in French IPOs: by method of issue, 1983–1993

Percentage of investment, over period of arbitrage (not annualised); holding costs of frozen funds at risk-free rate.

	Method of issue						*Test of variance*	
Return (%)	*(1) OPV*	*(2) PO*	*(3) MeV*	*(4) OPV + OPV*	*(5) PO/MeV + OPV*	*(6) PO/MeV + PO/MeV*	*F*	*X^2*
1	24.67	5.69	17.36	33.24	25.51	33.64	6.3	50.26
2	23.37	5.26	16.16	24.6	19.54	25.95	3.74	30.52
3	23.21	4.85	15.54	13.7	9.65	4.92	3.72	25.46
Number of issues	62	46	73	80		16		

Notes:

Return 1 is the average of gross abnormal return across issue period for the sample.

Return 2 is abnormal return net of holding costs of frozen funds, at risk-free rate for three days.

Return 3 is abnormal return net of holding costs for actual period of freeze for the issues involved.

OPV is the *offre publique de vente*; PO is the *procédure ordinaire*; MeV is the *mise en vente*; OPV + OPV is a suspended, then resumed IPO by OPV; PO/MeV + OPV are IPOs initially by PO or MeV which were suspended, then resumed by OPV; PO/MeV + PO/MeV are IPOs by PO or MeV which were suspended, then resumed by either repeated PO/MeV or by the alternative MeV/PO.

F is the *F* statistic test of significance in analysis of variance; X^2 is the Kruskal–Wallis test. All means statistically significantly different from zero.

groups made by various combinations of OPV, PO and MeV (see notes to Table 12.6). Second, the numbers in these various groups are dominated by the (single) OPV, which accounts for 62 IPOs, and the OPV/OPV combination (80 IPOs); the MeV on its own accounts for a further 73 and the PO on its own another 46 issues. Thus the definition of 'method' can be contentious. Here (as in Table 12.6) the joint methods are aggregated. Third, the non-normal distribution of abnormal returns across the sample makes parametric tests unreliable: hence the non-parametric Kruskal–Wallis test of variance is utilised here. Fourth, one method, the PO, was predominantly used in periods of falling market prices, when discounts in general were lower, which will distort the comparison with other methods. Finally, of course, the costs of frozen funds, as analysed in the previous section, may distort tests, since the various methods imply different arrangements for freezing applicants' funds during the application for and initial pricing of shares. This is particularly so where there are suspended and resumed issues by two methods or procedures.

Table 12.6 demonstrates that there is strong support for the hypothesis that the methods are associated with different discounting levels. At the level of raw abnormal returns, the OPV displays radically higher discounts than other methods, whether used singly or in combination. The other methods, used singly, exhibit lower discounting; although where the issue is referred and resumed under a second procedure, these crude returns are seen to rival those from OPV routes.

When costs of frozen funds are included, the picture becomes clearer. Realisable returns drop considerably, particularly in combined procedures where the PO or the MeV is involved (columns 5 and 6 of Table 12.6): clearly, where issues are suspended and resumed, the resulting gain in information on the market profits neither the issuer nor the investor, but rather the holder of the frozen funds.

CONCLUSIONS

This chapter has introduced studies of two second-tier equities markets in continental Europe which clarify as well as confirm some of the analysis of UK markets in earlier chapters. These markets have arisen during the 1980s for common reasons: widespread concerns with the inadequacy of traditional secondary markets in their provision of routes to quotation for growing, independent businesses. Second-tier markets have been established with the objectives of lowering regulatory and cost barriers to entry for the medium-sized firm. The Italian experience shows again that regulatory barriers are not the only barrier to growing firms' use of secondary markets. Instead the Mercato Ristretto in Italy largely attracted the equities of (mutual) banks, where only peculiarities in the transfer of their shares prevented them from entering the upper tier of the exchange. The numbers of commercial and industrial entrants attracted has been very small.

This has contributed to the reassessment of Italy's exchange framework, with detailed legislatory changes aimed at promoting a model of localised markets relevant to emergent enterprises. In France, the existence of the six provincial exchanges around the Paris metropolitan bourse did draw numbers of fast-growth firms into quotation. As in the UK, however, the process of introduction has been characterised by high price discounts and subsequent thin markets. Some, but not all of the price discounting is explicable in Rock's (1986) model of information asymmetry and adverse selection in IPOs. As in the UK's USM, however, the French experience suggests that IPOs on second-tier markets have been systematically underpriced.

NOTES

1 Mario Anolli is a faculty member of the Universitata Cattolica del Sacre Cuore in Milan. He has researched extensively in Italian capital markets with Professor Cesarini (also of the Universitata Cattolica del Sacre Cuore). Michel Dubois is Professeur de Finance at the Université de Neuchatel in Switzerland.

2 In the UK, for example, there were over 200 IPOs in 1987, a third of them on the USM; in 1992 the number had dropped to under 100, with less than 10 on the USM (Davis and Pointon 1994: p. 328).

3 Keasey and Short (1992), however, pose doubts as to the relevance of Rock's model to the institutional framework of IPO pricing in the UK, with its contemporary reliance upon share placings rather than by competitive offers for sale.

4 See, for example, the annual reports of the market's governing authority (CONSOB 1977: pp. 41–2, or 1979: pp. 59–60).

5 In some cases property rights are transferred by annulment of the security sold and subsequent issue of a new security registered with the name of the purchaser.

6 Of particular interest are the rules regarding concentration of all trading in listed securities in the hands of licensed brokers. From the

beginning of 1993 this will prevent banks from offsetting customers' buy and sell orders and from acting as a counterpart with them. Law no. 1/91 also enables CONSOB to create new local markets, dedicated to the trading of securities not listed on the stock exchange or on the Mercato Ristretto.

7 However, reliable data on this 'grey' market does not exist to support the contention.

8 Italian banks have shown as little enthusiasm as those in the UK for such a role.

9 Incorporating research first reported in Dubois (1989). We acknowledge the translation provided by Dr B Nicoulaud.

10 See, for example, MacDonald and Fisher (1972), Neuberger and Hammond (1974), Ibbotson (1975, 1982), Baron (1982) and Beatty and Ritter (1986).

11 Use of provincial exchanges is one factor; other key attractions of the regulatory relaxation, particularly for French family-controlled firms, are the lower threshold of public holdings and the looser reporting requirements. See Daigne and Joly (1986), Chevalier (1989) and Buckland (1989) for more detail.

12 Most studies assume that β is unity. For this data tests show that, for measurements of abnormal returns between the 1st and the 25th week following entry, the β of the sample firms is not significantly different from unity. In 79 out of 99 cases between 1983 and 1986 the unity hypothesis must be accepted; for the remaining 20 companies regression coefficients are statistically nil. (For such companies their risk was overestimated by considering $\beta = 1$ and the excess return was overestimated when market return was negative, underestimated in the opposite case. The average market return over the period was positive. Hence bias introduced by our measure slightly reduces the excess return.) See Dubois (1989); and also Brown and Warner (1980) for a discussion.

13 This reflects the French practice of gradual movement, limit-up or limit-down, towards equilibrium prices. Where there is substantial disequilibrium, it may take several days (*séances*) or weeks before all orders are cleared.

13

THE DEVELOPMENT OF FINANCIAL STRATEGY AND ACCOUNTABILITY AROUND QUOTATION

Roger Buckland and Edward W. Davis

INTRODUCTION

This chapter addresses two specific issues which might be argued to be at the core of the status change at first quotation of the firm's equity: the evolution of corporate governance, and the maturation of the management systems (including financial systems and controls) of the firm. This research forms part of a study sponsored by the Economic and Social Research Council (ESRC), of the financing behaviour and characteristics of newly quoted firms in the United Kingdom; it follows upon a survey-based study of all new entrants to the London Stock Exchange markets between 1980 and 1985, as reported in Buckland and Davis (1989). The second-stage research reported here, however, utilises 40 case studies of newly quoted firms which have also featured in Chapter 9 of this book. It follows a methodological approach now commonplace in research in finance and accounting, as it has long been in other aspects of business research (Jones 1992; Ryan et al. 1992; Scapens 1990, 1992). The processes by which systems of corporate governance evolve and are developed have attracted increasing attention (Cadbury 1992, for example). This first concern relates to the novel principal–agent relationships erected by outside shareholders and stock exchange oversight (concern expressed in, for example, Charkham 1989; Bank of England 1988; Tricker 1984). The second concern stems from the process of corporate maturation. The mid-sized firm is well known to face difficult periods when its management is mutating from the 'Type I', or entrepreneurial focus, to 'Type II' (functional or professionalised management), as well as any transition between

Type II and a 'Type III' (divisionalised) entity (see, for example, Brandt 1981: pp. 7ff; and Kuhn 1989: pp. 114–15). Quotation triggers a change in the firm's ownership, previously intertwined with management, to that of a new and more complex relationship: with the increase in public obligations and oversight, management must now report and answer to an additional set of principals. The typical newly quoted firm is seeking to sustain a strategy for continued abnormal growth, but it needs to communicate with and demonstrate this to a set of new and more remote principals.

The difficulties of development of financial and management control systems have been long recognised as a research issue (for example in Carsberg and Hope 1976 and Ray and Hutchinson 1983). Jones's empirical work (1985, 1992) stands out as contributing to our understanding of linkages between status changes and control issues. In this research it is apparent, from 40 completed case investigations, already cited in previous chapters, that the quotation process in the early 1980s did not assure investors, or the firms themselves, that financial and management systems had been effectively matured in ways that would promote the development of the business's organisation and the formulation of its strategy. Much case material suggests immaturity in financial and management control, and that immaturity persisted beyond quotation.

This suggests that the procedures for conditioning and reviewing entrants' financial and management systems at quotation are deficient, attending primarily to purely financial reporting rather than providing an assurance of management quality in the conduct of the firm's future financial performance.

SAMPLING FOR QUALITATIVE STUDY

The population

Firms were drawn from the comprehensive Buckland and Davis database of USM and OL entrants in the period between 1980 and 1985, as already described in Chapter 9. The nature of respondents and their firms is summarised in Table 13.1.

Methodological concerns in sampling

Several issues arise here. First, it is crucial in conducting longitudinal research on newly quoted firms to establish access to those

Table 13.1 Case status and respondent function

	Unlisted securities market	*Official list*	*All*
Continuing in market	5	6	11
Moved to OL	5		5
Taken over	9	14	23
In receivership/liquidation	1	0	1
Total	20	20	40
Founder shareholder/chairman/ chief executive officer	6	7	13
Finance director now[a] and at quotation	5	4	9
Finance director[b] now	9	7	16
Other director[c]		2	2
Total	20	20	40

[a] Includes 1 financial controller (OL)
[b] Includes 3 financial controllers (OL)
[c] One corporate affairs director in OL company; one non-executive director of (OL) business services company, since taken over by business now in receivership.

firms which have 'died' subsequently. The rate of attrition is very substantial. More than half this sample had died through take-over prior to being researched. Four of the businesses accessed were in receivership (three following take-over). In the USM, only 25 per cent of the sample remained in that segment: five transfers to the official list had occurred (all OL transfers retained independent quotes in that segment); of nine entrants taken over (to date), all but two were taken over within five years of entry. In the official list, overall attrition rates are very similar, but arise wholly from take-over in these cases. Of the fourteen firms taken over to date, nine had been lost within five years.

EVIDENCE ON DEVELOPMENT OF FINANCIAL AND MANAGERIAL CONTROL

In addressing the investment and financial management process within newly quoted firms we have been conscious that our original objectives, of examining the adoption of and attitudes towards traditional and 'new-technology' investment criteria, have been overtaken by the characteristics identified from the data. Methodologically, it is undesirable as well as difficult to control interview data on a subject as specific as investment appraisal, when the subject is enfolded within other key financial and managerial issues, and where respondents are not specifically selected for their detailed competence in or knowledge of that aspect of corporate affairs. Few respondents gave prominence to capital budgeting techniques in accounting for the development of their financial control systems around quotation: still fewer placed any emphasis on specific techniques such as Discounted Cash Flow. In this, of course, they reflect the findings of repeated survey research on the use of positive financial-management techniques in business: the informality of approach as well as the absence of rigorous application of 'correct' appraisal (Sangster 1992).

Corporate governance – imperfect adaptation to quotation

In the development of the business around quotation the governance of the firm is being reoriented, to strengthen the position of passive, external investors and to enable a dispersed community of investors to participate in the financing of the business. Trust-formation is central to the formation of these agency relationships, which will be crucial in the long-term survival of the growing firm. Arrangements for quotation are themselves bound together with the production and establishment of trust: either institutionally, by the issue of the prospectus and assurance of quality within a stock exchange (Neu 1991a, 1991b); or character-based trust (Zucker 1986). Governance, and the perception of directors' character and attributes, are used in prospectuses to establish these trust relationships between manager–agents and the new community of outsider investor–principals.

Prior to quotation, the corporate governance of the business is primarily determined by the presence of dominant owner–managers, often holding majority shareholdings in the business. Boards of directors are compact, often without explicit functional responsibility or external membership. There are isolated cases of firms with different characteristics: there are businesses which have been spun off from parents, in attempts to realise the value locked up in inappropriate organisational forms; the samples include a large privatised oil-exploration business; in the USM entrants, one firm was previously a subsidiary of a quoted business. There are also businesses whose pre-quotation development has been supported within a venture-capital framework: two electronics businesses revealed this, while several others had had significant institutional shareholdings prior to entry.

Most newly quoted firms are still being directed and managed by the people who established the firm: generational succession may be one factor in motivation for quotation. Founder–shareholders are a crucial element in entrants' governance: 27 of these 40 firms had a board of directors chaired by a founder–shareholder; in 24 cases the founder combined the roles of chairman and chief executive. There was no great difference between segments here: executive chairmen (there were no female chairmen) were equally split between USM and OL; in the official list, three further founders had taken a non-executive role. In fact, the OL firms showed rather higher numbers of founder–directors: 44 compared to 34 in the USM. USM boards were, however, likely to be somewhat smaller than those for OL entrants: Table 13.2 shows how board sizes were distributed, with higher numbers of executive members for the OL sample.

Table 13.2 Boards of directors at quotation (numbers of members)

Executive	*<4*	*4*	*5*	*6*	*>6*
Official list	5	4	2	4	4
USM	9	4	2	2	3

Non-executive	*0*	*1*	*2*	*>2*
Official list	2	6	7	5[a]
USM	3	10	3	3[b]

Total board	*<5*	*5*	*6*	*7*	*8*	*>8*
Official list	3	4	5	2	0	6
USM	6	5	1	2	3	3

[a] Includes 1 television company
[b] Includes 1 television company, 1 radio company

As has been recognised in the Cadbury Report (1992), non-executives on boards of directors can be one key element in trust formation vis-à-vis outsider investors. The role of the non-executive is, first, to provide board input from an external, alternative perspective, bringing expertise from other established firms. Second, where the firm moves to quotation and gains outsider equity investors, the non-executive can take an 'outsider' position within the board, safeguarding the interests of these new principals when set against the power and insider knowledge of the founders and management.

Most entrants had at least one non-executive director prior to entry: only five firms had none. However, for half of the USM sample there was only one non-executive on the board; and in addition nearly half of USM entrants had less than four executive members. This does not provide the complete picture, however. Certainly, in some cases, non-executive members had been appointed very recently, and explicitly in relation to impending quotation. Many respondents recounted the advice from sponsors, issuing houses and brokers to 'strengthen' non-executive board representation at the time of entry:

> Martin said, 'We've got to have a chairman, if we're going to be a public company we've got to have a chairman.' So, I don't know where he went, but we interviewed three actually, and one of them said he was fed up of going shopping for his wife, carrying the basket, and he wanted to do something else, another one fell asleep, he'd been chairman of a very big public company, and the other one was, you know, the other one, so, we said, 'Take him.'

This light-hearted expression of the style, rather than the substance, of non-executive representation was reflected throughout the cases. It was more apparent in the OL sample than among the USM firms: two-thirds of all non-executive members on OL entrants' boards had been appointed less than a year before entry, while a half of USM non-executives had been in place over two years. There is here evidence that newly quoted firms were being conditioned for entry by introducing non-executive board representation, a process which has now become mandatory for listed companies, following the Cadbury Committee Code of Practice (Cadbury 1992). Several

Table 13.3 Entrants' non-executive directors

	Time as director			*Previous experience*								
	<1yr	*1–2 years*	*>2yrs*	*Firm*	*Fam*^{y}	*Ins*^{t}	*Bank*	*Br*^{kr}	*Acc*^{y}	*plc*	*ltd*	*Other*
OL	30	5	10	5	1	10	6	2	1	8	7	10
USM	15	4	22	4	1	7	3	1	3	13	0	14

Legend: Fam^{y} = family member; Ins^{t} = representative of institutional shareholder; Br^{kr} = worked as stockbroker; Acc^{y} = professional accountant firms had identified quotation as a consequence of input from non-executives, too:

> We decided to recruit a non-executive chairman. The guy they approached ... said 'Yes, I'll come and join you but I'm not joining a private company, it must be a public company'; and that's how it all came about, because the first thing that everybody said was 'What's the USM?' and it all went from there.

Table 13.3 also gives some important information on non-executive directors' backgrounds. A small number were ex-managers and/or family members. Institutional shareholders constitute a major source, especially where there has been venture-capitalist involvement pre-quotation. This attention to the venture-capitalist interest also applies to individual 'Aunt Agathas' or 'business angels': private risk capital investors in the company who have been involved in financing its growth without direct participation in management. There the director is likely to have been involved in the early direction of the firm, and to have management experience in other public limited companies. It is clear that even in these most visibly successful growth small firms of the 1980s there were very few influential 'business angels': a position which the 1993 March budget sought to address through its provision for roll-over of Capital Gains Tax liability (see also, for example, Harrison and Mason 1993b and Chapter 5 in this volume). OL entrants were more likely to have representation from their merchant bank on the board, and more likely to have directors with experience of firms in related business activity (here long-standing non-executive appointments were mainly directors of other, private limited, companies in similar businesses).

Entrants' chairmen were predominantly drawn from the founder–shareholders, the entrepreneurial centre of the businesses. In Table 13.4 it can be seen that this was true in both market segments: indeed there was a slight bias towards company founders in the sample of bigger, OL entrants. The proportions of non-executive chairmen were identical in the two samples, at 40 per cent of the totals.

Present conventional wisdom on governance suggests that combining the roles of chairman with that of chief executive officer is unwise (Cadbury 1992: Interim Report; Kay 1992; for example). Here, the majority of new entrants were led by men who combined the two roles as the firm moved into quoted status. The argument developed in the Interim Report of the Cadbury Commit-

Table 13.4 The chairmen of newly quoted businesses

	Chair/CEO[a]	*Founder*	*Non-executive*	
			<1 year	*>1 year*
Official list	12	15	2	6
USM	12	12	2	6

[a] Combined post of chairman and chief executive officer

tee was that the dual role and responsibility lead to an over-concentration of power. In the context of new quotation, the danger is that there may not be full recognition of the novel responsibilities of the board to outsider, public investors. The continuity of executive chairman suggests a potential hazard for the entrant: control structures for the business may not be reappraised and the 'Type I' hierarchical, entrepreneurial leadership characteristic of rapid-growth small businesses might persist unchallenged. Respondents were asked to report on this aspect of their histories, and there were several cases where it was explicitly suggested that the direction of firms had suffered. One large and successful equipment lease broker was described as 'an entrepreneurial, marketing, sales-led company that was dreadfully managed'. In another, a computer equipment company, the entrepreneurial style persisted long after the shift to quoted status and responsibilities:

> [The company] was entrepreneurial to the end. I mean, [the chairman] was very entrepreneurial. It never really got to be a professionally managed company until [the take-over]. It was very entrepreneurial, and run by entrepreneurs.

and:

> The MD was the founder of the organisation. He was still trying to apply what was a start-up operation management stance to a much larger organisation, and not really perceiving as organisations become bigger they do need some sort of bureaucracy, some sort of financial control.

The development of planning and the long form report

Maturation of the organisation may be seen as closely linked to professionalisation of management and of corporate planning. In the Stock Exchange's Listing Agreement (or General Undertaking, for the USM) and in the rigorous accountants' examinations in the Long Form Report newly quoted firms are intended to review and revise their procedures and practices in order to assure investors of sound management: a classic attempt to anticipate and resolve new agency problems. One of the strongest threads running through these cases is the naivety of strategic planning, accompanied by failures of control, reappraisal, and revision of business strategy. This is in turn associated with the weakness of mechanisms to review strategy formation and implementation as businesses move into markets and into a size class where the previous centralised (and informal) control of the entrepreneur is unable to cope with the demands of the organisation and its activity. There are aspects of simple management failure in this, as expressed by one respondent:

> Once they floated the company, we were entering a different ball game, with different skills needed to manage it. No longer is the business actually driven by entrepreneurial flair, it needs to be driven by professional management, to the standard the Stock Market required. So maybe you needed to introduce another layer of management who would say, 'OK, you go and do wonderful things out there, we will take what we need from you, and make sure the Stock Market get their standard 15 per cent growth per annum on their investment, and anything else you give us we will just keep in the balance sheet, and when you get one wrong, we will balance the books for you', basically. They never really introduced that level of management.

Failure to recognise the requirements of changed status was accompanied in many cases by strategic failure. Entrepreneurs attempted to transfer 'proven' strategies to new markets (a trait particularly evident in expansion into US markets); and almost universally such new entrants found that such 'strategy' did not transfer with any great success, leading to a dissipation of resources and often to the eventual take-over of the firm.

The issue was not clear-cut, however. There are exceptional firms in this sample, where the pre-quotation management culture was already professionalised and where the business was already moving into a 'Type II' functional and professionalised structure. One example is that of a software business joining the OL, where its founder and executive chairman recounted in detail the considered strategy leading up to the decision to obtain a stock exchange quotation:

> All the way through we had mission statements. The mission, well, mission statement in 1969 was written down as to become the top real-time software house in the UK ... So you either keep as a smaller company, which is nice and secure and, job for the rest of your lives, and that kind of stuff, or you take the other route. And after a lot of debate we decided to take the other route [quotation].

In this case quotation was a stage in the maturing of the business, which was driven by five-year strategic plans, cast in financial terms and specifying markets, strategies, control factors and budgets.

That respondent was the exception rather than the rule. Quotation was indeed part of adopted strategy in other entrants. One brewer came to the USM after restructuring its business and reorienting its strategy: the USM was selected to maintain independence from the banking system and to permit the founder family to exit from management succession. A fast-growing design business saw quotation (first USM, then OL) as one key element of its expansion strategy. Through quotation the founder wished to achieve rapid growth through acquisition, and was prepared to accept the disciplines of quotation in doing so.

Another OL entrant, in engineering, came to the market after two years' planning, having searched for a non-executive, City chairman. For that company, however, quotation itself was the strategy, and it is this weakness that repeatedly strikes through the analysis of respondents' views. Management views quotation as an objective in itself, rather than as a risky, if potentially important, change of status. In drawing the distinction, one comes to the heart of the 'Type I'–'Type II' transition. In the entrepreneurial firm, quotation is not a natural component of the entrepreneur's strategy, because it strikes counter to the spirit of entrepreneurship. The quoted business takes on prime responsibilities to public stakeholders, while the entrepreneur maintains accountability only to him- or herself; if the entrepreneur holds and pursues a strategic view, a mission, it is not necessary to the firm's success or operation that the strategy be shared or co-owned. In the professionalised firm, on the other hand, the management team is collective in nature, and thus the transmission, challenge and justification of plans and information are entrenched in the management culture. Given the necessary acceptance of sharing the development of strategy in such a context, it is simpler to graft external stakeholders and responsibilities upon it.

Where the firm was as yet uncommitted to transition, the process of entry and adjustment to quotation would always be difficult in management terms. Where quotation itself constitutes the strategy, the business adjusts its control mechanisms only as directed by the market. As one (now taken-over) firm's finance director put it:

> [Quotation] did have some impact, in that the company appointed a non-executive director who was well-known to the City, and there were some disciplines. The company had to be more careful about what it did, what it announced to the press, how it faced the world externally, but I think the actual way that it was run, I don't believe it did have any impact whatsoever ... Disciplines weren't there, systems weren't changed and understood, information wasn't made available. I think it's, the outward-facing relationship with investors and Stock Exchange can be managed, but I think in this case there was very little substance behind it. Bullshitting the public, for want of a better word.

Such an entrant adopts procedures in line with the International Stock Exchange Quotation Committee regulations and arranges its affairs such that the Long Form Report from its auditors is acceptable. It has no rationale for reform of management control other than these formulae, and so one finds newly quoted firms introducing sophistication and key personnel in conventional finance-related areas while remaining unreflective and weak in others. This can be seen clearly in the people appointed to functional posts within newly quoted companies' boards. The single greatest pressure on corporate governance at quotation is to show strength of financial systems. A key concern is to have a 'qualified' head of the finance function: in fact the bulk of these samples did have finance directors on their boards at entry.

The Long Form Report prescribes an audited examination of entrants' systems of financial reporting and control; it is the locus of formal review of the firm's management quality. These respondents confirm that new quotation throws a searchlight upon control issues. Respondents associated the impetus for such development with quotation, and have an image of the business as attaining 'maturity'; but it is apparent that the instigators – and to a large extent, the shapers – of this restructuring of management function are the advisers and accountants to the firm at the time.

This is a point of some importance, since it is the classic expertise of the accounting-oriented auditor/adviser that defines the scope and penetration of the revision of management systems accomplished at quotation. Respondents accentuate the introduction of 'proper', or comprehensive, monthly financial reporting; the introduction of management control systems; the appointment of professionally qualified staff. It is clear from Table 13.5 that quotation and impending quotation brought qualified accounting-trained personnel into the finance function for most new entrants, in many cases for the first time. For several firms in this sample, quotation was the time at which hitherto chaotic internal accounting controls were first addressed; most attributed their current sophistication of control to the trigger of quotation and the rigours of conforming with the Long Form Report required by the London Stock Exchange Quotations Committee.

Table 13.5a The finance directors of newly quoted businesses

	None	*CEO*	*Time in post*[a]			
			<1 year	*1 year*	*2 years*	*>2 years*
Official list	1	1	7	0	1	12
USM	7[b]	2	7	0	1	9

[a] Where given in issue prospectus
[b] There were 3 non-executive FDs, 1 part-time FD

Table 13.5b Finance directors' qualifications and experience

	Qualified as:			*Previous experience:*			
	CA	*CCA*	*CMA*	*plc*	*ltd*	*acc*[y]	*bank*
Official list	15	1	1	6	4	8	1
USM	10	2	1	6	3	8	1

Legend: CA = chartered accountant; CCA = certified accountant; CMA = cost and management accountant

> With a public company coming along, we had to tighten a lot of controls and systems, and to be honest, before I arrived I felt that there was a lack of control, there was no qualified accountant in the place before I arrived, and therefore certain information that I regarded as fairly vital was lacking.
>
> How did flotation affect the company's controls? I guess they certainly increased them. And sort of part of that was that I had been recruited: prior to flotation, the company had gone through the classic, growing company, periodically bursting at the seams, in management control terms, particularly in the manufacturing area, which was where I was brought in.

On the other hand, respondents defined this reappraisal and maturation as one of control in score-keeping and 'keeping the finger on the pulse' of the firm: there was no concept of new quotation as a rite of passage in terms of non-financial systems/controls. Many respondents were explicit about this, and when interviews addressed the histories of manifest weakness in the generation, planning, and control or audit of corporate strategy it was commonplace for respondents to make clear that quotation had had little impact upon the development of these key maturational fields for the growing firm.

> In terms of actual management of the business and so on, the impact was very low.'
>
> That tends to address sort of mechanical issues rather than the board control of the operations of the company ... one stands and looks at what kinds of things could be done to improve the financial controls within a company. The flotation produced a lot more focus on short-term financial controls.
>
> Q: So there's a revolution, if you like, in the recording and record-keeping? A: Oh yeah. Q: How about other aspects of management, control of your personnel or your marketing or strategic planning or whatever? A: Didn't affect anything like that, that came later, I think.

We find it significant that professionalisation of financial control and management was not matched by any observable shift in other key functional areas. We expected to find evidence in these transitional organisations of a shift between 'left-' and 'right-handed' organisations: the spectrum of emphasis on marketing as opposed to financial control in the business (Doyle and Hooley 1991). Instead, we can report only a general absence of professionalised marketing, with a consequent asymmetry towards financial control in the organisation. While many businesses regarded themselves as 'marketing-led', this invariably reduced to entrepreneurial, intuitive exploitation of market opportunities: a reflection of the case firm's present dominance of their market segment. As Table 13.6 demonstrates, the formal marketing skills and relevant marketing experience in these entrants, at board level, compares poorly with the recruitment of accounting expertise during their accession to quotation.

This image, of the entrant's non-financial systems running through the period of management audit represented by the Long Form Report, recurs again and again. Respondents variously paid lip-service to the creation of financial controls, or they upgraded the financial reporting without attending to other functional aspects. The key once again is whether the firm was making the transition from a Type I to a Type II enterprise: whether the culture remained

Table 13.6a The marketing directors of newly quoted businesses

	None	*CEO*	*Time in post*			
			<1 year	*1 year*	*2 years*	*>2 years*
Official list	11	0	2	0	1	6
USM	7[a]	2	3	0	2	9

[a] Less 1, where there was a marketing director designated at quote

Table 13.6b Marketing directors' qualifications and experience

	Qualified as:		*Previous experience:*		
	MIM	*Other*	*plc*	*ltd*	*other*
Official list	1	4	2	3	2
USM	1	2	8	1	1

Note: MIM = member, institute of marketing

one of entrepreneurial derring-do, or of shared allegiance to a formulated strategy:

> The fact that they survived the [financial] difficulties was, if you like, fortunate that they'd been persuaded or had the wit to put in financial management controls at the time. The thing is that it didn't, putting the people in and putting the systems in didn't automatically change them as people. It seemed as though they had to run into some difficulties.

> The company has always been very, very entrepreneurial, and very much against controls, Very much open door policy, people could be trusted, people given marketing freedom and flair and creativity, opportunities to attack the market. In fact been very much opposed to financial management.

> [The firm] has never been very formal. It didn't get any more formal after [quotation]. I think there was a realisation that we had to be a little bit more formal, but it never actually got to formal business planning. Certainly we were driven to it in '85, '86 [with the collapse of the US subsidiary].

The contrast with the quotation of Type II firms is acute:

> Q: Do I sense that becoming listed made very little difference to you? A: Yes. None at all, none at all. We didn't change a thing. And I mean I could show you some of the, some strategic plans, it was always a five-year look ahead financially in round, a one-year look ahead in detail, which markets we were going in to, how we were going to get in to those markets, what the key control factors were going to be.

By mapping the 40 case companies onto the Type I/II axis of corporate structure, we can gain a broader view of the place of quotation in the maturation of these growing businesses. Table 13.7 presents the results of this mapping. The majority of newly quoted businesses in this sample were Type I, entrepreneurial firms, where strategy was initiated, assessed and implemented from the key (normally the founder) management. There were notable numbers of entrants whose organisations had moved beyond that stage of organisational development, particularly amongst official list entrants. There we examined one firm which had returned to quotation after a previous quoted passage that had ended in merger (it had at the time of the research again been subsumed in another

Table 13.7 Development of management control and strategy

	Pre-quotation		*Post-quotation*					
	Type I	*Post-entr.*[a]	*Point of transition:*				*Type II*	
			Pre-quote	*At quote*	*Post-quote*	*Stuck*	*Entr.*[a]	*Team*
Official list	10	7	8	3	1	5	5	7
USM	14	4	4	4	5	5	6	5

[a] Insufficient classification data on 3 official list firms, 2 USM firms.

Notes:

1. Type I' organisations correspond to the entrepreneurial model, 'Type II' to the functional model; after Kuhn (1989: p. 114).
2. Entry under 'point of transition' locates respondents' views of where the stimulus for any shift from Type I form was experienced; 'stuck' organisations are those which have not (by the time of research) broken out of their entrepreneurial form.
3. Type II organisations are divided according to the establishment of a functional team which plans and manages strategy, or the hierarchical command of management and strategic control by the continuing entrepreneur(s).

merger, with a business that was subsequently to pass into receivership). There was one large privatised business with professionalised management structures, but also five others where organisation had already passed into a transitional, or even wholly 'Type II' phase.

There were fewer examples of this in USM entrants: there was one reorganisation and requote of a broadcasting business; but here also there were isolated cases (two) of firms where management had been professionalised and strategic controls and procedures erected: once following crisis and near-bankruptcy, only once as conscious preparation for business growth and evolution.

More striking is the evidence that quoted firms can remain locked into Type I structures, with the associated restrictions on information flows, accountability and responsibility. Five OL entrants as well as five USM firms remained locked into that form, with little development even of financial control systems and a reliance upon discretionary, entrepreneurial management. All five such organisations in the OL sample had been taken over (three were now involved in receivership and voluntary liquidation); three of those in the USM had also been taken over, with the remaining two in severe financial crises at the time of the research.

The trigger for functional transition

This evidence upon the trigger for transition to professionalised, Type II structures highlights that large numbers of these entrants passed through the quotation process without being required to review and reform their management systems. Where transition had taken place, OL entrants appear to prepare for it prior to quotation: by careful attention to managerial systems, personnel and professionalism in strategy formulation and review. Thus eight of seventeen classifiable OL firms prepared their firms for quotation in such ways. For another three, quotation itself was the spur to reorganisation. In the USM sample, by contrast, in addition to the five businesses locked into a Type I structure, a further five were propelled out of it by business crises subsequent to quotation.

This could arise from the spectacular failure of a significant investment, such as in one case where the management attempted to transplant a successful domestic business strategy into the alien US context: having devoted some hundreds of millions of the business's cash to this adventure, the impact of this (relatively simple) strategic error forced the business into cash crises, attracted hostile take-over bids, and resulted in the business being absorbed into a 'white knight' friendly take-over (itself seen as a strategic mismatch both by respondents and by financial markets). In this sample, such poorly appraised overseas adventures were common, and almost universally damaging for the business in their outcomes. Or it might be that the search for quoted status, the 'maturity' label of stock exchange presence, resulted in the grafting on of expert financial controls to a business which was entrepreneurial and opportunistic in its (non-quoted) existence. In one such case, while quotation failed to provide a strategic plan to progress the firm into any Type II or Type III existence, it did float a cash-rich company into a position where the short-term fluctuations of earnings in its narrow product market left it prone to a succession of take-overs by financial conglomerates.

The potential for disruption and even catastrophe in strategic development is well known in such conditions. The benefits of the historic strengths in entrepreneurship may be lost, or become inappropriate: 'Companies do not set out to lose entrepreneurship ... the loss of entrepreneurship occurs gradually' (Stevenson and Jarillo-Mossi 1986). Kuhn (1989: p. 204) stresses: 'Organisations, like people, have mid-life crises ... What matters is *structure*: how the company is set up, who reports to whom, what the organisational chart looks like, the kinds of positions running the place' and 'The time of transformation often occurs at both ends of the medium-sized spectrum, first when the firm is maturing out of its entrepreneurial stage and next when the firm is establishing its large organisational posture'.

It would seem to be a matter of pragmatic necessity, then, for quotation to address these issues. On the contrary, respondents described the quotation process as addressing them only indirectly, from a financial perspective. It was commonplace to find respondents describing strategic planning failure in the post-quotation period, where management had been 'legitimised' by the quoted status of the firm, but they remained unprofessional in terms of leading the business through the post-entrepreneurial phase in its development. Cases where strategy and non-financial management systems were thoroughly addressed were notable first by their infrequency – there were arguably only a handful of these 40 firms where management at quotation demonstrated conscious attention to strategy issues – and second in that most respondents ascribed any attention to strategy as arising quite independently of quotation.

One respondent, after describing in detail the long-standing attention to forward strategic planning and review within his business, expressed amazement that we should find his account untypical. However, the evidence is that the active strategic stance within his company long pre-dated quotation (although quotation itself was an element in strategic planning from the outset), and that it had been seen as an essential element of professional management of the business at all stages, not simply one occasioned by the review of the management process at the stage of quotation.

CONCLUSION: STRATEGIC UNFITNESS IN UK NEWLY QUOTED FIRMS

Our research reported here highlights the key role of management systems review at the time of entry to quoted status. Not only are firms taking on crucial new groups of investor–principals, not only are they exposing their future to the influence of outsider–investors' judgement and sentiment, but they are also, typically, fast-growth businesses close to the point in their lives where they should mutate from one organisational type to another. The experience of failed 'star' companies in the late 1980s suggests strongly that company boards should be strong enough and management professionalised enough to carry the newly quoted firm through to independent existence. The evidence is that the entry procedures of the London Stock Exchange fail to assure investors that entrants are likely to be well equipped.

It is apparent that newly quoted firms' outcomes, in terms of their survival, the success of their strategies, the continuation of their growth, are associated with their development of managerial systems. Most respondents describe their pre-quotation businesses as having a culture of success, which promoted management slack: the firm was cash-generative, it was achieving and sustaining high rates of growth, and there was little or no external discipline to exert close managerial control. Often respondents associated the firm's success with the entrepreneurial freedom (or licence) that such margins allowed. The tendency was then for the business to career onwards, riding initially through commercial difficulties through the presence of cash and the self-confidence of successful entrepreneurs, until the strategic issues were highlighted by a crisis.

Such instances serve to point up the absence of attention to what might be termed 'strategic fitness' in candidates for quotation. The review of their systems by advisers, and the analysis of their prospects by analysts, do not attend to issues beyond the financial control sphere, or beyond the short-term financial prospects of the firm. Such attention as is paid – the search for non-executive influence on boards of newly quoted firms, the regard of management systems in the Long Form Report – were not regarded as significant, disciplined, or even useful by respondents. In retrospect, at quotation the firm is seen as passing through a crucial developmental phase: professionalising its management and coping with complexity and maturity in its environment. Yet quotation complicates that process still further by adding powerful new external interest groups, without either forcing attention to procedures whereby the maturational problems can be anticipated or overcome, or linking the new external forces to co-operative, participative assistance in management.

14

CONCLUSION

Roger Buckland and Edward W. Davis

In our final, concluding, chapter we provide a summary of the findings of our various authors, setting their work within the wider context of that of other studies on small-firm financial behaviour. In the overall picture, contemporary themes of short-termism, finance gaps, stress on financing structures and financial market innovation, of bankers' practices and policies towards small firms are common threads. In the context of financial developments, the contributions of this book relate to the dominant triple themes of contemporary finance: liberalisation, securitisation and internationalisation. In academic terms, the models whereby these issues have been illuminated are dominated by contemporary advances in information theory and the analysis of agency relationships between firms and their sources of finance.

GAPS: MARKET FAILURE AS IT AFFECTS GROWING FIRMS

A failure of supply or of demand?

The chapter by Bovaird, Hems and Tricker, Chapter 2, linked evidence of market failure in financing small-firm expansion with the offsetting advantages to be derived from the use of consultants. Their crucial observation is that the barriers to emergent enterprises, which can be inferred from skewed patterns of financing, are as much a failure of entrepreneurs – of their demands for appropriate financing assets and for relevant consultancy services – as they are indicative of any failure on the part of the financial community to supply finance. Their research is primarily concerned with smaller-scale firms, at the point of development where critical financing gaps have been adduced in the past. However, the finding is not without relevance also to those larger businesses which, having obtained a stock exchange quotation, remain essentially family businesses with associated underdeveloped managerial systems.

The first hurdle to be faced by the smaller firm is that of raising external capital. Most small firms, but especially fast-growth firms, are more vulnerable due to financial constraints. These constrain their ability to withstand short-term business difficulties and periods of adverse cash flows. Particularly in the UK, the most accessible source of finance is that provided by the firms' clearing banks, with the form of such borrowing usually based upon the traditional overdraft. Fast-growth firms' need for capital, however, is more likely to require additional 'permanent' or longer-term capital rather than just an increased overdraft: that should generally be regarded as working-capital finance. In Chapters 3 and 4 of this book the authors explicitly address the role of banks, and the studies reported here again suggest that one should be wary of blaming the suppliers of funds for the reluctance displayed by small firms' owners and managers in transforming their growing businesses into mature organisations, capable of withstanding the pressures and tensions inherent in the growth process.

Borrowing from the bank is particularly attractive to small firms in part because of the lower transactions costs involved, but also because of the preference (indicated, for example, through the pecking-order hypothesis) for using debt, even in a relatively unstable form, rather than to dilute equity or yield control by taking on additional investors as shareholders. The risks of interest-rate exposure and credit rationing are therefore preferred to that of yielding of control. Here, Binks and Ennew illuminate the essential problem. British deposit banks traditionally mount their lending on a secured asset backing, based primarily on the balance sheet. That approach is, of course, one of long standing in the UK (see, for example, Nevin and Davis 1971); but it has undeniably been reinforced by the experience of the severe recession of the late 1980s and early 1990s. Then, for the banks to do otherwise carried considerable risks of expansion of their bad debts. In this sense, therefore, the growing small firm, outstripping its own corporate and its owners' capacity to generate cash to meet its longer- (or even its shorter-) term capital requirement, may well find that its balance-sheet asset base falls far short of securing sufficient capital to meet its prospective cash-flow requirement. Rather than grasp the nettle of financial restructuring, entrepreneurs often elect to curtail the potential for further independent growth.

Another key characteristic of the finance available from firms' clearing banks is that the banker possesses timely, privileged information about the financial solvency and stability of the borrowers. This arguably permits a low-cost resolution of the contractual problems, the assurance and bonding costs, entailed in providing the firm with finance; and there may be 'gaps' and difficulties involved in supplanting that contract with another, drawn up with 'outsiders'. This is a particular concern when there is a switch from a lender–borrower relationship, with firm promise of a schedule of money returns to the lender, to one of equity participation, where the investors must construct and inform their expectations of future returns.

Gaps in finance, in institutions, or in information?

Chapter 5 by Harrison and Mason suggests that, while the supply and scale of venture-capital investment has increased, the nature of the market is such that the small firm requiring equity capital from such a source is subject to just such an information gap. While information about the institutional venture-capital markets' services to the small-growth firm has become much more developed, given the build-up of specialist intermediaries within the UK since 1970 and particularly in the 1980s, the requirements of the external investor mean that only a relatively small proportion of firms will be able, or will want, to meet their requirements. This is especially true in relation to the manner and timing of investors' exits from their investments. A particular concern, also highlighted by Murray in Chapter 6, illustrates the difficulty of obtaining seed capital for new investment, an experience not confined to the UK but evident elsewhere in Europe. It is hardly surprising, therefore, to find that bank borrowing is the most regularly used source of finance by growing small firms.

One effect of this has been that the UK venture-capital market has converged, not on the supply of finance to emergent, growth small firms, but on the provision of financing for the restructuring of existing businesses through management buy-outs and buy-ins. The proportions of 'venture' capitalists' funding devoted to small, independent enterprises is seen in Murray's work to be in chronic decline, driven by the relative certainties of exit routes from buy-outs and buy-ins and by perceptions of high failure rates and transitional organisational hazards faced by the truly small firm during its maturation. Indeed, the contemporary perception in the UK is that the existing institutional framework for venture capital provides adequately for firms' requirements of under £1 million and above (see, for example, the comments by Tulloch 1994). Attention is being focused on the key smaller firms through skewed taxation incentives ('Venture Capital Trusts', benefiting from capital-gains tax relief), and through accentuation of stronger local and regional dimensions to venture-capital funds (Robbie and Wright 1994). These attempt to securitise the financing problem, through a collectivisation of speculative and venture investment within funds that themselves constitute tradable investments for individuals: thereby circumventing one of the venture capitalist's sticking points, when illiquid investments in unquoted equities cannot be realised. This function of the intermediary investment fund is joined by economies in information. Information is, however, problematic in a different way: the growing firm and the eager venture capitalist may never make contact, or realise the existence of a match between investor and investee. Harrison and Mason uncover, in their path-breaking investigation of informal venture capital, evidence that information networks can impact upon the provision of risk finance to the growing enterprise, rivalling the efforts of financial institutions. The experience of the US informal venture-capital industry suggests that there is scope for mobilisation of significant 'new' venture capital for the emergent enterprise within Europe, based upon closure of this particular information gap.

Keasey and Watson indicate from their research in Chapter 4 that UK banks played a large role in financing the expansion of the small firms investigated by them during the six years to 1990. Indeed, short-term bank borrowing by these firms increased in importance over this period, to the extent that by 1990 the banks' stake in funding small firms almost equalled the book value of their equity capital. This was an unhealthy financial structure for firms in the UK, about to experience severe recession. Keasey and Watson find that the most common contractual solution adopted by the banks to reduce their risk exposure is to offer primarily short-term, frequently reviewed loans and overdrafts, secured on the personal estate of the small-firm owner–manager. A significant proportion (42 per cent) of the 100 firms investigated by Keasey and Watson were family-based, so that failure of the family business would forfeit not only net worth invested in that but family personal assets, given the banks' right of recourse to that property.

INTERNATIONAL EXPERIENCE OF SMALL-FIRM FINANCE

The overriding impression derived by Keasey and Watson is that eligible small firms were not being denied bank finance. The evidence does not support the view of discriminatory behaviour by bank lending officers. The nub of the problem is the overdependence on short-term debt by such firms in the UK; and their failure to attract sufficient longer-term capital, particularly equity, with which to ensure adequate funding in subsequent periods of severe recession. This is one structural reflection of the characteristic dichotomisation of financial provision to companies in the UK: the financial institutions are reluctant to assume a role in corporate governance, preferring to rely upon either contractual lending contracts, bonded by security and covenants over borrowers' behaviour, or on discipline via the threat of acquisition and take-over. The latter skews the equity involvement of institutions towards enterprises which are, or are close to being, exposed to the corporate-control market via the stock exchange. The former promotes reliance upon arm's-length contracting and a lack of participation in or understanding of the business and its prospects, often construed as and described by 'short-termism'.

A revealing comparison may be derived from the experience of other countries. The much greater dependence within 739 UK small companies on overdraft finance, at 58 per cent of total debt, compared with 31 per cent for France, 35 per cent for Italy and 14 per cent for Germany, was highlighted by the report from Cranfield Enterprise Centre (1992). Of equal interest was the fact that the UK small companies investigated by the Centre also recorded the highest proportion of firms reporting no debt within their capital structure. In other EU countries short-term finance was provided instead to a much greater extent by short-term loans, comprising formal agreements to lend for periods of up to five years. Long-term loans (at 11 per cent of total debt for the UK) were far lower than levels recorded for France, Germany and Italy. Of particular interest must be the activity of the Kreditanstalt für Wiederaufbau, owned by the Federal Government of Germany (80 per cent) and various state governments (20 per cent). This dedicated industrial bank, the tenth largest bank in Germany, provides medium- and long-term capital through the commercial banking system, mainly to small and medium-sized businesses in manufacturing.

In other European nations, too, financial systems and institutions take a different, often more participative view towards the finance of industry and of emergent firms. In Chapter 12 by Anolli, Buckland and Dubois, examining IPOs across EU markets, these differences were highlighted in relation to markets in new equity; but they appear also in relation to bank relationships (see, for example, the overview in Cox 1986). German banks, for example, directly and indirectly control about 50 per cent of all German equities. Both in France and Germany, and in other EU nations such as Italy as well, there has historically been much greater state involvement in the provision of bank finance. The nature of the German banking relationship may also help to explain why so few German businesses had recourse to the stock exchange (Mayer 1994) at a time when successful British firms did so in much larger numbers.

Cultural differences must also be taken into account. Successful German entrepreneurs appear to regard a commitment to their local community as part of the fulfilment of their corporate roles and eschew a market quotation which may compromise that relationship. By contrast the aura of success epitomised in the UK by the USM of the 1980s and in France by the 'milliardaires' of the Second Marché would seem a fair representation of the idealised successful entrepreneur. Beyond this we may also observe, following Hughes (1994), much greater emphasis within Europe upon Mutual Guarantee Schemes (MGS) which act as guarantors of loans to small firms in several European countries. The study by the European Commission revealed that there were 286 MGS in France guaranteeing an average of 11,000 ECU of finance to specific industries, while 28 German MGS, organised regionally, guarantee on average 87,000 ECU of funding across all industrial categories. Further, in Germany (but also in the USA, with a stronger small–medium-enterprise sector), much of the banking system is itself essentially regionally based. Sponsored and subsidised regional investment funds exist to close the institutional gap between the emergent firm and its eventual investors (see, for example, Green 1986). In Britain, by contrast, we find that deposit banking, while nominally organised on a regional structure, is essentially concentrated and centralised (Middleton et al. 1994) and has in effect been so since 1918. Improvements in the quality of management education within the banks have merely further standardised existing attitudes towards small-firm lending, which may not necessarily have been to the advantage of the growth-small-firm sector.

International differences taken at their face value can be misleading. In both France and Germany there are relatively unsophisticated capital (equity) markets, coexistent with banks that have developed into suppliers of long-term as well as short-term capital. The market in corporate control is uncompetitive, with hostile take-over bids almost unknown. The twin facets of bank and equity funding cannot easily be transferred into another (UK) context, which must develop its own solutions to the funding difficulties of the growing enterprise. This may involve banks in restructuring their attitudes toward commercial lending; but, equally, they may develop novel solutions which exploit the developed strengths of the UK financial system. For example, Keith Whitson of the Midland Bank has recently described departures involving the use of options (the 'Phantom Option' over equity, repurchased by the entrepreneur at the exit point from the bank's involvement in development funding), which can draw the bank into a secure, bonded relationship without the entrepreneur needing to cede control of the equity (Whitson 1994).

THE CONTINUATION OF THE MACMILLAN GAP

The critical question now, given that the British banking system continues to favour the overdraft basis (whether due to consumer or to supplier preference), is whether innovations in UK equity markets have lowered the threshold/transactions costs of obtaining new equity capital for those firms willing to make use of them. This is critically important for founder–owners and entrepreneurs, but equally so for the informal or formal venture capitalist, who must look forward to the exit values of realising their investments in a sale of shares (or options), either at quotation or in a trade sale. The most obvious instances of financial innovation within this category are the institutional venture-capital market and the Unlisted Securities Market. Chapter 6 (Murray) and Chapters 7 to 12 in this volume examine various aspects of this critical phase in company growth, but re-examination of the 'Macmillan Gap' is a common theme across all our contributors. It is not a uniquely British phenomenon: the Macmillan Gap has its counterparts, also, in the criticisms, changes and innovations across European capital markets. One notable feature of these research reports is the range of perspectives from which the financing gap can be viewed: from the discrimination alleged within banks' treatment of small firms during recession, to an institutional lacuna in banking products and institutions, through failures in information networks, to a reflection of fundamental difficulties in the contractual resolution of agency relationships at times of firms' status change.

In venture-capital provision Murray (Chapter 6) and Harrison and Mason (Chapter 5) have ably analysed the nature of contemporary provision and illuminated crucial issues inhibiting growing firms' access to risk capital. We may note the Report of the CBI Smaller Firms Council (*Finance for Growth*), which commented both 'That management buy-outs and buy-ins represent about a quarter of deals and over half of the value for investment in the UK by venture capitalists' and that 'Such deals are more likely to deliver short term performance to allow early distribution of gains sought by many institutional investors'. In short, the CBI conclude, 'The contribution of venture capital to the funding of small firms in the UK is likely to remain limited' (CBI 1993).

Indeed, there are strong grounds for arguing that analysis of funding gaps has skated around the real, underlying issues ever since the original Macmillan Report in 1931. Dense layers of myth obscure these issues. Keasey and Watson, along with Binks and Ennew, establish firmly the mythical nature of banks' 'discriminatory' practices, locating the experience of the smaller firm rather in entrepreneurs' reluctance to adopt appropriate financing structures that will be robust in the face of business instability. There is, indeed, little reason to suppose that in a liberalised financial marketplace the capital market would not offer competitive products, rates and terms to firms that wished to avail themselves of support. Likewise, Hall and Hutchinson in Chapter 8, and Buckland and Davis in Chapter 9, demonstrate that IPOs tend to arise from firms with relatively few financing difficulties and exhibiting little financing distress, rather than the reverse.

In IPO pricing practice, the 1970s demonology of the inefficient and ineffective adviser has been supplanted by the 1980s fashion for explanation of new-issue discounting. In the Rock (1986) model, IPOs are, on average, discounted in order to overcome the problems of adverse selection inherent in an insider–outsider polarisation of applicants at introduction. Chapters 9 by Buckland and 12 by Anolli et al. show this to be too simplistic a revision. While uncertainty resolution and information asymmetries play a part, there remain institutional rigidities in European IPO markets that are costly to the emergent firm's owners and which render the change of status at firms' first quotation unnecessarily costly, uncertain, and potentially destabilising.

Under these circumstances, increased segmentation of equities markets holds out the potential for enhanced focus and specialisation of capital markets, and of lower barriers to entry for the emergent enterprise. The unlisted securities market, pioneered within the UK in the 1980s, must be regarded as a notable innovation in the history of British business finance. What matters, of course, is whether it lowered threshold transactions costs of obtaining, or transferring, equity capital in a way which more than offset the disadvantage of smaller UK firms' continued dependence on bank borrowing. As Chapter 7 indicates, although entry costs have been reduced by the USM, economies of scale in the issuing process still discriminate against smaller issues. Evidence to the CBI report makes clear that there is still a considerable barrier to quotation arising from the administration and market-pricing costs involved (CBI 1993). Further the illiquidity of small-firm securities has had corresponding implications for the image of the USM, leading to the decision by the Stock Exchange to discontinue it. As Anthony Steele observes in Chapter 11 'Overreaction to a small number of transactions is a feature of thin markets, and the provision of an orderly junior market may involve more than the mere relaxation of official list requirements … "How should a thin market be organised?" Unless this issue is resolved, the public-policy aims of the junior market to enhance the supply of venture capital to fast-growing enterprises will be impeded by excess volatility, by bubbles and by crashes'. Steele's contribution, using forecasting and valuation methodology to unravel the market's irrational and almost hysterical reaction to the entry of a fast-growth stock, illustrates one danger of reliance upon the equilibrating mechanisms of the free, but thin market in the valuation of firms and the provision of their supporting finance for growth. Nevertheless, if the alternative offered by the Stock Exchange was that afforded by Rule 535(2) allowing shares to be traded on a matched-bargain basis, then flexibility would be reduced (Simms

1994). Anolli's account of segmentation in the Italian stock exchange, and that by Dubois in relation to France, confirm the flawed character of the stock-exchange solution. In Italy, a market targeted on the 'seasoning' of future main-market entrants was dominated by the securities of relatively large banks, themselves excluded from the main market by reason of their mutual organisation or by peculiarities of their share transfer and registration requirements. As with the UK's Business Expansion Scheme, the 1980s experiments with 'second-tier' markets sought to support the growing small firm in its independent future, but were subverted into support for other, established enterprises.

Given such an impasse, and pending the development of a wider European 'market' in unlisted securities, our attention is inevitably directed towards interim, bank-financed growth along the lines of the post-1945 German model. When, however, we consider banking relationships of those UK firms which obtained a quotation on the USM, from Chapters 8 and 9, by Hall and Hutchinson, Buckland and Davis, we find that for most such firms quotation had little connection with gearing problems. Most such new entrants were typically cash-rich, financing their rapid growth from their own funds on high-margin lines of business; and were in general conservative in their attitude to debt. This impression is consistent with the previously noted findings of the 3i/Cranfield European Enterprise Centre's survey of small companies. For this also to apply to relatively higher-growth and larger firms eligible for a stock exchange quotation is, however, rather surprising. It suggests that the standard overdraft-based model is rightly not favoured by risk-averse borrowers. Of particular concern, of course, is whether entrepreneurs and small-firm managers elect to constrain growth to that lower rate for which the firm's internally generated funds are sufficient. While debt instruments, through term loans and leasing, are available to smaller-firm bank customers, the question of security remains critical, together with a strategy favouring lending criteria based on balance-sheet evidence, and a specific focus on tangible assets eligible for security.

Given the limitations already identified for junior stock exchanges like the USM, together with corresponding exit implications for venture-capital provision, how then does the smaller firm finance its growth up to the stage where stock exchange quotation becomes a cost-effective, feasible strategy? Without an attractive form of bank finance, whether generated by the banks themselves, or in conjunction with government through a small-business loan scheme, together with the general preference on the part of many small firms for self-finance, the logical focus should be upon the supply of retained earnings, the tax treatment of such investment and the quality of management directed towards it.

TAX EFFECTS ON SMALL-FIRM FINANCE

The tax effect upon small high-growth firms must be considered in terms of both corporate and personal taxes, the interaction between them and between income and capital forms of personal taxes. The general UK corporation tax position is summarised in Davis and Pointon (1994). What matters for our purpose is the tax treatment of cash flows, depreciation and working capital for growth. Up until 1984, the UK corporation tax had for some time been characterised as neutral with respect to investment, by virtue of 100 per cent, full relief for eligible capital expenditure. After 1984, however, as part of a wide-ranging reform of the tax system, these 100 per cent first-year capital allowances were reduced, in stages, to a 25 per cent reducing balance system of depreciation. This change has led to a situation where the level of tax allowances reflects past rather than current levels of investment, thereby penalising growing companies investing from a low base (CBI 1993), an effect similar to that illustrated by Davis and Pointon (1984) with respect to working-capital investment under different corporate tax treatment of depreciation.

As part of this overall reform personal taxes were also changed, with capital-gains tax brought in at individuals' marginal income-tax rates. In terms of fiscal neutrality, biases arising from significant differences between income, capital-gains and corporate tax rates were reduced. In terms of the stance of the tax system towards the act of investment they were increased. Further, while a series of measures, ranging from the Business Expansion Scheme to PEPs, were introduced to encourage investors to shift savings into equities, direct relief on owners of small firms did not benefit to the same extent (eg Harrison and Mason 1990). Whereas the BES scheme provided for relief from income tax for personal investors in unquoted small firms, this did not apply to beneficial owners of small (or larger) companies. For the owner–entrepreneur wishing to finance investment partly from personal income no such relief was made. While no tax allowance was made for input investment, the eventual sale would incur capital-gains tax at the investor's marginal income-tax rate, on values generated by cash flows after corporation tax had been deducted. While important concessions to the treatment of capital gains have been made, these hardly compensate the direct owner–entrepreneur for the risk of capital losses being assumed. While other countries' tax systems may be no different, or are even more severe, in this respect (for example in the USA), they usually have compensating advantages in a different capital market structure.

ORGANISATION OF THE GROWING FIRM AND ITS FINANCING

Most chapters in this book have raised questions about the presence of barriers to the financing of growth, whether these be informational, institutional, or cultural. Finally, in our penultimate chapter we may note that Buckland and Davis raise the question of the managerial systems practised by successful firms which had obtained a stock exchange quotation. Earlier, Bovaird et al. in Chapter 2 had linked the question of market failure in the finance of growing firms with the quality of management available, proxied through consultants' services. The focus of Buckland and Davis's penultimate chapter (Chapter 13) is the relative lack of attention paid to newly quoted firms' managerial systems at the time of their entry to quoted status.

Given the critical issues of maturation of management systems in the growing enterprise, this is surprising, particularly when compared with the emphasis upon accounting-based financial records and prospectuses. Evidence from case studies of 40 newly quoted firms reported by these authors illuminated how rudimentary, on occasion, managerial systems could be. While that phenomenon is hardly unique, it helps one to understand the behaviour of both banks and the firms themselves in terms of their attitude to lending relationships. The overall impression of the British capital market is that of a relatively short-term-oriented stand-off relationship when compared with the seemingly longer-term participative involvement characterised by the German model.

This in turn may help to explain why the question of the strategic fitness of newly quoted UK firms' management is so little addressed. The closer relationship of the German banking system with its smaller corporate clients but also the generally higher standard of small-firm management qualifications in Germany and the USA has a correspondingly beneficial effect upon how their growing firms succeed. The research here suggests that the reluctance of banks to get involved in the governance of growing firms may well be matched by the equity markets' reluctance to require, provoke and cajole new entrants into attending to the maturation of firms' governance structures as new financing partnerships are entered into. Despite the key role of the prospectus in the formation of new trust relationships, new entrants and investors are not being assured of a proper framework for their future interdependence. This will be a matter of concern in the evolution of corporate governance practice and research, building upon the thrust of the first report of the Cadbury Committee (1992) in the UK and attempting to resolve the problematic linkages between investors, company boards and management teams.

REFERENCES

Abel, M. (1993) 'Helping Small Companies Raise Equity', *Stock Exchange Quarterly with Quality of Markets Review*, Spring, London: London Stock Exchange.

ACOST (1990) *The Enterprise Challenge: Overcoming Barriers to Growth in Small Firms*, Advisory Council on Science and Technology, Cabinet Office, London: HMSO.

Aggarwal, R. and Rivoli, P. (1990) 'Fads in the Initial Public Offering Market?', *Financial Management*, 19: 45–67.

Amemiya, T. (1981) 'Qualitative Response Models: a survey', *Journal of Economic Literature*, 19: 1483–1536.

Aram Research Associates Inc. (1987) *Informal Risk Capital in the Eastern Great Lakes Region*, Washington DC: US Small Business Administration, Office of Advocacy.

Ashton, D., Crossland, M. and Mozier, P. (1991) *The Performance Evaluation of Fund Managers*, paper presented at the annual conference of the British Accounting Association, Salford: University of Salford, April.

Aston Business School (1991) *Constraints on the Growth of Small Firms*, London: Department of Trade and Industry.

— (1992) *Evaluation of the Consultancy Initiatives Demonstration Effect*, Report to the Department of Trade and Industry, Aston University.

Bagguley, P. (1991) 'Post Fordism and Enterprise Culture', pp. 151–168 in R. Keat and N. Abercrombie (eds.) *Enterprise Culture*, London: Routledge.

Baiman, S. (1990) 'Agency Research in Management Accounting: a second look', *Accounting, Organizations and Society*, 15(4): 341–371.

Banca d'Italia (1991) *Relazione per l'anno 1990: considerazione finali*, Rome, Italy: CONSOB.

— (1992) *Relazione per l'anno 1991: considerazione finali*, Rome, Italy: CONSOB.

— (1993) *Relazione per l'anno 1992: considerazione finali*, Rome, Italy: CONSOB.

Bank of England (1988) 'Composition of Company Boards', *Bank of England Quarterly Bulletin*, 28(2), May: 242–245.

Bannock, G. (1987) *Britain in the 1980s: Enterprise Reborn*, London: 3i plc.
— (1991a) *Attitudes to Breaking Out in Europe*, London: 3i plc.
— (1991b) *Venture Capital and the Equity Gap*, London: National Westminster Bank/Graham Bannock and Partners Ltd.
— and Doran, A. (1991) *Business Banking in the 1990s: A New Era of Competition*, Dublin: Lafferty Group.
Barber, J., Metcalfe, J.S. and Porteous, M. (1989) *Barriers to Growth in Small Firms*, London: Routledge.
Barnea, A., Hangen, R. and Senbelt, R. (1981) 'Market Imperfections, Agency Problems and Capital Structure: a review', *Financial Management*, Summer: 7–22.
Baron, D. (1982) 'A Model of the Demand for Investment Banking Advising and Distribution Services for New Issues', *Journal of Finance*, 37: 955–976.
Batchelor, C. (1987) 'Equity Funding: the gap that shows stubborn persistence', *Financial Times*, 17 March: 9.
— (1988) 'Private Financing: money and time to offer', *Financial Times*, 19 July: 9.
— (1989a) 'Private Investors: not just a wing and a prayer', *Financial Times*, 24 January: 17.
— (1989b) 'The Banks Fight off their Critics', *Financial Times*, February 14: 21.
Bayliss, B.T. and Butt Philip, A.A.S. (1980) *Capital Markets and Industrial Investment in Germany and France: Lessons for the UK*, Farnborough: Saxon House.
Beatty, R.P. and Ritter, J. (1986) 'Investment Banking, Reputation, and the Underpricing of IPOs', *Journal of Financial Economics*, 15: 213–232.
Beesley, M. and Wilson, P. (1982) 'Government Aid to the Small Firm' pp. 181–199 in J. Stanworth, A. Westrip, D. Watkins and J. Lewis (eds) *Perspectives on a Decade of Small Business Research: Bolton Ten Years On*, London: Paul Chapman.
Bernanke, B.S. and Lown, C.S. (1991) 'The Credit Crunch', *Brookings Papers on Economic Activity*, 2: 205–239.
Bester, H. (1987) 'The Role of Collateral in Credit Markets with Imperfect Information', *European Economic Review*, 31(4): 887–899.
— and Hellwig, M. (1989) 'Moral Hazard and Equilibrium Credit Rationing: an overview of the issues', in G. Bamber and K. Spremann (eds) *Agency Theory, Information and Incentives*, Berlin: Springer-Verlag.
Bini, M. (1990) 'Le recenti modificazioni regolamentari del Mercato Ristretto e le prospettive per un suo rilancio', *Revista Milanese di Economia*, 36: 18–32.
Binks, M.R. and Coyne, J. (1983) *The Birth of Enterprise*, IEA Hobart Paper 98, London: Institute of Economic Affairs.
— and Vale, P.A. (1990) *Entrepreneurship and Economic Change*, London: McGraw-Hill.
—, Ennew, C.T. and Reed, G.V. (1988) 'The Survey by the Forum of Private Business on Banks and Small Firms', pp. 99–120 in G. Bannock

and E.V. Morgan (eds) *Banks and Small Businesses: A Two Nation Perspective*, London: Forum of Private Business/National Federation of Small Business.
—, — and — (1990) *Small Business and their Banks 1990*, Knutsford: Forum of Private Business.
—, — and — (1992) *Small Business and their Banks: An International Perspective*, London: National Westminster Bank.
—, — and — (1993) *Small Business and their Banks 1992*, Knutsford: Forum of Private Business.
Bisoni, C. and Ferretti, R. (1991) 'Legge amato 'e adeguamento patrimoniale delle aziende di credito', *Il Risparmio*: 747–776.
Blume, M. (1975) 'Betas and their Regression Tendencies', *Journal of Finance*, 30(3): 785–795.
Bolton, J.E. (1971) *Report of the Committee of Inquiry on Small Firms*, Cmnd 4811, London: HMSO.
Bovaird, T. (1993) 'Analysing Urban Economic Development', *Urban Studies*, 30(4/5): 631–658.
Bradford, J. (1993) 'Banks and Small Firms: an insight', *National Westminster Bank Review*, May: 13–16.
Brakell, J.R. (1988) 'Institutional Investor Expectations from Investment in Venture Capital', *Guide to European Venture Capital Sources*, London: Venture Economics Ltd.
Brandt, S.C. (1981) *Strategic Planning in Emerging Companies*, Philippines: Addison-Wesley.
Brealey, R. and Myers, S.C. (1991) *Principles of Corporate Finance*, New York: McGraw-Hill.
Briscoe, G. and Hawke, G. (1976) 'Long-term Debt and Realizable Gains in Shareholder Wealth: an empirical study', *Journal of Business Finance and Accounting*, 3: 125–135.
British Chamber of Commerce (1991) Department of Trade and Industry UK insolvency figures quoted in *Business Briefing* British Chamber of Commerce, February.
Brown, D. (1990) 'Venture capital networks: promise and performance', paper presented to the *Second Annual Small Firm Financial Research Symposium*, Fresno, Calif., April.
Brown, M. and Warner, J.B. (1980) 'Measuring Security Price Performance', *Journal of Financial Economics*, 9: 205–258.
Buckland, R. (1987) 'The Costs and Returns of the Privatisation of Nationalised Industries', *Public Administration*, 65(3): 241–257.
— (1989) 'Second Tier Markets in the UK and France', *British Accounting Review*, 21: 3–22.
— and Davis, E.W. (1984) 'The Unlisted Securities Market', *Lloyds Bank Review*, 154: 32–43.
— and — (1987) 'Barriers to Entry in the Unlisted Securities Market: the significance of administrative expenses', *Accounting and Business Research*, 17(68): 301–309.
— and — (1989) *The Unlisted Securities Market*, Oxford: Clarendon Press.
— and — (1990a) 'The Pricing of New Issues on the Unlisted Securities Market: the influence of firm size in the context of the information

content of new issue prospectuses', *British Accounting Review*, 22(3): 207–222.

— and — (1990b) 'Bank Borrowing, Small Firms, and the USM', pp. 126–140 in E.P.M. Gardner (ed.) *The Future of Financial Systems and Services*, London: Macmillan.

— and Yeomans, K.A. (1977) 'Market Efficiency: the role of issuing houses', *Journal of Economic Studies*, 4: 59–66.

—, Herbert, P.H. and Yeomans, K.A. (1981) 'Price Discount on New Equity Issues in the UK and their Relationship to Investor Subscription', *Journal of Business Finance and Accounting*, 8(1): 79–96.

—, Davis, E.W. and Yeomans, K.A. (1989) 'Debt Management by Companies Entering the Unlisted Securities Market', *Accounting and Business Research*, 19(74): 99–111.

Burns, P. (1987) 'Financing the Growing Firm', *Proceedings of the 10th National Small Firms Policy and Research Conference*, Cranfield: Cranfield Institute of Technology.

— and Dewhurst, J. (1983) *Small Business Finance and Control*, London: Macmillan.

BVCA (1984–93) *Annual Reports on Investment Activity*, London: British Venture Capital Association.

— (1992) *Directory 1992/93*, London: British Venture Capital Association.

Bygrave, W.D. and Timmons, J.A. (1992) *Venture Capital at the Crossroads*, Harvard: Harvard Business School Press.

—, Fast, N., Kholyian, R., Vincent, L. and Yue, W. (1989) 'Early Rates of Return of 131 Venture Capital Funds Started 1978–1984', *Journal of Business Venturing*, 4: 93–105.

Cadbury, Sir A. (1992) *Cadbury Committee on Financial Aspects of Corporate Governance: Interim Report* (May) and *Report* (December), London: Gee.

Caprio, L. (1989) 'Redditivita e struttura finanziaria delle imprese industriali nel periodo 1974–1986', in G.P. Barbetta and F. Silva (eds) *Transformazioni Strutturali delle Impresa Italiane*, Bologna, Italy: Il Mulino.

Carsberg, B. and Hope, A. (1976) *Business Investment Decisions under Inflation: Theory and Practice*, Institute of Chartered Accountants in England and Wales, London: ICAEW.

Cary, L. (1991) *The Venture Capital Report Guide to Venture Capital in the Europe* (5th ed.), London: Pitman.

CBI (1983) *Smaller Firms in the Economy 1983*, London: Confederation of British Industry.

CBI (1993) *Finance for Growth*, London: Confederation for British Industry.

Cesarini, F. (1979) 'Commentario alla legge 23 febbraio 1977 n. 49', *Le Nuove Legge*: 488–496.

Charkham, J. (1989) 'Corporate Governance and the Market for Control of Companies', *Bank of England Panel Paper*, no. 25, London: Bank of England.

Cherin, A.C. and Hergert, M. (1988) *Do Venture Capitalists Create Value? A Test from the Computer Industry*, paper presented at the Babson Entrepreneurship Conference, Calgary.

Chevalier, A. (1989) 'Le Second Marché: outil de la transmission d'entreprise', *Les Petites Affiches*, 56: 89–97.

Chiampou, G.F. and Kallett, J.J. (1989) 'Risk/Return Profile of Venture Capital', *Journal of Business Venturing*, 4:1–10.

Chrystal, K. (1992) 'Don't Shoot the Messenger: do banks deserve the recent adverse publicity?', *National Westminster Bank Review*, May: 44–54.

Citron, E.B. (1992) 'Financial Ratio Covenants in UK Bank Loan Contracts and Accounting Policy Choice', *Accounting and Business Research*, 22(8): 21–30.

Clayman, M. (1987) 'In Search of Excellence: the investor's viewpoint', *Financial Analysts Journal*, 43(3): 54–63.

Clifton, R. and Tatton-Brown, C. (1979) *Impact of Employment Legislation on Small Firms*, Research Paper No. 6, Department of Employment, London: HMSO.

CMBOR (1992) *UK Management Buy-Outs 1992*, Nottingham: Centre for Management Buy-Out Research.

Conlin, E. (1989) 'Adventure Capital: where America's new businesses really get their money', *INC Magazine*, 11(9): 32–48.

CONSOB (1977) *Relazione Annuale*, Rome, Italy: CONSOB.

— (1979) *Relazione Annuale*, Rome, Italy: CONSOB.

Coopers and Lybrand (1990) *Local Support to Growing Businesses*. (A survey on behalf of Business in the Community and with the support of the Confederation of British Industry), London: Coopers and Lybrand.

Coopers and Lybrand Associates (1980) *Provision of Small Industrial Premises*, Department of Industry, London: HMSO.

Cosh, A.D. and Hughes, A. (1994) 'Size, Financial Structure and Profitability: UK companies in the 1980s', pp. 18–63 in A. Hughes and D. Storey (eds) *Finance and the Smaller Business*, London: Routledge.

Cousins Stephens Associates (1991) *Constraints on the Growth of Small Firms: A Report of a Survey of Financial Institutions and Other Organisations*, Department of Trade and Industry, London: HMSO.

Cowling, M., Samuels, J. and Sugden, R. (1991) *Small Firms and Clearing Banks: Report*, London: Association of British Chamber of Commerce.

Cox, A. (1986) *The State, Finance and Industry: A Comparative Analysis of Post-War Trends in Six Advanced Industrial Countries*, London: Wheatsheaf Books.

Cranfield Enterprise Centre (1992) *Report of 3i/Cranfield Enterprise Centre*, Cranfield: Cranfield Institute of Technology.

Cross, M. (1981) *New Firm Formation and Regional Development*, Farnborough: Gower.

Curran, J. (1986) *Bolton Fifteen Years On: A Review and Analysis of Small Business Research in Britain 1971–1986*, London: Small Business Research Trust.

— and Blackburn, R. (1990) *Small Business 2000*, Milton Keynes: Small Business Research Trust.

—, Stanworth, J. and Watkins, D. (eds) (1986) *The Survival of the Small Firm* (in 2 volumes), Aldershot: Gower.

Daigne, J-F. and Joly, X. (1986) *Le Second Marché: un atout pour l'entreprise*, Paris, France: les editions d'organisation.

Dautresme (1983) *Rapport Dautresme*, Paris, France: la documentation française.

Davie, J. (1991) 'Finding and Keeping Good Venture Capital Managers', *Venture Capital Journal*, July: 21–26.

Davies, W.K.D. and Yeboah, I.E.A. (1990) 'Capital Demand and Small Businesses: the development and impact of the Alberta Opportunity Company', *Area*, 22(2): 159–167.

Davis, E.W. and Pointon, J. (1984) *Finance and the Firm*, Oxford: Oxford University Press.

— and — (1994) *Finance and the Firm* (2nd edn), Oxford: Oxford University Press.

— and Yeomans, K.A. (1976) 'Market Discount on New Issues of Equity: the influence of firm size, method of issue and market volatility', *Journal of Business Finance and Accounting*, 3(4): 27–42.

—, — and Buckland, R. (1974) *Company Finance and the Capital Market: The Effects of Firm Size*, Department of Applied Economics Occasional Paper 39, Cambridge: Cambridge University Press.

Day, T., Stoll, H. and Whaley, R. (1985) *Taxes, Financial Policy and Small Business*, Lexington, Mass.: Lexington Books.

de Meza, D. and Webb, D.C. (1987) 'Too Much Investment: a problem of asymmetric information', *Quarterly Journal of Economics*, 102: 281–292.

Dimson, E. (1979), 'The Efficiency of the British New Issue Market for Ordinary Shares', unpublished doctoral thesis, London Business School.

Dixon, R. (1989) *Venture Capital and Investment Appraisal*, Report for the Chartered Institute of Management Accountants, London: CIMA.

— (1991) 'Venture Capital and the Appraisal of Investments', *Omega*, 19(5): 333–344.

Doyle, P. and Hooley, G.J. (1991) 'Strategic Orientation and Corporate Performance', *Special Edition on Strategic Marketing of the International Journal of Research in Marketing*, 9(1): 59–73.

DTI (annually), *Business Monitor MA3*, London: HMSO.

Dubini, P. (1989) 'Which Venture Capital Backed Entrepreneurs Have the Best Chance of Succeeding?', *Journal of Business Venturing*, 4: 123–132.

Dubois, M. (1989) 'Les entreprises qui s'introduisent en bourse sont-elles sous évaluées?', *Journal de la Société de Statistique de Paris*, 130(1): 4–16.

— and Dumontier, P. (1988) 'La sous-évaluation des actions lors de leur introduction en bourse: motifs et conséquences', *Économie et Société*, 12: 43–56.

Economists Advisory Group (1971) *Problems of the Small Firm in Raising External Finance: The Results of a Sample Survey*, Committee of Inquiry on Small Firms, Research Report No. 5, London: HMSO.

Eisenhardt, K.M. (1989) 'Agency Theory: an assessment and review' *Academy of Management Review*, 14(1): 57–74.

Ennew, C.T. and Binks, M.R. (1993) 'Financing Entrepreneurship in Recession: does the banking relationship constrain performance?', paper presented to *12th Babson Entrepreneurship Research Conference*, Houston, March.

—, Reed, G.V. and Binks, M.R. (1993) 'Importance–Performance Analysis and the Measurement of Service Quality', *European Journal of Marketing*, 27(2): 59–70.

ESRC (1993) *Small Businesses in Britain*, Report by the Economic and Social Research Council, Swindon: ESRC.

EVCA (1992) *1992 Yearbook: Venture Capital in Europe*, European Venture Capital Association, London: KPMG.

Falk, N. (1978) 'Growing New Firms: the role of the social entrepreneur', *Built Environment*, 4(3): 204–212.

Fama, E. (1970) 'Efficient Capital Markets: a review of theory and empirical work', *Journal of Finance*, 25: 383–417.

Finn, F.J. and Higham, H. (1988) 'The Performance of Unseasoned New Equity Issues-cum-Stock Exchange Listings in Australia', *Journal of Banking and Finance*, 12(3): 333–351.

Flood, R.P. and Garber, P.M. (1980) 'Market Fundamentals versus Price-level Bubbles: the first tests', *Journal of Political Economics*, 88(4): 745–770.

Foss, D.C. (1985) 'Venture Capital Network: the first six months of an experiment', pp. 314–324 in J. Hornaday, E. Shils, J. Timmons and K.H. Vesper (eds) *Frontiers of Entrepreneurship Research 1985*, Wellesley, Mass.: Babson College.

Fothergill, S., Monk, S. and Perry, M. (1987) *Property and Industrial Development*, London: Hutchinson.

Fredriksen, O., Olofsson, C. and Wahlbin, C. (1990) 'The Role of Venture Capital in the Development of Portfolio Companies', paper for the SMS Conference Strategic Bridging, Stockholm, September.

Freear, J. and Wetzel, W. (1988) 'Equity Financing for New Technology-based Firms', pp. 347–367 in B.A. Kirchhoff, W.A. Long, W.E. McMullen, K.H. Vesper and W.E. Wetzel (eds) *Frontiers of Entrepreneurship Research 1988*, Wellesley, Mass.: Babson College.

— and — (1989) 'Equity Capital for Entrepreneurs', paper presented to the *9th Babson Entrepreneurship Research Conference*, St. Louis, April.

Fruhan, W.E. (1979) *Financial Strategy: Studies in the Creation, Transfer and Destruction of Shareholder Value*, Chicago: Irwin.

Fuller, R.J. and Hsia, C.C. (1984) 'A Simplified Model for Estimating Stock Prices of Growth Firms', *Financial Analysts Journal*, 40(5): 49–56.

Furlong, P. (1986) 'State, Finance and Industry in Italy', pp. 142–171 in A. Cox, *The State, Finance and Industry: A Comparative Analysis of Post-War Trends in Six Advanced Countries*, London: Wheatsheaf Books.

Garman, M.B. and Ohlson, J.A. (1980) 'Information and the Sequential Valuation of Assets in Arbitrage-free Economies', *Journal of Accounting Research*, 18(2): 421–440.

Gaston, R.J. (1989) *Finding Private Venture Capital for your Firm: A Complete Guide*, New York: Wiley.

— and Bell, S.E. (1986) *Informal Risk Capital in the Sunbelt Region*, Washington DC: US Small Business Administration, Office of Advocacy.

— and — (1988) *The Informal Supply of Capital*, Washington DC: US Small Business Administration, Office of Advocacy.

Gill, J. (1985) *Factors Affecting the Survival and Growth of the Smaller Company*, Aldershot: Gower.

Glyn-Jones, A. (1982) *Small Firms in a Country Town*, Exeter: University of Exeter.

Golby, C.W. and Johns, G. (1971) *Attitude and Motivation*, Committee of Inquiry on Small Firms, Research Report No. 7, London: HMSO.

Goodman, J.P. and Allen, K.R. (1992) 'The Credit Crunch: are Federal policies putting entrepreneurial firms on a debt diet?', paper to *12th Babson Entrepreneurship Research Conference*, INSEAD, Versailles.

Gorman, M. and Sahlman, W.A. (1989) 'What Do Venture Capitalists Do?', *Journal of Business Venturing*, 4(4): 231–248.

Goslin, N.L. and Barge, B. (1986) 'Entrepreneurial Qualities Considered in Venture Capital Support', *Frontiers of Entrepreneurial Research*, Wellesley, Mass.: Babson College.

Government of Ontario (1990) *The State of Small Business: 1990 Annual Report on Small Business in Ontario*, Toronto: University of Industry, Trade and Technology, Government of Ontario.

Green, D.M. (1983) 'Strategic Management and the State: France', pp. 161–192 in K. Dyson and S. Wilks (eds) *Industrial Crisis*, Oxford: Martin Robertson.

— (1986) The State, Finance and Industry in France', pp. 80–117 in A. Cox, *The State, Finance and Industry: A Comparative Analysis of Post-War Trends in Six Advanced Industrial Countries*, London: Wheatsheaf Books.

Greenhow, F. (1982) 'The Banks and Bolton Ten Years On', pp. 31–43 in J. Stanworth, A. Westrip, D. Watkins and J. Lewis (eds) *Perspectives on a Decade of Small Business Research: Bolton Ten Years On*, Aldershot: Gower.

Gregory, R. (1991) 'An Examination of the Fund Raising Environment of UK Venture Capitalists 1989–91', unpublished MBA dissertation, Warwick Business School, University of Warwick, England.

Grenier, R. (1988) *Le Second Marché: règles et fonctionnement*, Paris, France: EDIC/Economica.

Grinblatt, M. and Hwang, C.H. (1989) 'Signalling and the Price of New Issues', *Journal of Finance*, 37: 393–420.

Grossman, S.J. and Shiller, R.J. (1981) 'The Determinants of the Variability of Stock Market Prices', *American Economic Review*, 71: 222–227.

Gupta, M.C. (1969) 'The Effect of Size, Growth and Industry on the Financial Structure of Manufacturing Companies', *Journal of Finance*, 24: 517–529.

Haar, N.E., Starr, J. and Macmillan, I.C. (1988) 'Informal Risk Capital Investors: investment patterns on the east coast of the USA', *Journal of Business Venturing*, 3: 11–29.

Hakim, C. (1988) 'Self Employment in Britain: recent trends and current issues', *Work, Employment and Society*, 2(4): 421–450.

— (1989) 'Identifying Fast Growth Small Firms', *Employment Gazette*, 97(1): 29–41.

Hall, G.C. and Hutchinson, P.J. (1993) 'A Probit Analysis of the Changes in the Financial Characteristics of Newly Quoted Small Firms 1970–73 and 1980–83', *Journal of Small Business Economics*, 5: 207–214.

Hamilton-Fazey, I. (1993) 'CBI chief calls for changes in financing for small businesses', *Financial Times*, 6 May: 18.

Hanna, L. (1992) *The Finance of Innovation 1880–1980*, Economic and Social Sciences Research Council funded project, London: ESRC.

Harrison, R.T. and Mason, C.M. (1986) 'The Regional Impact of the Small Firms Loan Guarantee Scheme in the UK', *Regional Studies*, 20: 535–550.

— and — (1988) 'Risk Finance, the Equity Gap and New Venture Formation in the United Kingdom: the impact of the Business Expansion Scheme', pp. 595–609 in B.A. Kirchhoff, W.A. Long, W.E. McMullen, K.H. Vesper and W.E. Wetzel (eds) *Frontiers of Entrepreneurship Research 1988*, Wellesley, Mass.: Babson College.

— and — (1990) 'The Role of the Business Expansion Scheme in the UK', *Omega*, 17(2): 147–157.

— and — (1992a) *The Roles of Investors in Entrepreneurial Companies: A Comparison of Informal Investors and Venture Capitalists*, Venture Finance Research Project Working Paper No. 5. University of Southampton/Ulster Business School.

— and — (1992b) 'International Perspectives on the Supply of Informal Venture Capital', *Journal of Business Venturing*, 7: 459–475.

— and — (1993a) 'Finance for the Growing Business: the role of informal investment', *National Westminster Bank Quarterly Review*, May: 17–29.

— and — (eds) (1993b) *Informal Venture Capital: Information Networks and Public Policy*, Hemel Hempstead: Woodhead-Faulkner.

Hay, M. (1992) 'Barriers to Small Firm Growth', paper presented at *12th Babson Entrepreneurship Research Conference*, INSEAD, Versailles, June.

Henderson, R.F. (1950) *The New Issue Market and the Finance of Industry*, Cambridge: Cambridge University Press.

Henry, N. (1992) 'The New Industrial Spaces: locational logic of a new production era?', *International Journal of Urban and Regional Research*, 16: 377–396.

Hughes, A. (1994) 'The "Problems" of Finance for Smaller Businesses', pp. 209–236 in N. Dimsdale and M. Prevezer (eds) *Capital Markets and Corporate Governance*, Oxford: Oxford University Press.

Hutchinson, P.J., Meric, I. and Meric, G. (1988) 'The Financial Characteristics of Small Firms which Achieve Flotation on the UK Unlisted Securities Market', *Journal of Business Finance and Accounting*, 15(1): 9–20.

Ibbotson, R.M. (1975) 'Price Performance of Common Stock New Issues', *Journal of Financial Economics*, 3: 235–272.

— (1982) *Common Stock New Issues Revisited*, Working Paper no. 84, Chicago: Chicago Graduate School of Business, July.

—, Sindelar, J. and Ritter, J. (1988) 'Initial Public Offerings', *Journal of Applied Corporate Finance*, 1: 37–45.

Industrial and Market Research (1984) *Market Research Report*, unpublished research report for the Department of Trade and Industry.

Inland Revenue (1991) *Inland Revenue Statistics 1991*, London: HMSO.

Investors Chronicle (1987) 'Sock Shop: Thatcher Clone', *Investors Chronicle*, 1 May.

Isaac, D. (1987) 'Sophie Socks it to the City', *Daily Telegraph*, 9 May.

Jackson, P. (1993) 'Taxation, Public Choice and Public Spending', in P. Jackson (ed.) *Current Issues in Public Sector Economics*, Basingstoke: Macmillan.

Jenkinson, T.J. and Espenlaub, S. (1991) 'Costs of Capital Raising on the USM', *Stock Exchange Quarterly*, Autumn: article 2, 7–11.

Jensen, M.C. and Meckling, W. (1976) 'Theory of the Firm: managerial behaviour, agency costs and capital structure', *Journal of Financial Economics*, 5, October: 11–25.

Jog, V.M. and Ryding, A.L. (1987) 'Underpricing in Canadian IPOs', *Financial Analysts Journal*, 43(6): 48–55.

John, K. (1987), 'Risk-shifting Incentives and Signalling through Corporate Capital Structure', *Journal of Finance*, 42(3): 623–642.

Jones, C.S. (1985) 'An Empirical Study of the Role of Management Accounting Systems following Take-over or Merger', *Accounting, Organisations and Society*, 10(2): 177–200.

— (1992) 'The Attitudes of Owner–Managers towards Accounting Control Systems following Management Buy Out', *Accounting, Organisations and Society*, 17(2): 151–168.

Kay, W. (1992) *The Times*, December 10: 27c.

Keasey, K. and McGuinness, P. (1991) 'Prospectus Earnings Forecasts and the Pricing of New Issues on the unlisted securities market', *Accounting and Business Research*, 21(82): 133–145.

— and — (1992), 'An Empirical Investigation of the Role of Accounting in the Valuation of Unseasoned Equity Issues', *Accounting and Business Research*, 22(86): 133–142.

— and Short, H. (1992) 'The Winner's Curse Model of Underpricing: a critical assessment', *Accounting and Business Research*, 23(89): 74–78.

— and Watson, R. (1991) 'The State of the Art of Small Firm Failure Prediction: achievements and prognosis', *International Small Business Journal*, 9: 11–30.

— and — (1992) *Investment and Financing Decisions and the Performance of Small Firms*, London: National Westminster Bank.

— and — (1993a) *The Management of Small Firms: Ownership, Finance and Performance*, Oxford: Blackwell.

— and — (1993b) 'Banks and Small Firms: is conflict inevitable?', *National Westminster Bank Review*, May: 30–40.

— and — (1994) 'The 1986 UK Insolvency and Company Directors' Disqualification Acts: an evaluation of their impacts on small firm financing decisions', *Small Business Economics*, 6: 257–266.

Keeble, D. (1990) 'Small Firms, New Firms and Uneven Regional Development in the United Kingdom', *Area*, 22(3): 234–245.

—, Tyler, P., Broom, G. and Lewis, J. (1992) *Business Success in the Countryside: The Performance of Rural Enterprise*, Department of the Environment, London: HMSO.

Kindleberger, C. P. (1978) *Manias, Panics and Crashes: A History of Financial Crisis, New York: Basic Books.*

— (1992) 'Bubbles', pp. 20–22 in P. Newman, M. Milgate and J. Eatwell (eds) *New Palgrave Dictionary of Money and Finance*, London: Macmillan;

King, M. (1977). *Public Policy and the Corporation*, London: Chapman and Hall.

Kuhn, R.L. (1989) *Creativity and Strategy in Mid-Sized Firms*, Englewood Cliffs, J: Prentice-Hall.

Landstrom, H. (1991) 'Private Investors in Sweden: an agency theory approach', paper presented to *RENT V- Research in Entrepreneurship*, Vaxjo University, Sweden, November.

Lee, T.A. (1983) 'Funds Statements and Cash Flow Analysis', *The Investment Analysts Journal*, July: 13–21.

Lehmann, B.N. (1990) 'Fads, Martingales, and Market Efficiency', *The Quarterly Journal of Economics*, 105(1): 1–28.

Leland, H. and Pyle, D. (1977) 'Information Asymmetries, Financial Structure and Financial Intermediation', *Journal of Finance*, 32: 261–275.

Lemée, H. (1983) 'Observations comparatives sur l'Unlisted Security Market et le Second Marché', *Analyse Financière*, pp. 35–47.

LeRoy, S.F. and Porter, R.D. (1981) 'The Present-Value Relation: tests based on implied variance bounds', *Econometrica*, 49: 555–574.

Levis, M. (1990) 'The Winner's Curse Problem, Interest Costs, and the Discounting of IPOs', *The Economic Journal*, 100: 76–89.

— (1992) 'The Long-Run Performance of Initial Public Offerings: the UK experience 1980–1988', paper at the British Accounting Association Annual Conference, Warwick University, April, mimeo.

LINC (1990) *LINC Bulletin*, No. 138, June.

Lisle-Williams, M. (1982) 'Changing Social Organisation and Market Conduct in the English Merchant Banking Sector', unpublished doctoral thesis, University of Oxford, Oxford.

Lloyd, S. (1989) 'Special Report: an industry on the brink of the 1990s', *UK Venture Capital Journal*, 10 November.

Lonie, A.A., Lonie, R. and Power, D.M. (1989) *The Overreaction Effect: Some UK Evidence*, Working Paper, University of Dundee, June.

Lorenz, T. (1989) *Venture Capital Today* (2nd edn), London: Woodhead-Faulkner.

Lovering, J. (1990) 'Fordism's Unknown Successor: a comment on Scott's theory of flexible accumulation and the re-emergence of regional economies', *International Journal of Urban and Regional Research*, 14: 159–174.

McCloskey, D. (1986) *The Rhetoric of Economics*, London: Wheatsheaf Books.

MacDonald, J. and Fisher, A.K. (1972) 'New Issue Stock Price Behaviour', *Journal of Finance*, 27: 97–102.
— and Jacquillat, B. (1974) 'L'efficacité de la procedure française d'introduction en bourse', *Banque*, pp. 31–39.
—, — and Rolfo, J. (1978) 'French Auctions of Common Stock New Issues, 1966–1974', *Journal of Banking and Finance*, pp. 305–322.
McKay, G. and Corke, A. (1986) *The Body Shop: Franchising a Philosophy*, London: Pan Books.
Macmillan, Lord (1931) *Report of the Committee on Finance and Industry*, Cmd 3987, London: HMSO.
MacMillan, I.C., Siegal, R. and Subba Narishima, P.N. (1985) 'Criteria Used by Venture Capitalists to Evaluate New Venture Proposals', *Journal of Business Venturing*, 1(1): 126–141.
—, Kulow, D.M. and Khoylian, R. (1989) 'Venture Capitalists' Involvement in their Investments: extent and performance', *Journal of Business Venturing*, 4(1): 27–47.
Malkiel, B.G. (1963) 'Equity yields, growth and the structure of share prices', *The American Economic Review*, 53(5): 1004–1031.
Marsh, P. (1982) 'The Choice between Equity and Debt: an empirical study', *Journal of Finance*, 37: 121–144.
— (1990) *Short-Termism on Trial*, London: Institutional Fund Managers' Association.
Martin, R. (1989) 'The Growth and Geographical Anatomy of Venture Capital in the United Kingdom', *Regional Studies*, 23: 389–403.
Mason, C.M. (1989) 'Explaining Recent Trends in New Firm Formation in the UK: some evidence from south Hampshire', *Regional Studies*, 23: 331–346.
— and Harrison, R.T. (1989) 'Small Firms Policy and the North–South Divide in the United Kingdom: the case of the Business Expansion Scheme', *Transactions, Institute of British Geographers*, 14: 37–58.
— and — (1991a) 'Venture Capital, the Equity Gap and the North–South Divide in the United Kingdom', pp. 207–247 in M. Green (ed.) *Venture Capital: International Comparisons*, New York: Routledge.
— and — (1991b) 'The Small Firm Equity Gap since Bolton', pp. 112–150 in J. Stanworth and C. Gray (eds) *Bolton 20 Years On: The Small Firm in the 1990s*, London: Paul Chapman.
— and — (1991c) 'Informal Investors', *CBI Smaller Firms Economic Report*, January: 12–18.
— and — (1992a) *Promoting Informal Investment Activity: Some Operational Considerations for Business Referral Services*, Venture Finance Research Project Working Paper No. 4, University of Southampton (Urban Policy Research Unit) and University of Ulster (Ulster Business School).
— and — (1992b) *The Financing of Technology Based New Firms in the UK: The Role of Informal Venture Capital*, paper presented to the Anglo-German Workshop on Seed Capital and New Technology Based New Firms, Oxford.
— and — (1993a) *The Role of Venture Capital in the Financing of Technology-based SMEs in the United Kingdom*, paper to the

Conference on New Technology Based Firms, Manchester Business School, June.

— and — (1993b) 'Promoting Informal Venture Capital: an evaluation of a British initiative', paper presented to *13th Babson Entrepreneurship Research Conference*, Houston, March.

—, Harrison, J. and Harrison, R.T. (1988) *Closing the Equity Gap? An Assessment of the Business Expansion Scheme*, London: Small Business Research Trust.

—, Harrison, R.T. and Chaloner, J. (1991) *Informal Risk Capital in the UK – A Study of Investor Characteristics, Investment Preferences and Investment Decision-Making*, Venture Finance Research Project Working Paper No. 2, University of Southampton (Urban Policy Research Unit) and University of Ulster (Ulster Business School).

Mayer, C. (1994) 'Stock Markets, Financial Institutions, and Corporate Performance', pp. 179–194 in N. Dimsdale and M. Prevezer (eds) Capital Markets and Corporate Governance, Oxford: Clarendon Press.

Mayes, D.G. and Moir, C.B. (1989) 'Small Firms in the UK Economy', *Royal Bank of Scotland Review*, December: 15–33.

Mayoux (1979) *Le Développement des initiatives financières locales et régionales (Rapport)*, Paris, France: Documentation française.

Merrett, A.J., Howe, M. and Newbould, G.D. (1964) *Equity Issues and the London Capital Market*, London: Longman.

Merrett Cyriax Associates (1971) *Dynamics of Small Firms*, Committee of Inquiry on Small Firms, Research Report No. 12, London: HMSO.

Merton, R.C. (1987) 'On the Current State of the Stock Market Rationality Hypothesis', pp. 93–129 in R. Dornbush, S. Fischer and J. Bossons (eds) *Macro Economics and Finance: Essays in Honour of Franco Modigliani*, London: MIT Press.

Middleton, M., Cowling, M., Samuels, J. and Sugden, R. (1994) 'Small Firms and Clearing Banks', pp. 141–160 in N. Dimsdale and M. Prevezer (eds) *Capital Markets and Corporate Governance*, Oxford: Clarendon Press.

Miller, M. and Rock, K. (1985) 'Dividend Policy under Asymmetric Information', *Journal of Finance*, 40: 1031–1051.

Mirman, S. (1987) 'Sock Shop', *Management Week*, 27 November.

Modigliani, F. and Miller, M. (1958) 'The Cost of Capital, Corporation Finance, and the Theory of Investment', *American Economic Review*, 48(2): 261–297.

Monck, C.P.S., Porter, R.B., Quintas, P.R., Storey, D.J. and Wynarczyk, P. (1988) *Science Parks and the Growth of High Technology Firms*, Beckenham: Croom Helm.

Monti, M., Cesarini, F. and Scognamiglio, C. (1983) 'Report on the Italian Credit and Financial System', *Banca Nazionale del Lavoro Quarterly Review* (special issue, June): 174–257.

Morgan, E.V. and Harrington, R.L. (1977) *Capital Markets in the EEC*, London: Economists Advisory Group.

Murray, G.C. (1991a) *Change and Maturity in the UK Venture Capital Industry 1991–95*, Warwick Business School, University of Warwick.

— (1991b) 'The Changing Nature of Competition in the UK Venture Capital Industry: a competitive force analysis', *National Westminster Bank Quarterly Review*, November: 65–80.

— (1992a) 'A Challenging Market Place for Venture Capital', *Long Range Planning*, 25(6): 79–86.

— (1992b) 'An Evaluation of the First Three Years of the European Seed Capital Fund (ESCF) Scheme', paper presented to *Conference on Studies in the New Europe*, University of Nottingham, April.

— and Francis, D. (1992) *The European Seed Capital Fund Scheme: Review of the First Three Years*, Report to the Commission of the European Community (DGXXIII), Warwick Business School, University of Warwick.

— and Lott, J. (1992) 'Have Venture Capital Firms a Bias Against Investment in High Technology Companies?' Paper at the *12th Babson Entrepreneurial Research Conference*, INSEAD, Versailles, France, July.

Muscarella, C. and Vetsuypens, M. (1989) 'A Simple Test of Baron's Model of IPO Underpricing', *Journal of Financial Economics*, 15: 187–212.

Myers, D.D. and Moline, M.D. (1988) 'Networks and Participation Interest in Missouri Informal Investors', paper presented to the *8th Babson Entrepreneurship Research Conference*, Calgary, May.

Myers, S.C. (1984) 'The Capital Structure Puzzle', *Journal of Finance*, 39: 575–592.

— and Majluf, N. (1984) 'Corporate Financing and Investment Decisions when Firms Have Information Investors do not Have', *Journal of Financial Economics*, 12: 187–222.

Nahmijas, A. and Pera, A. (1988) 'Capital Market Efficiency and Newly Issued Common Stocks: an analytical study of Italian data', *Review of Economic Conditions in Italy*, 1: 49–74.

Nash, T. (1993) 'Britain's Unsung Heroes', *Director*, 46(12): 32–38.

NEDC (1986a) *External Capital for Small Firms*, London: National Economic Development Office.

— (1986b) *Finance for Growth: A Study of Small and Medium-Sized Firms in the Electronics Sector*, London: National Economic Development Office.

— (1986c) *Lending to Small Firms*, London: National Economic Development Office.

Neiswander, D.K. (1985) 'Informal Seed Stage Investors', pp. 142–154 in J.A. Hornday, E.B. Shils, J.A. Timmons and K.H. Vesper (eds) *Frontiers of Entrepreneurship Research 1985*, Wellesley, Mass.: Babson College.

Neu, D. (1991a) 'New Stock Issues and the Institutional Production of Trust', *Accounting, Organisation and Society*, 16(2): 185–200.

— (1991b) 'Trust, Contracting, and the Prospectus Process', *Accounting, Organisation and Society*, 16(3): 243–256.

Neuberger, B.M. and Hammond, C.T. (1974) 'A Study of Underwriters' Experience with Unseasoned Common Stock New Issues', *Journal of Financial and Quantitative Analysis*, 9(March): 165–177.

Nevin, E. and Davis, E.W. (1971), *The London Clearing Banks*, London: Elek Books.

NVCA (1992) *Annual Report 1991*, Arlington Va: National Venture Capital Association, Venture Economics Inc.

Ohlson, J.A. (1983) 'Price Earnings Ratios and Earnings Capitalisation under Uncertainty', *Journal of Accounting Research*, 21(1) 141–154.

— (1988) *Accounting Earnings, Book Value and Dividends: The Theory of the Clean Surplus Equation (Part 1)*, Working Paper, Columbia University, November.

— (1989a) 'Ungarbled Earnings and Dividends: an analysis and extension of the bearer, Lambert and Morse valuation model', *Journal of Accounting and Economics*, 11(2/3): 109–115.

— (1989b) *A Synthesis of Security Valuation Theory and the Role of Dividends, Cash Flows and Earnings*, Working Paper, Columbia University, April.

— (1989c) *The Theory of Value and Earnings, and an Introduction to the Ball–Brown Analysis*, Working Paper, Columbia University, October.

Peat, Marwick, Mitchell and Co. (1980) *Entering the Unlisted Securities Market*, London: Peat, Marwick, Mitchell and Co.

Peek, J. and Rosengren, E.S. (1992) 'The Capital Crunch in New England', *New England Economic Review*, May/June: 21–31.

Perry, M. (1986) *Small Factories and Economic Development*, Aldershot: Gower.

— (1988) 'The Supply and Demand of Small Business Finance in a Rural Region', *Tijdschrift voor Economische en Sociale Geografie*, 79: 188–198.

Peters, I. (1989) 'Small Business Growth: spatial and non-spatial aspects of development', unpublished doctoral thesis, University of Southampton.

Peterson, R. and Shulman, J. (1987) 'Capital Structure of Growing Small Firms: a 12 country study on becoming bankable', *International Small Business Journal*, 5: 10–22.

Pettengill, G.N. and Jordon, B.D. (1990) 'The Overreaction Hypothesis, Firm Size, and Stock Market Seasonality', *The Journal of Portfolio Management*, 16(3): 60–64.

Pettit, R.R. and Singer, R.F. (1985) 'Small Business Finance: a research agenda', *Financial Management*, Autumn: 47–60.

Piore, M. and Sabel, C. (1984) *The Second Industrial Divide: Possibilities for Prosperity*, New York: Basic Books.

Planning Exchange (1986) 'Enterprise Agency Marriage Bureaux', *LEDIS*, B35.

Pointdexter, J.B. (1976) 'The Efficiency of Financial Markets: the venture capital case', unpublished doctoral dissertation, New York University, New York.

Porter, M.E. (1979) 'How Competitive Forces Shape Strategy', *Harvard Business Review*, 57(2): 137–145.

— (1980) *Competitive Strategy: Techniques for Analysing Industries and Competitors*, New York: Free Press.

Postma, P.D. and Sullivan, M.K. (1990) *Informal Risk Capital in the Knoxville Region*, Knoxville, Tenn.: College of Business Administration, University of Tennessee.

Pratt, G. (1990) 'Venture Capital in the United Kingdom', *Bank of England Quarterly Bulletin*, 30(1): 78–83.
Puxty, A.G. (1985) 'A Critical Overview of Agency Theory', *Issues in Accountability*, 12(1): 1–24.
Radcliffe Report (1959) *Report of the Committee on the Working of the Monetary System*, Cmnd 827, London: HMSO.
Ray, G.H. and Hutchinson, P.J. (1983) *The Financing and Financial Control of Small Enterprise Development*, Aldershot: Gower.
Rickwood, C., Coates, J.B. and Stacey, R. (1987) 'Managed Costs and the Capture of Information', *Accounting and Business Research*, 17(68): 319–326.
Riding, A.L. and Short, D.M. (1987a) 'Some Investor and Entrepreneur Perspectives on the Informal Market for Risk Capital', *Journal of Small Business and Entrepreneurship*, 5(2): 19–30.
— and — (1987b) 'On the Estimation of the Investment Potential of Informal Investors: a captive–receptive approach', *Journal of Small Business and Entrepreneurship*, 5(3): 26–40.
Riley, B. (1992) 'The Long View', *Financial Times*, 6/7 July: 1.
Ritter, J.R. (1991), 'The Long-run Performance of IPOs', *Journal of Finance*, 46: 3–27.
Robbie, K. and Wright, M. (1994), 'Regional Expertise Comes to the Fore', *The Times, Focus on Venture Capital*, 22 June: 33.
Roberts, J. and Scapens, R.W. (1985) 'Accounting Systems and Systems of Accountability: understanding accounting practices in their organisational contexts', *Accounting, Organizations and Society*, 10(4): 443–456.
Robson Rhodes (1984) *A Study of Business Financed Under the Small Firms Loan Guarantee Scheme*, Department of Trade and Industry, London: HMSO.
Rock, K. (1986) 'Why New Issues are Underpriced', *Journal of Financial Economics*, 15: 187–211.
Roddick, A. (1992) *Body and Soul*, London: Vermillion.
Rothwell, R. (1986) 'The Role of Small Firms in the Emergence of New Technologies', pp. 114–139 in J. Curran, J. Stanworth and D. Watkins (eds) *The Survival of the Small Firm*, vol. 2, Aldershot: Gower.
Ryan, R., Scapens, R.W. and Theobald, M. (1992) *Research Method and Methodology in Finance and Accounting*, London: Academic Press.
Sahlman, W.A. (1989) *The Changing Structure of the American Venture Capital Industry*, National Venture Capital Association Conference, May.
Sangster, A. (1992) 'Capital Investment Appraisal Techniques: a survey of current usage', *Journal of Business Finance and Accounting*, 20(3): 307–332.
Sapienza, H.J. (1992) 'When do Venture Capitalists Add Value?', *Journal of Business Venturing*, 7: 9–27.
— and Timmons, J.A. (1989) 'The Role of Venture Capitalists in New Ventures. What Determines their Importance?', *Academy of Management Best Papers Proceedings*: 74–78.
Scapens, R.W. (1990) 'Research in Management Accounting Practice: the role of case study methods', *British Accounting Review*, 22(3): 259–281.

— (1992) 'The Role of Case Study Methods in Management Accounting Research: a personal reflection and reply', *British Accounting Review*, 24(4): 369–383.

Schaeffer, R.E. and Pulver, G.C. (1985) 'Regional Variations in Capital Structure of New Small Businesses', pp. 166–192 in D. Storey (ed.) *Small Firms in Regional Economic Development*, Cambridge: Cambridge University Press.

Schell, D.W. (1984) 'The Development of the Venture Capital Industry in North Carolina: a new approach', pp. 55–72 in J.A. Hornday, F.A. Tardley, J.A. Timmons and K.H. Vesper (eds) *Frontiers of Entrepreneurship Research 1984*, Wellesley, Mass.: Babson College.

Schmidt, H. (1984), *Special Stock Market Segments for Small Company Shares*, EEC Publications: Luxembourg.

Scholes, M.S. (1972) 'The Market for Securities: substitution versus price pressure and the effects of information on share prices', *Journal of Business*, 45(2): 179–211.

Scott, A.J. (1988) *New Industrial Spaces*, London: Pion.

Segal, Quince, Wicksteed Ltd (1989) *Evaluation of the Consultancy Initiatives*, Department of Trade and Industry, London: HMSO.

Shiller, R.J. (1981a) 'Do Stock Prices Move too much to be Justified by Subsequent Changes in Dividends?', *American Economic Review*, 71: 421–436.

— (1981b) 'The use of volatility measure in assessing market efficiency', *Journal of Finance*, 36: 291–311.

— (1984) 'Stock Prices and Social Dynamics', *Brookings Papers in Management*, July: 457–498.

Short, D.M. and Riding, A.L. (1989) 'Informal Investors in the Ottawa–Carleton Region: experience and expectations', *Entrepreneurship and Regional Development*, 1: 99–112.

Simms, J. (1994) 'Is it Time for a Replacement for the USM?', *Quarterly Enterprise Digest*, May.

Small Business Research Trust (1989) *Risk Capital for Small Firms: A Guidebook and Directory*, London: Barclays Bank plc.

— (1991) *NatWest Quarterly Survey of Small Business*, No. 4, Milton Keynes: SBRT.

Solnik, B. (1991) *International Investments* (2nd edn), Reading, Mass.: Addison-Wesley.

Stanworth, J. and Curran, J. (1976) 'Growth and the Small Firm: an alternative view', *Journal of Management Studies*, 13(2): 95–110.

— and Gray, C. (eds) (1991) *Bolton 20 Years On: The Small Firm in the 1990s*, London: Paul Chapman.

—, Westrip, A., Watkins, D. and Lewis, J. (eds) (1982) *Perspectives on a Decade of Small Business Research: Bolton Ten Years On*, Aldershot: Gower.

Steed, G.P.F. and De Genova, D. (1983) 'Ottawa's Technology-oriented Complex', *Canadian Geographer*, 27: 263–278.

Steele, A. (1990) *How Well Do Share Prices Reflect Accounting Fundamentals?* Warwick Papers in Management, Warwick Business School, July.

Stevenson, H.H. and Jarillo-Mossi, J.C. (1986) 'Preserving Entrepreneurship as Companies Grow', *Journal of Business Strategy*, 7(1).

Stiglitz, J.D. (1988) *Economics of the Public Sector* (2nd edn), New York: W.W. Norton & Co.

— and Weiss, A. (1981) 'Credit Rationing in Markets with Imperfect Information', *American Economic Review*, 71: 393–410.

Stock Exchange (1986), *Flotations and Pre-emption: A Discussion Paper*, London: London Stock Exchange Quotations Department, January.

Storey, D. (1982) *Enterpreneurship and the New Firm*, London: Croom Helm.

— and Johnson, S. (1987) *Job Generation and Labour Market Change*, London: Macmillan.

— and Strange, A. (1992) *Entrepreneurship in Cleveland 1979–1989: A Study of the Effects of the Enterprise Culture*, Sheffield: Department of Employment, Employment Department Research Series No. 3.

—, Keasey, K., Watson, R. and Wynarczyk, P. (1987) *The Performance of Small Firms: Profits, Jobs and Failures*, London: Routledge.

—, Watson, R. and Wynarczyk, P. (1989) *Fast Growth Small Business: Case Studies of 40 Small Firms in North East England*, Research Paper No. 67, Department of Employment.

Sullivan, M.K. and Miller, A. (1990) 'Applying Theory of Finance to Informal Risk Capital Research: promise and problems', paper presented to the *10th Babson Entrepreneurship Research Conference*, Wellesley, Mass.: Babson College, April.

Syron, R.F. (1991) 'Are we Experiencing a Credit Crunch?', *New England Economic Review*, July/August: 3–10.

Taylor, T.W. (1985) *The Financing of Industry and Commerce*, London: Heinemann.

Thomas, K. (1978) *Small Firms in Birmingham: An Analysis of their Operating Environment*, Working Paper 6, Department of Planning and Landscape, Birmingham: City of Birmingham Polytechnic.

Tickell, A. and Peck, J.A. (1992) 'Accumulation, Regulation and the Geographies of Post-Fordism: missing links in regulation research', *Progress in Human Geography*, 16: 190–218.

Timan, S. and Wessels, R. (1988) 'The Determinants of Capital Structure Choice', *Journal of Finance*, 43(1): 1–9.

Tinic, S.M. (1988) 'Anatomy of Initial Public Offerings of Common Stock', *Journal of Finance*, 43(4): 782–822.

Tomkins, C. and Groves, R. (1983) 'The Everyday Accountant and Researching his Reality', *Accounting, Organizations and Society*, 8(4): 361–374.

Tricker, M. and Bozeat, N. (1983) 'Encouraging the Growth of Small Firms in Rural Areas', *Regional Studies*, 17: 201–204.

Tricker, T.I. (1984) *Corporate Governance: Practices, Procedures and Powers in British Companies and their Boards of Directors*, London: Gower.

Tulloch, I. (1994), 'Fight the Equity Gap', *The Times, Focus on Venture Capital*, 22 June: 34.

Turok, I. and Richardson, P. (1989) *Supporting the Start-up and Growth of Small Firms: A Study in West Lothian*, Strathclyde Papers On Planning, Glasgow: University of Strathclyde.

Tyebjee, T.T. and Bruno, A.V. (1984) 'A Model of Venture Capital Investment Activity', *Management Science*, 30: 1051–1066.

Tymes, E.R. and Krasner, O.J. (1983) 'Informal Risk Capital in California', pp. 347–368 in J.A. Hornday, J.A. Timmons and K.H. Vesper (eds) *Frontiers of Entrepreneurship Research 1983*, Wellesley, Mass.: Babson College.

Urry, M. (1990) 'When a Niche Becomes a Tomb', *Financial Times*, 24 February.

US Small Business Administration (1987) *The State of Small Business: A Report of the President*, Washington DC: US Government Printing Office.

Vaughan, G.D., Grinyer, P. and Birley, S. (1977) *From Private to Public*, London: Woodhead-Faulkner.

Venture Economics Canada Ltd. (1990) *Financing Early Stage Companies*.

Venture Economics Ltd. (1991) 'Special Report: Venture Capital Investment in Quoted Companies', *UK Venture Capital Journal*, March/April.

Vickery, L. (1989) 'Equity Financing in Small Firms', pp. 204–236 in P. Burns and J. Dewhurst (eds) *Small Business and Entrepreneurship*, London: Macmillan.

Vyakarnam, S. and Jacobs, R. (1991) 'How Bank Managers Construe High Technology Entrepreneurs', paper to *National Small Firms Policy and Research Conference*, Lancashire Enterprise Ltd/Manchester Business School, November.

Walker, D.A. (1989) 'Financing the Small Firm', *Small Business Economics*, 1: 285–296.

Walker, E.W. and Petty, J. (1978) 'Financial Differences between Large and Small Firms', *Financial Management*, 7: 61–68.

Waller, D. (1987) 'Sophie Socks it to you', *Investors Chronicle*, 17 April.

Water Services Association (1992) *The Cost of Capital in the Water Industry*, London: Water Services Association.

Watkins, D. and Morton, T. (1982) 'Small Firms in Britain and Europe: the perceived environment', pp. 164–179 in D. Watkins, J. Stanworth and A. Westrip (eds) *Stimulating Small Firms*, Aldershot: Gower.

Weber, W. (1993) Die Relevanz kleiner und mittlerer Betriebe für die Struktur und Entwicklung ländlicher Räume, Arbeitsmaterialen zur Raumordnung und Raumplanung, Book 125. Bayreuth: Lehrstuhl Wirtschaftsgeographie und Regionalplanung, Universität Bayreuth.

Welch, I. (1989) 'Seasoned Offerings, Imitation Costs, and the Underpricing of IPOs', *Journal of Finance*, 44: 421–449.

Wells, S. (1991) 'Less-Liquid Market', *Stock Exchange Quarterly with Quality of Markets Review*, Autumn: article 6, 27–32.

— (1992) 'Developments in the Smaller Companies Market', *Stock Exchange Quarterly with Quality of Markets Review*, Autumn: article 4, 19–24.

Wells, W.A. (1974) 'Venture Capital Decision Making', unpublished doctoral dissertation, Carnegie-Mellon University.

WEMTECH (1990) *Survey of SMEs in Engineering*, Birmingham: West Midlands Regional Technology Centre.

Weston, J.F. and Brigham, E.F. (1978) *Managerial Finance* (6th edn), Chicago: Dryden Press.

Wetzel, W.E. (1981) 'Informal Risk Capital in New England', pp. 217–245 in H.M. Vesper (ed.) *Frontiers of Entrepreneurship Research 1981*, Wellesley, Mass.: Babson College.

— (1983) 'Angels and Informal Risk Capital', *Sloan Management Review*, 24: 23–34.

— (1986a) 'Entrepreneurs, Angels and Economic Renaissance', pp. 119–139 in R.D. Hisrich (ed.) *Entrepreneurship, Intrapreneurship and Venture Capital*, Lexington, Mass.: Lexington Books.

— (1986b) 'Informal Risk Capital: knowns and unknowns', pp. 85–108 in D.L. Sexton and R.W. Smilor (eds) *The Art or Science of Entrepreneurship*, Cambridge, Mass.: Ballinger.

— (1987) 'The Informal Risk Capital Market: aspects of scale and efficiency', pp. 412–428 in N.C. Chevwill et al.. (eds) *Frontiers of Entrepreneurship Research 1987*, Wellesley, Mass.: Babson College.

— (1992) 'Starting a Private Investor Network: reflections on the history of VCN', paper presented at the *Department of Employment/Training and Enterprise Councils Informal Investment Match-making Seminar*, Knutsford, Cheshire, January.

— and Seymour C. (1981) *Informal Risk Capital in New England*, Washington DC: US Small Business Administration, Office of Advocacy.

— and Wilson I.G. (1985) 'Seed Capital Gaps: evidence from high-growth ventures', pp. 221–240 in J.A. Hornday, E.B. Shils, J.A. Timmons and K.H. Vesper (eds) *Frontiers of Entrepreneurship Research 1985*, Wellesley, Mass.: Babson College.

Whitson, K. (1994), 'How Banks Could Come to Appear Positively Angelic', report of *Guardian* Mittelstand Conference, *Guardian*, 27 June: 13.

Williams, H., Bozeat, N., Cook, A. and Hardy, B. (1980) *Industrial Renewal in the Inner City: An Assessment of Potential and Problems*, London: Inner City Directorate, Department of the Environment.

Wilson H. (1979) *The Financing of Small Firms*, Interim Report of the Committee to Review the Functioning of Financial Institutions, Cmnd 7503, London: HMSO.

— (1980) *Committee to Review the Functioning of Financial Institutions: Report*, Cmnd 7937, London: HMSO.

Woodcock, C. (1986) 'The Financial and Capital Environment of the Small Firm', pp. 39–52 in J. Curran, J. Stanworth and D. Watkins (eds) *The Survival of the Small Firm*, Aldershot: Gower.

Yadzipour, R. (1990) 'An Empirical Analysis of the Market for Formal Venture Capital: evidence from the US', *Small Business Economics*, 2(2): 89–94.

Yao-Su Hu (1984) *Industrial Banking and Special Credit Institutions: A Comparative Study*, London: Policy Studies Institute.

Zarowin, P. (1990) 'Size, Seasonality and Stock Market Overreaction', *Journal of Financial and Quantitative Analysis*, 25(1): 113–125.

Zucker, L. (1986) 'Production of Trust: institutional sources of economic structure, 1840–1920', *Research in Organizational Behaviour*, 53–111.

INDEX

www.ingramcontent.com/pod-product-compliance
Lightning Source LLC
LaVergne TN
LVHW011113300926
849160LV00008B/371
* 9 7 8 1 1 3 8 6 7 9 9 4 8 *